Reasonable Doubt

Reasonable Doubt

Learning to Dwell in Biblical Ambivalence and Paradox

HANZ GUTIERREZ SALAZAR

Foreword by Rubén Rosario Rodriguez
Preface by Miguel A. De La Torre

WIPF & STOCK · Eugene, Oregon

REASONABLE DOUBT
Learning to Dwell in Biblical Ambivalence and Paradox

Copyright © 2024 Hanz Gutierrez Salazar. All rights reserved. Except for brief quotations in critical publications or reviews, no part of this book may be reproduced in any manner without prior written permission from the publisher. Write: Permissions, Wipf and Stock Publishers, 199 W. 8th Ave., Suite 3, Eugene, OR 97401.

Wipf & Stock
An Imprint of Wipf and Stock Publishers
199 W. 8th Ave., Suite 3
Eugene, OR 97401

www.wipfandstock.com

PAPERBACK ISBN: 979-8-3852-2947-5
HARDCOVER ISBN: 979-8-3852-2948-2
EBOOK ISBN: 979-8-3852-2949-9

10/16/24

To Francesca, Daniel, Bryan, Linda, and Melody

To Peru, land of ambivalences, paradoxes,
and abundant life.

Contents

Foreword by Rubén Rosario Rodriguez | ix
Preface by Miguel A. De La Torre | xiii
Introduction: The Value of An Elusive Sense | xv

I. From Reading to Interpretation and the Other Way Round | 1

II. The Birth of a Reader-Centric Hermeneutics | 20

III. The Text and Distantiation: The Value of a Slow Interpretation | 61

IV. The Reader and Imagination: The Value of a Transgressive Interpretation | 83

V. A Sober and Inclusive Language | 108

VI. A Hermeneutics of Paradox | 137

VII. Neutralizing the Paradox by an "Excess of Text": Textual Positivism | 174

VIII. Neutralizing the Paradox by a "Deficit of Text": Anthropocentric Subjectivism | 196

Conclusion: Reasonable Doubt: Learning How to Prolong the Power of Questions | 216

Bibliography | 221

Author Index | 229

Foreword

ANY SCHOLARLY DISCIPLINE STANDS within a tradition of interpretation. One such interpretive tradition, scientific rationalism, rose to prominence during the Enlightenment and proved so successful at quantifying and predicting natural processes that in the popular imagination the scientific method became the standard for truth. Scientists accept that the scientific method is extremely successful within a limited range of application, but they also recognize that science cannot make moral and aesthetic judgments with the same degree of certainty, cannot prescribe how scientific knowledge and technological advances ought to be used, and can neither prove nor disprove the transcendent claims of the world's many religions. Still, the misconception persists that moral and spiritual claims exist outside the realm of knowledge and continue to be denigrated as opinion instead of fact.

The issue is compounded within the discipline of Christian theology, relegated as it is to confessional seminaries and a few departments of theology at religiously affiliated colleges and universities, where certain ossified ideas narrowly define the task of theology as preserving tradition by repeating past formulations. Not only does this naïve view of tradition fail to make theological doctrines relevant in new cultural and historical contexts, but it also ignores the role of the interpreter in the creation and transmission of knowledge. Or, in the words of Hanz Gutierrez Salazar, the "interpreter is expected to leave his or her own imprint on the biblical language. Indeed, to add to that language something that it does not have" (p. 9). As historian Jaroslav Pelikan has noted, "Tradition is the living faith of the dead; traditionalism is the dead faith of the living."[1]

---

1. Pelikan, *Christian Tradition*, 9.

With the rise of secular modes of reasoning during the Enlightenment, theology and biblical hermeneutics were viewed with suspicion within the academy, so much so that some scholars considered non-canonical sources as more reliable than the canonical texts embraced as sacred Scripture by the community of faith. Thankfully, the dialogue between theological and philosophical hermeneutics has reached a sort of détente to the point that noted champion of secularization, Jürgen Habermas, acknowledges that the Enlightenment's exclusion of religion from the public discourse was misguided.[2]

Hanz Gutierrez Salazar's contribution to this conversation manages to take the Bible seriously as a source of divine self-communication while also recognizing the inherent ambivalent and polyvalent quality of biblical texts. In other words, doubt, uncertainty, and plurality are part of both the interpretive process and the personal journey of faith, to the chagrin of both the biblical literalist and the modern rationalist who desire the solace of "absolute certainty" (whatever that is). In place of epistemological certainty, Gutierrez offers ambivalence and paradox, a hermeneutics which does not aim at "a final and resolving synthesis of meaning" (p. 10) but embraces the unfinished and open-ended quality of human existence. In *Being and Time* (1927), Martin Heidegger argues that human beings are best conceived as *Dasein* ("being there"), not autonomous thinking selves or isolated rational minds, since the human experience is that of constantly negotiating one's identity in conversation with other beings within a given context, such that one is always uncovering and disclosing as much as hiding and concealing. That is why I have always thought that Heidegger's concept of *Dasein* as "being-in-the-world" is like finding yourself on a stage in the middle of the third act of a play: you have no script, and another actor has just given you your cue. Human beings are not passive receivers of knowledge but active creators and interpreters, and unlike the age of Enlightenment, the present moment welcomes faith as one of the ways of being authentically human in the world.

In *Reasonable Doubt: Learning to Dwell in Biblical Ambivalence and Paradox*, Hanz Gutierrez Salazar gives the religious believer and the non-religious observer a hermeneutical framework for engaging the Bible not as a dead letter forever stuck in the past, nor as an authoritarian moral compass from which there is no deviation, but as an encounter with the Other circumscribed by this simple paradox: a text written, preserved,

---

2. See Habermas et al., *Awareness of What Is Missing*.

and disseminated by human acts is also the Word of God. The author concludes, "Truth is only in the search for truth, and the engine of that search is reasonable doubt" (p. 206). Echoing the wisdom of past sages like Blaise Pascal and Søren Kierkegaard, Gutierrez reminds the patient reader that the journey is its own reward and that truth is a target one constantly aims at, even when all our efforts fall short of the mark. Given this open-ended and unfinished dimension of the hermeneutical task, a sense of humility, a receptiveness to differing perspectives, and a tolerance for multiple voices within a single text is needed to read the Bible in a way that moves beyond rote memorization. If, as Pelikan contends, doctrine is "what is believed, taught, and confessed,"[3] then Gutierrez's biblical hermeneutics of paradox challenges the dogmatic theologian to rethink the very nature of Christian doctrine. And that is a good thing.

Rubén Rosario Rodríguez, PhD
Clarence Louis and Helen Steber Professor of Theological Studies
Saint Louis University
St. Louis, Missouri
USA

---

3. Pelikan, *Christian Tradition*, 3.

Preface

"The Bible said it; I believe it; and that settles it!" For some, this simplistic hermeneutical methodology drives away doubts one might have about the Bible and masks contradictions embedded within the text. A universal interpretation is presented which is clear as to what is expected of believers, regardless of their social location and/or context. To question said universal interpretation is akin, at best, to heresy; at worse, to disbelief. In either case, such supposed heterodoxy requires silencing, lest others also be led astray. And it is this silencing which is responsible for some of the greatest abuses known to humanity. Think of the religious wars waged between Christians interpreting the text from different perspectives, or the cruelties of the Inquisition unleashed upon those deemed to be falling short of orthodoxy, or the countless people, mainly women, banished from their communities and murdered on charges of being witches, or the ships launched in pursuit of new colonial ventures for Christ, or the genocide of indigenous populations who stood in the way of colonialist Bible-thumpers. It seems that more dangerous than any army is the one person in authority who believes they hold the true and inerrant interpretation of Scripture.

What do we do when the text is misused to say what we want it to say, specifically proof-texting a spiritual justification for unearned power, privilege, and profit? The danger that humanity faces is how the interpretation of Scripture by the privileged is fused and confused with universal truth: dangerous because they possess the necessary power to make their subjective interpretation objective for everyone else, dangerous because there is no room for either suspicion or doubt of their interpretations. And yet, instructive are the words of father who came to Jesus asking for his son to be healed. When Jesus told him to believe in the healing, the father replied, "I do believe; help me overcome my doubt" (Mark 9:24). The biblical witness presents doubt as neither a sin nor an act of disbelief. Rather, doubt and suspicion are healthy hermeneutical tools which can be employed to make the biblical text relevant and useful for different communities occupying different contexts.

For this reason, Hanz Gutierrez Salazar's book—*Reasonable Doubt*—is an important contribution to the discourse. Understanding the complexity of faith, his hermeneutics of paradox moves us beyond simply a suspicion of interpretations, leading us to instead wrestle with the difficulty of ascertaining certainty from an ambivalence and at times contradictory text which is read by an ambivalent and a contradictory person. Rather than glossing over textual ambiguities or the internal tensions which exist, these contradictory texts, along with all their complexities, are preserved by choosing the mediation of the text to construct the meaning of the Christian faith.

While a scholarly attempt is usually made to find the so-called objective interpretation of the text, Gutierrez Salazar unabashedly embraces and encourages the interpreter of the text to leave their mark, providing biblical meaning relevant to the interpreter's specific social location. Rather than dismissing the interpreter as a threat to biblical meaning, Gutierrez Salazar empowers the interpreter to provide textual meaning, which leads to new hermeneutical perspectives rooted within different realities. This matrix of interpretative meanings raises healthy questions rather than providing a straitjacket of closed arguments, pregnant with definitive universal answers. Such an approach to the biblical text provides us with a methodology by which we can move away from a history of biblical interpretations that has spurred more harm than good.

Miguel A. De La Torre
Professor of Social Ethics and Latinx Studies
Iliff School of Theology/Denver University
Denver, Colorado
USA

Introduction
The Value of An Elusive Sense

BIBLICAL HERMENEUTICS IS COMMONLY conceived in Christianity as an event of clarification, as from an ambivalent—and even obscure—text, we arrive, through the act of interpretation, at a clarity of meaning.

Christianity introduces this desire for clarity, even before the act of interpretation, at an even more fundamental level and applies it to God himself. The God of the Bible, in fact, is conceived as a God who wants to reveal himself and make his will manifest.

If we consider a third dimension in which this engagement with clarity is visible and manifest—in the understanding of the nature of the Bible and then in the understanding of the Bible as a clear and unambiguous book—then the sequence is completed. God, the Bible, and the act of interpretation would be three moments of clarity that describe spiritual experience as an intelligible, coherent, and transparent event. This is what Catholic theologian Bruno Forte[1] calls the obsession with clarity and what Protestant theologian Dietrich Bonhoeffer[2] calls *Offenbarungpositivismus*, "the positivism of Revelation."

This way of thinking about the act of interpretation, seemingly legitimate and the basis of the believer's spiritual journey, however, denies the true nature of the Bible, the complexity of the experience of faith, and also ignores the way God and his action are articulated in history.

---

1. This is, for example, Bruno Forte's critique of the Protestant concept of *Offenbarung* (revelation), where the sense of concealment and mystery inherent in the biblical conception of revelation is lost and which the Latin equivalent, "Revelatio," instead keeps intact. Forte, "Sacred Scripture and Theology," 30–42.

2. See the complete letter written from Tegel Prison on April 30, 1944. Bonhoeffer, *Widerstand und Ergebung*, 137–142.

In this essay, we will propose a different conception of hermeneutics that starts from thinking of the Bible as an ambivalent text and thinks of hermeneutics as an event in which this ambivalence is not annulled or overcome, but preserved. It is what we call the "Hermeneutics of Paradox." To grasp this central feature of Hermeneutics, its structural "ambivalence," let us begin with a brief comparison of two kinds of knowledge, that promoted by Plato in Book VII of the Republic and that presupposed by Hermeneutics.

Plato[3] not only upholds the superiority of *episteme* (reason) over *doxa* (opinion) but, within *episteme* itself, the superiority of intellect (*nòesis*) over analytical reason (*dianoia*). Argumentative reason (*dianoia*) in use, for example, in mathematics, still finds too many footholds, according to Plato, in the sensible world, since it starts from unproven assumptions drawn from objects perceived by the senses. In contrast, intellectual knowledge (*nòesis*) is supreme precisely because it proceeds only by intuition and does not resort to any kind of mediation. It is direct and immediate through contemplation.

Hermeneutics, compared to the Platonic intellect, is completely different in nature. It rejects the immediate path of intellect and deliberately chooses the path of sense mediated through a text. For Plato, hermeneutics is inferior and unreliable knowledge because it relies on mediation in a structural way. For hermeneutics, however, immediate knowledge, the contemplative knowledge of the mystics or Plato's intellectual knowledge, is riddled with stumbling blocks and recurring risks. This is why it introduces an additional step that serves as a corrective filter and a place of verification of the meaning that is arising. This place of verification and filter is represented by the passage through the text.

Hermeneutic knowledge recognizes its own slowness in the construction of meaning, conditioned by an additional step in the cognitive process, which is that of the text. The text necessarily slows down the articulation of meaning. At the same time, hermeneutics makes a claim. It is able to offer better meaning because it is filtered through an additional step. The passage through the text actually does not restrict meaning, but enhances and expands it through what Paul Ricœur calls the mechanism of "distantiation."[4]

---

3. Plato, *Republic*, Book VI, 509d-511e.
4. Ricœur, *Philosophical Hermeneutics and Biblical Hermeneutics*, 53–78.

This mechanism creates separation and detachment between the author and his message, between the author and the original addressee, and between the dialogists and the immediate external reality (reference). These three forms of distancing are possible only because of the text. This detachment (distancing), introduced at these three levels by the text, is not a negative detachment (*verfremdung*).[5] It is a mechanism that ensures the enhancement of meaning through a positive detachment of otherness (*entfremdung*).[6]

Hermeneutics bases its claim to validity on the bet of the text as "distantiation," as a mechanism for the expansion of meaning. We now turn our attention to the validity of this claim of biblical hermeneutics, which is based on a mechanism opposite to that of intellectual knowledge (*nòesis*) articulated by Plato.

Hermeneutics is the choice of mediation as a means of constructing the meaning of the Christian faith. Not only Catholic Christianity but also Protestant Christianity, with its strong reference to the Bible, is a religion of mediation. As such it requires a hermeneutic that takes seriously the ambivalence of the text and the ambivalence of the reader (Hermeneutic Circle).

Interpretation is not the repetition of the biblical language and its message as the reader found them. That would be pure tautology and, as an interpretive event, perfectly useless. No, interpretation adds specification to the Bible read. The interpreter does not stand before the biblical message as a purely decorative element, as an ornamental hermeneutical element with no real impact on the meaning-making process.

The interpreter is expected to leave his or her own imprint on the biblical language. Indeed, to add to that language something that it does not have. By his intervention, the interpreter ennobles the Bible because he converts its latency of meaning into something specific. The interpreter is not only a potential deformer from whom to protect the sacred text, but he is also a necessary enhancer of the sacred text. And he does so as a ferryman of meaning that, from latent, becomes explicit by virtue of extra-textual events that allow one to look at the Bible from new perspectives. In this sense, it is as if the Bible awaits the creative hand of

---

5. *Verfremdung* in German, translated as alienation in the sense of estrangement or estrangement. For a description of the role of "distantiation" in the process of Interpretation, see Gadamer, *Truth and Method*.

6. Translated as alienation, but in the sense of otherness or detachment.

the interpreter to deliver to the world meanings that, without this hand, would remain purely potential and in a state of latency.

This is what we mean by the hermeneutics of ambivalence and paradox. Among ambivalence and paradox, the common element is given by the synchronic existence of different possible meanings. Both are thus declensions in the plural. In ambivalence and paradox, plurality is not lost, but becomes the hallmark of the interpretive act in all its stages. The interpreter is required to maintain and reproduce in his interpretation the plurality he has found in the Bible and which is not to be overcome in the new meaning found.

Derived meaning does not mark the disappearance or exhaustion of biblical language and its plurality. How to maintain the biblical message and language without being tautological and without denying the necessary addition of the interpreter and his creative intervention? The challenge is therefore daunting and can be summed up in this maxim: the exuberance and sobriety of biblical language must be prolonged in the interpretation that the interpreter constructs from the Bible.

Ambivalence and paradox, while similar, are not entirely identical. Ambivalence refers to a plurality of senses that coexist together and may eventually converge until they overlap. In paradox, on the other hand, there is a plurality that does not assimilate but remains in tension. In paradox, the senses present remain asymmetrical and unassimilated, but it is this structural tension that provides the space in which the senses manifest and confront each other, thus opening up a horizon of meaning. Ambivalence and paradox are thus two looks at the plurality of meaning, similar but different.

This is the essence of a hermeneutics of paradox. A hermeneutic that aims to prolong questions rather than to close them with final and resolving answers. The biblical hermeneutics of paradox does not aim at a final and resolving synthesis of meaning. It is not identified with a hermeneutic of transparent clarity. It remains, from the beginning to the end of the interpretive process, linked to the complexity and productive tension it can create.

This dynamic complexity, i.e., of paradox,[7] is expressed at three levels.

1. At the intratextual level, bringing out in the text itself a tension of meaning that is the cradle of all meaning.

---

7. Galimberti, *Footsteps of the Sacred*, 35–61. See also Galimberti, *The Body*, 11–27.

INTRODUCTION   xix

2. At the extra-textual level, highlighting that even in the life of the person reading the text there are paradoxes that create existential tensions parallel to those in the text.
3. At the level of linkage, the non-synthetic comparison and juxtaposition between paradoxes inside and paradoxes outside the text: it is in the tense space between inside and outside the text that meaning occurs and is given.

Biblical hermeneutics is not only complex in the sense of its plurality. This plurality is not always complementary. Sometimes it presents itself as irreducible. It does not integrate but resists synthesis. Paradox is thus a guarantee of truth. The Bible works with a structural tension that does not wear it down but makes it possible. It is in essence a hermeneutics of paradox.

But paradox is not easily identified. Therefore, a hermeneutics of paradox cannot be immediate. It presupposes legitimate prior levels of interpretation that cannot claim to express the main perspective of the text. Only when one discovers the paradox that grounds a text can one claim not to exhaust the text, but to follow its horizon. A text reveals its message and offers itself to the reader only from its central paradox. This is why all texts of the Bible are difficult, because the paradox that grounds them is not immediately traceable. Below we list four levels at which paradoxes can emerge.

a. Proximal-immediate paradox

The proximal-immediate paradox is given when it emerges in proximity, in the same verse, but it does not mean that its understanding is instantaneous. It just means that the paradox is closer spatially than one might imagine. It is found in the same verse. An example is Psalm 119:105. Here we find the paradox of a light that more than illuminates the path illuminates the foot of the walker.

b. Proximal-deferred paradox

The proximal-differential paradox is given when this emerges not in the same verse but within the entire passage or entire chapter of reference. This means that reading, let alone hasty application, is not sufficient to grasp the central address of the passage. Since it is deferred, this paradox is grasped only later, after much reading and reflection, which, however, should not create habit or habituation. The challenge is to maintain repeated and recurrent reading without erasing the imagination. An example of this kind of paradox can be found in Psalm 23, where the first metaphor (the shepherd) is a theocentric metaphor, while the second (God-homemaker) is an anthropocentric metaphor that contrasts with the first making possible a dual version of the identity and action of both God and the human.

c. Distal intratextual paradox

Distal intratextual paradox occurs when it does not emerge in the same verse nor in the same chapter, but at a distance (distal), either in other chapters of the same book or in a different book of the Bible. This means that reading, much less hasty application, is not sufficient to grasp the central address of the passage read. Because it is distal, one grasps it only later, after several readings not only of the passage in question, but of the whole book in which it is found. Reading the whole book should be neither scattershot nor monolithic, for it is a matter, through familiarity with style, typing of themes and imagination, of finding connections and highlighting them. An example of this kind of paradox is found in the thematic parallelism between these two verses: Lk 14:26 and Eph 6:1,2, where two contrasting calls coexist in tension, the first, Luke's call to leave the family to follow Christ, and the second, that of the epistle to the Ephesians, which instead calls to follow him by remaining in the very family.

d. Distal extratextual paradox

The extra-textual distal paradox occurs when this emerges not in the same verse, nor in the same chapter, nor even in the Bible, but at a distance (distal) and in relation to a non-biblical fact or event occurring in reality itself. This requires a different effort. A different reading of the Bible. A knowing how to read not only the Bible, but also reality and everyday common life. This extra-textual distal paradox reminds us that the Bible cannot be read alone. We must, along with it, know how to read reality and the world. Being distal, this paradox is grasped only later, after various readings, which also include non-Biblical readings.

INTRODUCTION

The Bible is not the whole of reality but only an important part of it, therefore, to grasp its message we cannot escape but must confront the reality to which the Bible is a witness, guide and reflection. It is the Bible itself that pushes us toward reality. If this does not happen, it is a clear sign that we are reading it wrongly. The Bible is a map of reality, not reality itself. And this extra-textual distal paradox reminds us of this very essential fact. To read the Bible well, we must read it together and not instead of reality. We find an example of this kind of paradox in the contrast of a biblical text, 1 Corinthians 14:34,35, where a clear limitation of women's freedom is articulated, with today's world where awareness and respect for women's rights, compressed with the right of speech, have found a full and across-the-board recognition that can hardly be recused.

The "hermeneutics of paradox,"[8] characterized by its "plurivocity" (complexity), is nothing but the extension of biblical language and its corresponding plurivocity to the level of the interpreter. It is the plurivocity (complexity) that characterizes the two terms of the "hermeneutic circle." The plurivocity of the text must also remain as the plurivocity of the reader reading that text called the Bible. The plurivocity of the text cannot resolve itself into the univocity of the reader and the interpretation he or she processes. The reader is not the locus of the ultimate epiphany of meaning. The legitimate transport that each reader experiences in discovering a sense of the text, but certainly not of the totality of possible senses, is and must remain a partial and transitory transport. Hermeneutic messianism is not a reality that is consummated in the present, but always refers forward and describes a meaning that is always on the way.

The reader is not an endpoint of the text, but a continuation of it and as such must prolong the essential datum of the text, which is its plurivocity. For this reason, hermeneutics as an interpretive act must necessarily be as paradoxical as the reading text is. Interpretive resumption cannot be limited to resuming only the content. It must also take up and prolong the form in which that content is expressed in the text. That is, its plurivocal form.

It is true that every interpretive take must add a clarification that the text does not have, otherwise that interpretation would remain a tautology of the text. Such clarification legitimately added by the interpreter, however, cannot liquidate and make caducous the formal plurivocity of the text. This is the challenge. The plurivocity of the read text must be

---

8. See Chapter VI of this essay entitled "A Hermeneutics of Paradox," pp. 121–181.

able to be transcribed into the new language that the interpreter uses to express what he or she has drawn from the read text. In other words, the interpreter must be able to ensure the transcription of the content into a new context, but at the same time also be able to extend the plurivocal linguistic form of the biblical text into the new languages in which the interpreter transcribes the collected message.

The plurivocity of interpretation is given and guaranteed by certain elements. The first is the impermanence of the sense found. The sense found cannot be a definitive sense, otherwise the interpretation becomes more important than the text it interprets. The second is the plurality of meanings worked out by the interpreter himself. The interpreter's interpretation must never be monolithic: not only out of constraint to the subjective openness of the reader, but especially out of obligation to objective fidelity to the interpreted text (Bible). Every good interpretation creates its own alternatives. Finally, the plurality of interpreters. The interpreter and his or her system of reference (church, community, ideology) must recognize and coexist with other systems and with the different senses that these differentiated systems have worked out.

The biblical hermeneutics of paradox does not aim at the answer but at the extension and enrichment of the question. Biblical hermeneutics is not and cannot be a synthetic and resolving instance of meaning. It is not a hermeneutics of clarity but of complexity. Indeed, of dynamic complexity—that is, of paradox.[9] The meaning sought thus always remains an elusive meaning, both in the text from which one starts (the Bible), the account taken of its structural ambivalence, and in the interpretation to which the reader arrives because that legitimate and necessary interpretation nevertheless remains partial and transitory, capable of touching the meaning only tangentially and provisionally.

---

9. Galimberti, *Footsteps of the Sacred*, 35–61. See also Galimberti, *Body*, 11–27.

I

From Reading to Interpretation and the Other Way Round

HERMENEUTICS EXPRESSES A PARTICULAR way of knowledge. This is knowledge through a text. The text is the element that qualifies a knowledge as hermeneutic. The center of hermeneutics is thus the act of interpreting a text.[1] While it is true that the obligation to go through a text slows down and problematizes the process of sense articulation, it is equally true that the sense gained becomes better. It creates the mechanism of its own verification and filter, which in this case is provided by the text itself, its projection, and the "alternative and experimental world"[2] that each text tries to delineate and suggest.

There is no immediate or automatic meaning. Meaning is the product of a struggle, which many times becomes an open adventure. Meaning is an earned result and not a presupposed intuition. Meaning is not arrived at immediately through an intuition, a stroke of genius, or an illumination. It is earned through the suffered, slow, and demanding passage of reading and close confrontation with a text.

---

1. Zimmermann, *Hermeneutics*, 1–18.

2. Paul Ricœur calls the project that each text suggests the "world of the text," and it represents for him the center of every interpretive act because it encloses the main axes of the proposition that each text articulates and carries. Cf. *Dal testo all'azione* . . . Ricœur, *Philosophical Hermeneutics*, 121–25.

Hermeneutics is a praise of the text as a mediator of better meanings. The text serves as a positive obstacle in the face of the craving and enthusiasm for immediate, clear, and functional meanings. Hermeneutics is a typical cognitive strategy that makes mediation a value and an obligatory step. This mediation is provided by the passage through the text.

Various conceptions subsist on the text. Essentially, there are two.

The first is a weak conception of the text. It considers the text merely as a supporting element to a thought or idea without touching them or even changing their essence.

The second is a strong conception of text. In this case, a text is not limited to being a mnemotechnical support of the oral message. Its function is more central. The message itself is profoundly altered when it becomes text.

There survives in all of us the nostalgia for the spoken word and the belief that the best communication is verbal communication. Writing, one is convinced, must still be surpassed by the warmth and immediacy of the spoken word. The word preceded the text, and it is still the word redeemed by the reading of a text in the process of understanding and assimilating the message. Writing is cold, anonymous, and too formal, one thinks. Instead, the word behind it, which must be resurrected, carries the force and persuasion of a warm and immediate message. It is as if the text is only a necessary evil.

The idea is adduced that talking face-to-face, *viva voce*, avoids misunderstandings related to text mediation. The more direct the communication, the better. Clearly, the advantage of oral communication lies in its freshness and overwhelming immediacy. However, this does not erase misunderstandings. Indeed, at another level, oral communication, through speech, increases these misunderstandings. In oral communication, which necessarily takes place in real time, words and replies to words cannot be stopped. The communicative flow must be guaranteed because it is that flow in its immediacy and naturalness that is the strength of oral language.[3]

In the freshness and immediacy of this flow of orality, spoken words find their strength but also their limitation. That flow overwhelms them, overlaps them, jostles them, bumps them, halves them, exasperates them, accelerates them. Indeed, they are forced by this flow to become fast

---

3. Ong, *Orality ad Literacy*, 5–15.

words, less thought-out words, instinctive words, words that are easy and immediate but not necessarily the best.

The undoubted greater coolness of the text brings with it necessary corrective benefits. The written word which becomes text can become a thought, a verified and filtered word—that is, a text. The text is a written word, therefore a thought, and for this reason is balanced, becoming an objective sign that communicates better, even if more slowly, the intentions and will of those in dialogue. This is the bet of hermeneutics and its praise of the text as a tool for better communication.

Hermeneutics is not the only possible way of knowing. Life in general, and religious life in particular, continually confront us with a variety of ways of knowing. It is true that some specific experiences tend to privilege a particular kind of knowledge, that which is most akin, relevant, and functional to the area involved. But the best human experiences are never monolithic and always introduce a diversity of approaches and perspectives. These various ways of knowing are not always complementary. Sometimes they are called to coexist in tension. For this reason, two basic principles should generally be kept in mind about the Bible and Christian knowledge.

1. The approach to the Bible must be able to make room for a variety of ways of knowing. It would be reductive to want to exhaust the relationship with the Bible by limiting it to a single cognitive strategy. Nor can biblical hermeneutics alone ascribe this prerogative to itself. Various types of biblical hermeneutics[4] are possible, but so are strategies that will be critical of the hermeneutic cognitive model as such. It is well that it should be so, because hermeneutics, while representing an important mode of reading, in our opinion the best,[5]

---

4. Grondin, *Introduction to Philosophical Hermeneutics*, 124–39.

5. In this sense we make our own the conviction, expressed by Claude Geffré, that in today's historical period, with the limitations and side effects that must be continually monitored, theological reason has become structurally hermeneutic. And it would become so in rupture with "speculative reason," which for centuries has characterized theology in a clear connection with Greek thought. The distancing from this metaphysical reason prompted us to approach theology from a "historical understanding." To think of theology as hermeneutical would be uniquely to draw the consequences from this shift from a "metaphysical understanding" to a "historical understanding" of reality. Geffré writes, "When, however, the notion of order is challenged in the modern era, we necessarily move from a still axiomatic understanding to an empirical and historical conception of science that is defined by experiment: its object, in effect, is not eternal truth but history and the totality of phenomena. Since, by definition, God escapes the limits of reason, the object of theology will be transformed. Theology tends to

nevertheless does not have a monopoly on reading the Bible. In defending its own legitimacy, hermeneutic knowledge will also have to defend the legitimacy of this cognitive diversity in which it itself fits.

2. These various cognitive modes sometimes complement each other, sometimes they do not. They can create a tension which is given by their non-assimilability. This tension is not in itself negative. On the contrary, tension makes sense possible and guarantees it in its articulation. Sense emerges within that tension, which one must know how to keep alive. The arc that that tension creates must never disappear even when the final sense, which is always a provisional sense, has been achieved. Sense can occur and survive only within that tensional arc.

A THEOLOGICAL-CULTURAL LOOK AT HERMENEUTICS[6]

Hermeneutics is not the only form of knowledge. To better identify its specificity, we will try to parallel it with a different and even opposite kind of knowledge. The opposition between different ways of knowing is classically expressed, for example, by Blaise Pascal in one of his most famous thoughts:

> The heart has its own reasons that reason does not know.[7]

---

understand itself not simply as a discourse about God, but as a discourse that reflects on language about God, language that speaks humanly about God. Everyone recognizes the prerogative that is now given to the humanities of religion in the study of religion, in particular, to a linguistic approach to religious language. There is no direct knowledge of reality outside of language, and language is always an interpretation." Geffré, *Credere e interpretare*, 19–21.

6. Reflection on the scope and validity of hermeneutics is part of the discipline that goes by the name "theory of knowledge," a philosophical discipline that deals with problems related to the nature, acquisition, and growth of different forms of human knowledge. See Cevolanti et al., "Dalla filosofia alla scienza," 5–14. Although the classical formula expressed in the "tripartite definition" of propositional knowledge formulated by Plato in the Theaetetus (206–208) as "a true and justified belief," has lately been the subject of criticism (Gettier, "Is Justified True Belief Knowledge?"), the underlying questions all remain, and all of them directly concern the purported validity of hermeneutic knowledge. See Piazza, *Che cos'è la conoscenza*, 27–35; Audi, *Epistemologia*, 8–24; O'Brien, *Theory of Knowledge*, 10–21; Vassallo, *Teoria della conoscenza*, 30–41.

7. Pascal, *Pensieri*, 277.

Human intelligence is not only analytical-discursive but also synthetic-intuitive. This intuitive capacity Pascal attributes to the heart. It is obvious that, in this sense, the heart has its own reasons that reason must merely presuppose with respect and docility because they are foreign to it. To honor the legitimacy of this cognitive diversity and try to understand its deeper meaning, we will try, in this introduction, to compare two kinds of knowledge: the hermeneutic way of knowing and the rational "intellectual" way that Plato calls *noesis*. We will try, by grasping the difference, to understand the specificity of each, particularly that specificity that distinguishes the nature and scope of hermeneutic knowledge.

Plato compares knowledge to a line.[8] This line is then divided into two segments, corresponding respectively to lower sensible knowledge (*dòxa*) and higher rational knowledge (*epistéme*), which are divided in turn into two other subspecies of knowledge. Four types of knowledge are thus delineated. At the lowest level we find sensible knowledge (*dòxa*), also called opinion. On the one hand, it includes conjecture (*eikasia*) or knowledge by images, which has for its object the shadows of things that remain unrelated to each other. On the other hand, again in an ascending sense, there is belief (*pistis*), or knowledge through visible objects, which aims at grasping sensible things in their mutual relations.

At a higher level, we have rational knowledge, also called science (*epistéme*). This includes discursive reason (*diànoia*), which has mathematical ideas as its object, It also includes, at the highest level, "intellectual reason" (*nòesis*) or philosophical intelligence, which has immutable ideas as its object and proceeds only through intuition.

Plato not only argues for the superiority of *episteme* (reason) over *doxa* (opinion) but, within *episteme* itself, the superiority of intellect (*nòesis*) over analytical reason (*dianoia*). Argumentative reason (*dianoia*) in use, for example, in mathematics, still finds too many footholds, according to Plato, in the sensible world, since it starts from unproven assumptions drawn through objects perceived by the senses. In contrast, intellectual knowledge (*nòesis*) is supreme precisely because it proceeds only by intuition and has no recourse to any kind of mediation. It is direct and immediate through contemplation.

We might call Platonic and ancient idealism "objective" because it does not make ideas dependent on the knowing subject. This is different in kind from modern idealism, i.e., ours, which is instead a "subjective"

---

8. Plato, *Republic*, Book VI, 509d-511e.

idealism characterized by the dependence of ideas on the knowing subject. This is why modern idealism is constructivist and pragmatic, while Platonic idealism is a contemplative, intuitive idealism and does not resort to any mediation.

Hermeneutics, in comparison with the Platonic intellect, is of an entirely different nature. It rejects the immediate path of the intellect and deliberately chooses the path of sense mediated through a text. For Plato, hermeneutics is inferior and unreliable knowledge because it relies on mediation in a structural way. For hermeneutics, immediate knowledge, the contemplative knowledge of the mystics, or the intellectual knowledge of Plato is seeded with stumbling blocks and recurring risks. For this reason it introduces an additional step that serves as a corrective filter and a place of verification of the sense that is arising. This place of verification and filter is represented by the passage through the text.

Hermeneutic knowledge recognizes its own slowness in the construction of meaning, conditioned by an additional step in the cognitive process, which is that of the text. The text necessarily slows down the articulation of meaning. At the same time, hermeneutics articulates a claim. This is that it is able to offer a better sense because it is filtered by an additional passage. The passage through the text does not actually narrow the sense but enhances and expands it through what Paul Ricœur calls the mechanism of "distanciation."[9]

This mechanism creates separation and detachment between the author and his or her message, between the author and the original addressee, and between the dialogists and the immediate external reality (reference). These three forms of distancing are possible only because of the text. This detachment (distanciation), introduced at these three levels by the text is not a negative detachment (*verfremdung*).[10] It is a mechanism that guarantees the enhancement of meaning through a positive detachment of otherness (*entfremdung*).[11]

Hermeneutics bases its claim to validity on the bet of the text as "distanciation" as a sense-expanding mechanism. We now turn our attention to the validity of this claim of biblical hermeneutics, which is

---

9. Ricœur, *Ermeneutica filosofica*, 53–78.

10. *Verfremdung* is a German word, translated to English as "alienation" in the sense of estrangement.

11. In English this is also translated as "alienation" but in the sense of otherness or detachment.

founded on a mechanism opposite to that of the intellectual knowledge (*nòesis*) articulated by Plato.

Hermeneutics is the choice of mediation as a means of constructing the meaning of the Christian faith. Not only Catholic but also Protestant Christianity, with its strong reference to the Bible, is a religion of mediation. As such it requires a hermeneutic. What is hermeneutics?[12] Let us try to describe it through the path of some stages.

READING[13] THE BIBLE

Since it is a book, the Bible can be approached from two strategies that are complementary but different in nature. One is through reading, which leads immediately to application. The other is through interpretation, which, moving from reading, also reaches application but more slowly. Those who choose the first option tend to be wary of interpretation and see it not only as a mechanism for slowing down the achievement of meaning but also as a space of risk for meaning itself. Those who choose the second, on the other hand, will see the interpretive slowdown as a positive mechanism for verifying meanings, which from a simple reading almost always arrive one-sided and distorted.

These two moments should be sequential and complementary.[14] Today there is a large cohort of Christians, especially in the most dynamic and high-growth churches and groupings, who in reaction to an overly rational approach to the Bible choose the short route from reading to application. This hermeneutical choice, naïve though often well-intentioned (because even those who choose not to interpret are actually interpreting anyway), is doubly short-sighted. First, it accedes to and follows the implicit traditional interpretation, the least current and therefore the worst, which it mistakenly identifies with the Bible itself, illegitimately imposing it as incontrovertible fact. Second, it forgoes constructing a current interpretation, which is the one most likely to become the best by virtue

---

12. Ricœur, *Dal testo all'azione*, 11–34. Ferraris, *Storia dell'ermeneutica*, 5–7.

13. In this section and throughout our text, we will assume two types of readings. One that is closed in on itself and another that instead is open to interpretation. When this happens, then we are talking about a successful reading, as Werner G. Jeanrond does. Jeanrond, *Ermeneutica teologica*, 157–201.

14. In this regard, Jeanrond put it this way: "Hermeneutics is most interested in the analysis of the dialectic between reader and text, and the effects of this dialectic on the self-understanding of the individual reader or groups of readers." *Ermeneutica teologica*, 17–18.

of its respect for the addressee, the projection of the text, and the challenges present in the context.

The setting aside of interpretation in favor of reading and its immediate application unfortunately does not give birth to the best meanings, whether those present in the text itself or those that could be created from the text in its interaction with the current context. Haste, which tends to become an obsession to achieve meaning quickly, prevents one from seeing the complexity of the text with its richness and variety of possible meanings. It is still the same haste in application that also drives the reader to overlook the opportunities offered by the external context as stimuli for looking at the text from different perspectives.

The intended self-sufficient reading to grasp the meaning of the text hides yet another more insidious and distorting anomaly. This is the presumption and certainty behind the rush for immediate meaning that the text is transparent and unambiguous. This is the most important error of disallowing the nature of the biblical text, of thinking that the biblical text is a clear text whose meaning is immediately and automatically within the reach of the reader's sincerity and zeal.

These readers presume that the only task to be accomplished is to assume an attitude of listening and waiting in the face of a text that alone gives itself and delivers itself limpidly to the sincere reader. The complexity and difficulty, they think, comes not from the text but from the reader, from his or her laziness or prejudices. This is a very common hermeneutic fallacy. Unfortunately, very often, it is directly proportional to the sincerity and spiritual eagerness of the believer on duty.

This reductive gaze with respect to the text is subsequently prolonged and validated also in the reductive gaze with respect to reality itself. Even external reality, with which the text always tries to compare itself (linguistic reference), becomes, in this kind of reading, a crushed reality because it is reduced to its clarity. It is a non-reality, a falsified reality. The result is the implicit and unconscious hermeneutic union and fellowship between a "textual reductionism" and a "reductionism of the reality." The path of sincere reading of the Bible, with its immediate application, does not offer a horizon of authentic growth. It represents at its base a paradoxical form of spiritual involution. "Read and apply" seems the best and most direct option. Certainly, it is the fastest. It is not necessarily the best.

INTERPRETING THE BIBLE

Hermeneutics is the art of interpreting a text.[15] Every text represents an otherness, an obstacle, a challenge. If the Bible is the text par excellence, this means that the difficulty in confronting it will be even greater. This is probably why euphoric Christians in constant search of spiritual sugars of immediate assimilation not only tend to run away from the arduous path of hermeneutics; it often happens that they also end up calling it the very antithesis of truth. But it is easy to see which side is common sense and which side is the "chaff that the wind scatters."[16]

In the hermeneutic way, reading is not erased. It becomes a necessary but not unique step and, even less, a conclusive step. Rather, reading opens the reader to the complication of the relationship with another text that is external to them and that they do not possess. It is as the presence of a person whom I find in my path and who in no way belongs to me. Indeed, the other person I find on my path offers me a difficult but more direct relationship than a text requires of me, because with the other person the relationship is articulated in the immediacy of verbal dialogue without interposition or mediation. Text, on the other hand, represents an even more indirect way of dialogue and consequently slows down the communicative process more markedly. In this sense, the interpretation of a text is typically a mediated route to meanings.

This fact invites us to a different reflection on Protestantism. Various times Protestantism is described as the religion of immediacy in the face of the typically Catholic and medieval burdening of religious experience that tends instead to create countless steps. In reality, this is not the case. Protestantism, like Catholicism and like Christianity in general, is a typical religion of mediation, not immediacy. God is not reached directly. The mediator is Christ and with him his Word, the Bible.

The true religions of immediacy radically combat the idea that to get to God one must go through a book. Even those Christian forms of mysticism throughout history that have had a critical look at religious formalities have never been able to truly detach themselves from the foundational Christian text, the Bible. The difference between Catholics and Protestants, in their common defense of religious mediation as the foundational mechanism of Christianity, lies elsewhere. It concerns the nature and quantity of necessary mediations, not their denial.

15. Ferraris, *Ermeneutica*, 3–31.
16. Ps 1:4.

This fundamental trait of the Christian religion emerges and becomes visible in the choice of interpretation as a way to approach the Bible. Biblical hermeneutics is the linguistic way of expressing the very essence of Christianity as mediation. On the other hand, reading[17] represents a deformation of it with immediate application Wanting to limit oneself to only reading the Bible with the corresponding immediate application is not only a hermeneutical deformation; even more fundamentally, it is a theological deformation because it dispenses with and denies the structurally mediated character of Christian faith. The obsession with a reading and its immediate application is a typically modern deformation.

The rush to read, understanding just what's necessary to apply it with a view to a visible and quick result, is a typical deformation of our times that is nefarious and dangerous. Besides being abnormal, it claims to be the model to follow. In addition to this harm, it also represents a mockery of the text. This interpretative dysfunction is typical of our times because of the pragmatism it expresses. We could call it the way of "practical mysticism." This oxymoron expresses well the two components of this modern anomaly. On the one hand, there is the desire for immediacy typical of any mysticism; on the other hand, there is the desire for concreteness typical of contemporary pragmatism. Biblical pragmatism, a plague of our time as much as biblical indifference is, is a phenomenon that we moderns have given birth to and cannot transfer to other eras.

The simplicity of access to the Bible certainly existed in other eras and was also widespread. But this simplicity of approach to the Bible in other ages was an enchanted and mysterious simplicity. The simplicity claimed by today's biblical pragmatism is disenchanted and manipulative. This introduces an immediacy without mystique that, as such, could only arise in our time.

This passage through the text is therefore central to hermeneutics.[18] Text is strictly defined as a writing produced by an author and intended for a reader. This does not mean that the meaning of the text is circumscribable only to the author's intention or that the scope of the meaning

---

17. Reading is essential in the interpretive process, that reading which does not close in on itself but turns into a dialogue with the text. This reading embodies the essence of interpretation. See Schökel and Bravo Aragon, *Appunti di ermeneutica*, 83–102.

18. This shift from text is essential in hermeneutics. Not only in the sense that without text there would be no trace of what needs to be interpreted, but the text is the true goal of interpretation beyond the author who wrote that text and its intentionality. See Schökel and Bravo Aragon, *Appunti di ermeneutica*, 25–38.

conveyed is exhausted in the interpretive logic of the original recipient. On the contrary, the meaning of what hermeneutics is and what it implies is at stake in the extension of meanings beyond the original author's intention and in the broadening of the interpreting community into potential recipients not included in the primary addressee.

The guiding question is to try to understand what the text really is and what the reader in fact represents. Can a text, which tends to make itself autonomous from its original author, consult circumstantial readers not envisaged in the initial configuration of the primary recipient, without distorting and altering the basic text? Or is hermeneutics precisely the legitimization of this alteration?

For the Christian, understanding this process is vitally important because Christianity has tied its destiny in an irreversible and primary way to understanding a text, the Bible. Many religions reconnect with a text to recount their origin, to think about the reality around them, and to articulate their own response to it. Although many religions develop reflections from a sacred text, not in all religions does that sacred text have the importance and primary status that the Bible has for Christianity. Christianity is necessarily, and across the whole spectrum of its manifestations, a hermeneutical religion from its inception and not by historical accident.[19]

The need to understand what interpretation is imposes itself on the twenty-first century believer not only from the essence of his own religion but also from the profoundly changed external cultural context. Contemporary culture, modern and postmodern, has made the book the privileged mechanism for gathering information about reality and on this to build one's own way of standing before the world.

Today the Christian is forced to interpret not only his Bible but also all the texts that accompany the natural and secular development of his life. Within one's own faith community, Bible commentaries, community organization manuals, catechetical texts, institutional statements, newspapers, magazines and the various texts produced within it are to be read as well as the Bible.

From this brief introductory description, the reader comes to a rather clear perception that hermeneutics, and the interpretation of texts, is not a secondary component of being a Christian today. It represents its central node. Without close confrontation with one's foundational text,

---

19. Geffré, *Credere e interpretare*, 11–43.

the Bible, the resulting faith profile is already born deformed, although the effects will only be visible over time. It is therefore required of the believer to understand as best he can what is at stake when he reads and interprets a text such as the Bible. Let us pause now to consider some important implications that this wager on interpretation carries.

THE DUAL HERMENEUTICAL NATURE OF CHRISTIANITY[20]

A first element to be taken up and carefully considered is the extent of the interpretive dimension in the very structure of Christianity. Christianity is a religion closely linked to a book, the Bible; this fact necessarily sets in motion an interpretive process. We often hear that interpretation undermines the Word of God because, through interpretation, one would like to make the Bible say not what it really says but what one thinks it says. Effectively, interpretation carries a risk. But it must not be forgotten that non-interpretation also carries with it other risks. On the balance of risks of interpreting and non-interpreting, the risks of non-interpreting probably weigh more heavily.

The risks of interpreting are essentially two. The first is weakening the Bible by making it an interpreted word. The Bible becomes a more relative and therefore less binding and definitive Word. Second is elevating to a binding word a word that is instead only an interpretation, replacing the Word of God with a human word.

The risks of not interpreting are also essentially two. First, making it irrelevant by not updating it. Second, making the absolute a relative interpretation of the past. The risks are certain in both cases. Fundamentally, through different mechanisms, they consist in elevating what is purely circumstantial to a binding word. In the case of non-interpretation, the problem is to make binding not only a human word that passes itself off as divine but also a word that has in addition the sin of not being actual and relevant.

20. This dual characterization of Christian hermeneutics is described by Jeanrond in the following terms: "The early Christians thus had a twofold hermeneutical problem: 1. Initially almost always of Jewish background, they reinterpreted their Hebrew scriptures in the light of their experience of Jesus, his proclamation, death and resurrection; 2. They themselves put together, as time went on, a second body of scripture—New Testament—which, as it became increasingly canonical, that is, normative, ended up requiring appropriate interpretive strategies as well" (Jeanrond, *Ermeneutica teologica*, 33–41).

Interpretation cannot be replaced by pure application. This is not only because interpretation has the merit of making an ancient word present. It is also because interpretation becomes the true site of verification of relative words that want to pass themselves off as absolute. Beyond these undoubted benefits of the interpretive process, Christianity is a hermeneutical religion for two structural reasons.

First, because it starts from an ancient book that needs to be interpreted to ground a faith. Christian faith is not born in the individual, needing legitimization from the Bible. On the contrary, it arises only from hearing the Word of God that finds a hook in the human being. There is no other way to give birth to faith except through the reading of that book called the Bible.

In this sense, interpretation is not an anomalous or intrusive act in the Christian faith. It is its true and proper fulfillment. Only in contact with that text does faith have the possibility of its birth. We will call this first mechanism "exogenous interpretation." It is the interpretation which arises outside the Bible in the Christian community, in history, as a legitimate experience of the arising of faith through contact with the foundational text. The second mechanism can be called the "endogenous interpretation" because interpretation in this case precedes the believer's interpretation. The foundational text of Christianity, the New Testament, is itself already an interpretation of the Old Testament, so from extra-biblical, interpretation becomes intra-biblical.[21] Interpretation then is not only legitimate because we have to interpret a text to found our faith: it is also legitimate for a more structural reason. The text that grounds us, the Bible, is itself already an interpretation of an earlier text. We call this second mechanism "endogenous interpretation." This is because it arises within the Bible itself.

This double foundation of Christian hermeneutics allows us to assert that Christianity is thus doubly hermeneutical because it legitimately and necessarily generates an interpretation (exogenous) but also because it arises genealogically from an interpretation (endogenous). This double fact carries with it two consequences. On the one hand, it gives legitimacy to the interpretation and the interpreter. Interpretation, therefore, is welcome. It is structurally necessary. It needs to be there. When the Christian interprets, he does not commit a crime but honors his faith. The obligation to interpret is placed in the wake and logic of the

---

21. See Barr, *Old and New in Interpretation*, 103–48.

Christian faith. No one can be born as a Christian if he does not interpret. Interpretation represents the way into Christianity. This is why no one within Christianity has to ask permission to interpret. This is required of them as an obligation.[22]

On the other hand, the Word of God is conceived in its relationality as a Word that deserves and needs interpretation. Being conceived as a revealed Word, the Bible was constructed relationally; therefore, it needs and strongly calls for interpretations. The Bible bears all possible interpretations well and does not wear out at all in the face of them. Interpretations only succeed in enhancing, empowering, and highlighting its many latent meanings. If there were no interpretations, the Bible would easily become a shrunken and insignificant book.

Interpretations give it muscle and vigor. Interpretations make it flourish. In its typical perspective of gift and exchange, the Bible does not fold in on itself but aims to make readers who approach it flourish, recognizing in them legitimate interlocutors, legitimate interpreters. The Bible has deliberately chosen to depend, in the construction of meaning, on external readers. How is the interpretive process configured in its essence?

THE "HERMENEUTIC CIRCLE"[23]

Any hermeneutics presupposes that the starting point for a cognitive process or articulation of meaning is the presence of a text. Only the presence of a text guarantees the emergence of a true interpretive process. In the Christian context, biblical hermeneutics strongly and irrevocably affirms the necessity and obligation to move from the biblical text. There is no Christian faith that is not simultaneously a reading of the biblical text.

This first structural element of hermeneutics, the text, is actually connected to a second foundational element: the reader. This second element is less visible, and even when it is made visible, it tends to be considered more secondary. The reader is a reader only because he is qualified by the text that grounds him as such. If the text is a sacred text such as the Bible, the Word of God, this sub-valorization of the reader tends to be even greater. The more sacred a text is, the stronger the tendency to delegitimize the reader and not grant him or her a full and relevant status.

22. See Geffré, *Credere e interpretare*, 17–19.
23. See Jeanrond, *Ermeneutica teologica*, 16–17.

In the hermeneutic process, the reader is just as important as the text. There is no reader without a text that qualifies him as such, but synchronically there is never a true text that is not written for someone.

Christianity is configured as a strongly legitimating religion of the reader because that foundational book, the Bible, though inspired by God, is intended and shaped by virtue of the human beings who read it. There is no hermeneutics without a reader who reads the text. Apparently this second hermeneutical claim takes away from the prominence of the Bible because it makes it overly dependent on the reader who reads it. That the reader-believer depends on the Bible as a text is understandable and theologically necessary. That, on the other hand, the Bible also depends on the reader, seems heterodox and appears a bit extreme. If we tried to understand the deeper meaning of this statement, we would find that it fully agrees with the nature and meaning of what the Bible claims to be.

The Bible, while being "Word of God," is first and foremost the "incarnate Word of God." It is Word addressed to man and incomprehensible without its ultimate recipient, the human being. The fact that it is relational does not make it more comprehensible. The absolute words, those "in and of themselves" (those without a recipient), are those which after all are reachable. Although they may be difficult, they are always attainable in their meaning.

Although they are the closest and the most familiar, relational words are truly unreachable in their total meaning because they are based on the mystery of the other. This structural unattainability and impenetrability is the guarantee of their relationality and, paradoxically, of their openness and gift. Every relational word is articulated in this systole and diastole of the presence of the other that offers and withdraws, delivers and subtracts.

The Bible is Word near and far. Word revealed and hidden, Word that comes and goes. The relational Word is never fully transparent. The Bible is *the* Word but it is also *a* Word. The Bible does not express all and every word of God. There are other words of God that are not included in the Bible. The Bible is *the* Word of God in that it is *a* Word of God. For us Christians it is the most important but not the only one. It is the most important because it is a relational Word in a specific context of salvation.

Biblical hermeneutics is both the affirmation of the text and the affirmation of the legitimacy of the reader. Text and reader are the two structural elements of any sound hermeneutics. In the hermeneutical process, the reader does not arrive at the meaning of life except through that text (the Bible), but at the same time that text is meant to flourish only through the reader's interpretation.

Why is the relationship between text and reader not linear?[24] Hermeneutics speaks of a "hermeneutic circle" and not "line" or "hermeneutic pair." We talk about the hermeneutic circle because entry to the interpretive process has various routes, and this is not solely of quantitative and organizational importance. The hermeneutic circle qualitatively describes and justifies the multi-directionality of the interpretive process. The interpretive process can be accessed from the side of the text (the most common route) but also starting from the reader.

It usually begins with the text that the reader reads and then applies. In what he applies, he takes into account what the text tells him. This is the "epistemological" way that presupposes the division, in the cognitive process, between the subject (reader) who knows and the object (text) that is known. Subject and object are separate and, in the process of their approach, only a cognitive, epistemological relationship occurs.

The interpretive process can also begin with the reader, before the reader reads the text. Is this possible? Certainly. The reader is never a *tabula rasa* when approaching the text. When the reader comes to the text with preconceived ideas and these are rigid, then the relationship breaks down because the reader will not feel challenged by the text but will impose his or her own biases on the text. The text will only be a pre-text to legitimize their own thoughts. The text will not change or transform them. But not every prior idea is a prejudice. A prior idea that does not manipulate the text is what in hermeneutics is called "pre-understanding."

"Pre-understanding" is legitimate and necessary for correct interpretation. If we did not have a pre-comprehension about the text we are reading, that text would become alien, unfamiliar, and incomprehensible. Pre-understanding is the affinity that binds us readers as humans to what the text describes as a human text. Pre-comprehension has not only an epistemological dimension. It has and presupposes above all an "ontological" dimension related to life, because it reminds us that before reading a text the reader is already rooted in the life and reality that the text tries to describe.

---

24. It is not, as Alexander S. Jensen points out, precisely because the connection between text and reader, can occur in various ways; hence the category of "hermeneutic circle." See Jensen, *Theological Hermeneutics*, 4–5.

Between text and reader, pre-understanding implies not a separation but a belonging. This belonging or rootedness, which binds reader and text together, represents the dimension of being and the bond of life by virtue of which all subsequent analytical, informational, and epistemological knowledge is possible. The text speaks of reality but is not the total reality. A good reader, in addition to paying attention to the text he or she is reading, must pay attention to its rootedness in life, which is a pre-textual experience that does not destroy but ensures a healthy relationship with the text.

In this sense, the hermeneutic circle adds two other important mechanisms to the valuable mechanism of mediation and interpretive slowdown:

1. The mechanism of balancing the instances at stake. Hermeneutics is not only the text, even though that text may be sacred. Hermeneutics is also the reader and what this represents in the articulation of meaning. The interpretive process is successful not when meaning is reached at any cost but when the hermeneutic circle is balanced and manages to ensure the survival of these two poles in creative tension.

The tension between the two poles is a guarantee, not an obstacle, to the manifestation of meaning. We find in the hermeneutic circle a kind of balancing of powers in a hermeneutic key. The health and truth of meaning are given not only by the linguistic and operational result but by the process by which it is arrived at. Neither the text nor the reader is absolute king. Or, put another way, both are kings but such that they know how to create convergence and consensus.

2. The hermeneutic circle corrects the excessive rationalization into which biblical interpretation can run, uniting subject (reader) and object (Bible) at the base in a pre-textual partnership. This is the meaning of pre-comprehension. In it, the typical separation of subject-knower and object-known is overcome. It is preceded through the affirmation of a bond prior to the more linear relationship between reader and biblical text. Reading will only enrich, orient, and correct this bond but will not create it in the strict sense.

The Bible can direct faith and correct it, but it cannot create it. Or it creates it in the relative sense, that is, that correcting it is like bringing it into existence. If the Bible created faith in the absolute sense as a capacity and attitude, then it would be the product of a book, a byproduct.

Even those who do not read the Bible, by virtue of this ontological link to life, which is a pre-textual link, understand, know, and experience what it means to be human in a more immediate and spontaneous way. We first are born and live as human beings, then we learn to read and follow what the Bible points us to. There is an ontological priority of being human over claiming and justly defending the value of a book. This ontological priority is neither secular nor denominational; it is simply human. In Christianity it is guaranteed by the call to the creator God.

Hermeneutics as a slow way, because it is mediated by interpretation, embodies and articulates a tension that is its own and which it cannot do without. Interpretation is realized and possible only within this tension. It is actually a threefold tension. It is at the intersection of these three tensions that hermeneutics is configured as such. Only within can meaning arise. The first is an "endogenous" tension, within the text. In the text a meaning coexists with other meanings that it cannot erase. There is never in the text an isolated meaning, much less a single imperial and totalizing meaning. A textual tension ensues.

The second is a tension exogenous to the text, in the reader. Conflicting and ambivalent attitudes to the text, conscious and unconscious, coexist in the reader. The result is a tension in the reader that is structural and indelible. When we desire the reader to be unitary and monolithic, we immediately move to the terrain of ideology. The third tension is a tension between the text and the reader. Neither pole can be erased in the intent to diminish the tension. Both are legitimate and necessary. The result is an interpretive tension that is the very guarantee of meaning.

Hermeneutics is not a monolithic process in the acquisition of meaning. It is articulated in the tension of the "hermeneutic circle." It tries, on the one hand, to de-emphasize the arrogance of a reader who wants to be independent of the text. On the other hand, it equally tries to de-emphasize the claim of a text that wants to be full of meaning regardless of the reader.

This mechanism, open and tensional in the articulation of meaning, guaranteed by the "hermeneutic circle," has become structural for theology today. By virtue of this fact, theological hermeneutics is not a section, much less an appendix, of theological work. It is not reduced to the interpretation of the Bible. Today, all theology has become hermeneutics. Geffré writes in this regard:

> It can be said that not only in the case of the humanities, but also in the case of the experimental sciences, the so-called natural sciences, any scientific knowledge today is interpretive knowledge. There is no learning, immediate approach of reality

outside of language, and language is already necessarily a certain interpretation. Thus, there is a consensus that all sciences are interpretive sciences. In fact, we have distanced ourselves from positivism or a certain scientism. It is in function of this epistemological break that the relevance of a hermeneutic model in theology should be understood.[25]

---

25. Geffré, *Credere e interpretare*, 15.

II

The Birth of a Reader-Centric Hermeneutics

THE HISTORY OF BIBLICAL hermeneutics[1] is at first a description of the various forms of interpretation that have followed one another over time according to various schools, denominations, territories and historical periods. As such, it aims to fulfill two important tasks.

The first consists in proposing a unified and integrative view of the different interpretative forms. It intends to create a certain sequentiality and organization of events which, were it not so, would appear excessively dispersed, disconnected, and elusive to a comprehensive gaze. The value of this first synoptic glance is not immediate because the connection between interpretive schools does not necessarily follow either the criterion of their territorial or their temporal proximity. Only a trained and discerning gaze can identify familiarity or common directions beyond apparent differences and contrasts.

The second intends to propose a differentiated view of the various interpretive proposals, which would otherwise appear as mere repetitions or extensions of pre-existing patterns. The value of this second look is valuable because it allows us to differentiate interpretive proposals that seem to belong to a common historical or territorial strain and instead contain *in nuce* a specific and differentiating element. Only in the

---

1. Jensen, *Theological Hermeneutics*, 9–37.

THE BIRTH OF A READER-CENTRIC HERMENEUTICS

evolution of history will this become more explicit and evident, creating true interpretive alternatives.

The history of biblical hermeneutics[2] is not a purely descriptive act. It is not reduced to the effort of registering and cataloguing well-organized various interpretative forms of the past. The history of biblical hermeneutics is itself an exercise in theological reflection. No description is completely aseptic. Neither is ours. Assumptions, affinities, and unconfessed and unconscious preferences condition the choice and manner of dealing with the chosen material.

The theological-reflexive component from which this brief historical synopsis starts, which we try to elaborate in this chapter, is summed up in a thesis that identifies the shift from a "strong text" to a "weak text" as the most significant event in the history of biblical hermeneutics. This transition corresponds to a very specific event: the birth of modernity.

This might appear as a far-fetched and overly compact thesis, for it escapes no one that there are no monolithic historical epochs. Within historical periods there always exist positions that quantitatively and qualitatively are well-differentiated. It would take little to point out this incontrovertible fact. Yet, there is a common trait that binds premodern interpretations. This is that they share, beyond even marked differences, a certain, almost sacred respect for the "stability of meaning." This element has led us to call premodern hermeneutics "text-centered hermeneutics," because in them, through respect for the text, respect for the stability of meaning predominates.

The hermeneutics that arose with the emergence of modernity are of an entirely different bent. Here, too, there is no shortage of sometimes radical differences between opposing positionings. Yet, there is a common element that seems to link the interpretive proposals that arose in our historical period: the "fluidity of meaning."

This recurring element, present in different proportions, prompts us to call modern hermeneutics "reader-centric hermeneutics," because in them, through the emphasis on the fluidity of meaning, the centrality of the reader is made explicit as a destabilizing element of traditional meaning. The reader is the one who, by virtue of the validity and relevance he ascribes to himself and his own projects, deconstructs, critiques, overthrows, dismantles without much scruple, and with a spontaneous

---

2. Jeanrond, *Ermeneutica teologica*, 25–75.

glee and freedom, the meanings and texts that the past has catalogued as sacred and unchanging.

"Text-centric hermeneutics" and "reader-centric hermeneutics" represent, in our historical review of interpretive schools, two central categories. Our historical look is not neutral. It starts, as mentioned earlier, from a well-typed theological reflection. This does not take the form of an ironclad prejudice but rather a flexible historical-theological hypothesis. This will allow us to describe, list, organize, and analyze the different interpretive proposals that have emerged in history, trying to give them a theological and cultural intelligibility.

What are the mechanisms that prepare, announce, and determine this epochal shift from the centrality of the text to the centrality of the reader? What are the effects, foreseen and unforeseen, expected and unexpected, that result from this shift? Does this shift have a purely historical significance? Does it mark a structural change in the interpretive enterprise itself? Do its effects also press upon theology and force it to alter its outlook on God, faith, the church, and the Bible? What is the history of hermeneutics? What is important in this history? How could it be organized? How could it be understood theologically? What category, perspective, or event should we choose as a starting point?

These are some of the theological questions that will be behind the scenes as we try to briefly list some of the most significant schools and hermeneutical perspectives in the history of Christianity.

A THEOLOGICAL-CULTURAL LOOK AT THE HISTORY[3] OF HERMENEUTICS

We will take the theological key to read this story from a non-theological event. It is a non-theological moment of modernity to which we still

3. The history of hermeneutics, not solely in a chronological sense but in a qualitative sense, can only be understood by connecting it to the nodes, transitions, and ruptures of culture taken as a historical whole. This connection points out that hermeneutics in general, but also the particular hermeneutics related to the reading of the Bible, is always rooted in, and thus influenced and conditioned in, the essentials of its emphasis and focus by the culture in which it is embedded. See Ong, *Orality and Literacy*, 136–52. This was true for the medieval period where sense predetermined by the group predominates over sense created by the individual, as in a broader perspective the group predominates over individual consciousness. See Ullmann, *Individuo e società nel medioevo*, 1–43; Le Goff, *Civilisation de l'occident médiéval*, 234–89. And the same thing happens with the advent of modernity, where the sense created by the individual will win out over the sense emerging in the community, as in a broader

belong. We will start from a historical figure, from Descartes. It will be a story told from our present, not in the exposition of the stages, as we will follow the traditional historical sequence. In this basic perspective, we will aim to grasp from the beginning the specificity of modern hermeneutics. To grasp it, we will necessarily look to the past but starting from the present, because, as Benedetto Croce well remembered, "All history is contemporary history."[4]

To be compact and direct, our historical reading hypothesis is articulated in the following way. Modern hermeneutics, both philosophical and theological, marks an important shift from a way of connecting to the sense of a text, in this case the Bible, as a "stable" and already given sense, typical of the Middle Ages, to a "fluid" sense that has yet to be constructed, at least in its final form. The mediator of that sense to be constructed is the interpreter. The interpreter, the "reader," becomes in the modern world, the mainstay of the interpretive enterprise. Although philosophical hermeneutics will formalize this with F. Schleiermacher in the early 1800s, who gave birth to philosophical hermeneutics, the shift in perspective certainly took place earlier. We have chosen, somewhat atypically and symbolically, to trace it back to Descartes. In Descartes, the extremes of what will become the perspective, the nature and the paradoxes of modern hermeneutics are already found in synthesis, but in a very clear way.

This pairing is all the more unusual and strange when one considers that hermeneutics is par excellence an exercise in mediation. Though hermeneutics is mediation, in Descartes we find expressed the persistent effort to disassociate itself from any mediation, so that it can come to construct an immediate and transparent knowledge. This is a knowledge that chooses to disassociate itself, through systematic doubt, from any sensory mediation in order to make its certainty rest solely in the immediacy of the *cogito*. Only the cogito, by virtue of its own doubt, arrives at the only possible certainty, which is that of its own thinking. Only thus does one arrive at "clear and distinct ideas," the only possible basis for new and irrefutable knowledge.

How can Descartes then be the starting point for a cognitive enterprise such as hermeneutics that makes the mediation of the text its strong

---

perspective the individual will take over from the group. See Gourevitch, *Naissance de l'individu*, 141–193; Cassirer, *Individual and the Cosmos*, 73–122; Cavicchia Scalamonti, *Morte*, 9–56.

4. Croce, *Storia come pensiero*. See also de Certeau, *Écriture de l'histoire*

point? He does this through an atypical but quite clear shift in its extremes and address from the very outset. A new cognitive and anthropological perspective based on two pillars comes with the rationality introduced by Descartes.[5] First, there is trust in the autonomous individual who with his reason (*res cogitans*) makes reality and the world transparent. Reason, with its order, analytical power, and organizational capacity, imposes itself for the first time in a massive way on external reality, erecting itself as an unquestionable guarantor over all that is real and true. The *cogito* as a cognitive instance detaches itself from the rest of reality that had hitherto contained, accompanied, limited, and even oppressed it. It claims the status of an autonomous subject capable of knowing only from itself, resting only on the power of its own reason.

Second, in order to give the cogito its power, an operation necessarily had to be accomplished first. Like any mechanism of domination and hegemony, the external reality or thing to be known necessarily had to be neutralized and demystified. No domination is exercised in a vacuum. Every conquest carries the trophy of a conquered territory. In Descartes, the controlled reality that guarantees the domination and rational supremacy of the cogito is the external world, reality, the cosmos and even that cosmos closest to the cogito which is one's own body. Reason must be able to control the distant and external cosmos and the near and familiar body. In order to control it, it needs to neutralize it. Descartes neutralizes far and near external reality by reducing it to one of its dimensions: measure (*res extensa*). Thus reduced, reality becomes predictable. It has no motion of its own. It has become a machine, a disenchanted reality. In order to move, it needs an element external to it, that is, the cogito. Having to depend on an external element, nature then becomes easily controlled by it. Nature becomes a reality subservient to the cogito.

Thanks to a new anthropology that overvalues the thinking subject as the determining element in ordering reality with its omnipotent reason, and thanks to a new cosmology that devalues nature because it reduces it to one of its dimensions and in so doing "disenchants" it, this new world is ordered. Here the order of the world expresses the measure of its disenchantment. The Cartesian scheme thus expresses two truths, two claims. On the one hand, there is the power of the knowing subject. On the other, there is the impotence and subservience of the known object. Because the object has lost its mystery, it appears devalued. Meanwhile,

---

5. Descartes, *Meditazioni metafisiche*; see especially the first and second meditations.

the subject has gained it beyond what it would be allowed. It intoxicates itself with an illusion that improperly overvalues it.

Here are the two extremes of the Cartesian system that we will later find at the heart of modern hermeneutics and its anomalies. The reader, the mainstay of modern hermeneutics, is a direct descendant of the Cartesian cogito (*res cogitans*) in an interpretive key, just as the text deciphered and controlled in its meaning and emptied of its mystery (*res extensa*) is a direct descendant of the reality and nature neutralized by Descartes.

We have seen so far that Christianity is a radically hermeneutic religion. In Christianity, interpretation is not a concession. It is "required" by moral and theological obligation. It is urged as a hallmark of those who claim to be truly Christian. The Christian believer, even before being a witness or a morally reliable person, is essentially an interpreter whose legitimacy is grounded in a text he is asked to read and understand before he can apply it. The nature and destiny of the foundational word of Christianity, the Bible, is not to keep it pure and aseptic. It is rather to contaminate it positively and continually with innumerable and ever new interpretations. Christian Scripture for this reason is not "interpretation-phobic." It is structurally "interpretation-philical." It does not flee or distrust interpretation. It willingly accepts and seeks interpretation as something inherent in it. Interpretation is for the Christian believer his amniotic fluid. It is that vital space that nourishes him and keeps him alive and without which his spiritual life would begin to perish and contract. It is in interpretation that the Bible finds its fullness.

Christianity has given rise to a multiplicity of hermeneutics that would be impossible to present in a summary chapter such as this one. The history of Christianity is the history of different hermeneutics that have been inspired by and originated from the stimulus derived from its founding book. Christian communities may vary in adding accompanying elements external or internal to the faith in order to better understand the meaning of Scripture. At the base is the common conviction that the text, and the divine event it grounds, remains. This is the starting point of all Christian experience. This is why interpretation in Christianity has always existed abundantly.

Let us look broadly at how these interpretations have followed and articulated themselves throughout history and, most importantly, at what, if anything, is the trait in it that distinguishes contemporary hermeneutics[6] from premodern hermeneutics.[7]

PREMODERN PERIOD: "TEXT-CENTRIC HERMENEUTICS"

The basic hypothesis we will try to articulate in this section is that all premodern hermeneutics, beyond their differences in school or methodology, are united in a common trait, which is that of "sense stability." Premodern hermeneutics, ancient and medieval, finds this stability of meaning not only in the text but in life in general. Therefore, our hermeneutic hypothesis starts from a cultural hypothesis. The stability of meaning in life in general finds in the stability of meaning in the text its natural extension. This is why the text is the guarantor of this stability. The guarantor of this stability is not the reader in the focus of premodern hermeneutics. This is why we describe these hermeneutics as "text-centered" hermeneutics.

Jewish Hermeneutics

In contrast to Greek thought, which is articulated as philosophical interpretation and reflection on the logos, with secondary reference to texts, Hebrew hermeneutics instead starts from a written text that becomes the inescapable starting point of knowledge of God and his will, which, through that text, becomes binding on faith. The believer must assimilate and make that text his own through reading and understanding its message. The reader is recognized as the rightful recipient of that message. Jewish hermeneutics is thus configured as the reading experience that affirms on the one hand the centrality of the text and on the other the concrete historicity of the interpreting community.[8]

---

6. Ricœur, *Dal testo all'azione*, 71–95.

7. Ferraris, *Storia dell'ermeneutica*, 5–14.

8. One should not project into the past categories that are of our time, such as those of *text* and *reader* as we moderns have conceptualized and described them from the central and primary category of the "hermeneutic circle." However, one should not disregard the affinities and similarities either. That of the *text* and that of the *community that reads* and hears that text are in Judaism two essential components that reconnect and foreshadow our own. Judaism is not a mystical or orgiastic community but an interpreting community.

THE BIRTH OF A READER-CENTRIC HERMENEUTICS

These two elements are discernible from the very first chapters of Genesis and will become transversal and recurrent throughout Scripture. One of the most characteristic passages with respect to this is the one that recounts the experience of Ezra who, as a spiritual leader, reconstructs the identity of the people after exile from the rediscovery of the Torah, its reading and interpretation:

> He read the book on the square that is in front of the Gate of Waters, from early morning until noon, in the presence of the men, women and those who were able to understand; and all the people strained their ears to hear the book of the law. Ezra, the scribe, stood on top of a wooden box, which had been specially made; beside him stood, on the right, Mattitiah, Semaiah, Ananias, Uriah, Chilchiah and Maaseiah; on the left, Pedaiah, Misael, Malchiah, Casum, Casbaddana, Zechariah and Mesullam. Ezra opened the book in the presence of all the people, for he stood in the highest place; and as soon as he opened the book, all the people stood up. Ezra blessed the Lord, the great God, and all the people answered, "Amen, amen," lifting up their hands; and they bowed down and prostrated themselves with their faces to the ground before the Lord. Iesuah, Bani, Serebiah, Iamin, Accub, Sabbetai, Odiah, Maaseiah, Chelita, Azariah, Iozabad, Anan, Pelaiah and the other Levites explained the law to the people, and they all stood in their places. They read in the book of God's law in an understandable way; they gave the meaning, so that the people would understand what they read. Nehemiah, who was the governor, Ezra, priest and scribe, and the Levites, who were teaching, said to all the people, "This day is consecrated to the Lord your God; do not be sad and do not weep!" For all the people wept, listening to the words of the law. Then Nehemiah said to them, "Go, eat fatty food and drink sweet drink, and send portions to those who have prepared nothing for them; for this day is consecrated to our Lord; do not be sad; for the joy of the Lord is your strength." The Levites calmed all the people, saying, "Be silent, for this day is holy; do not be sad!" All the people went out to eat, drink, send portions to the poor, and make a great feast, for they understood the words that had been explained to them" (Neh 8:3–12).

Jewish hermeneutics is condensed into the categories this passage introduces: read, explain, understand, listen, act, rejoice.[9] The goal is not a theoretical understanding but a personal and existential understanding

---

9. Throntveit, *Esdra e Neemia*, 104–8.

that leads to and puts us in touch with life. Understanding the text does not appear here as a speculative experience, nor is it limited to being a mere explanation of words. It includes all registers of human existence and leads the reader to action and joy. We find in this short narrative the perfect articulation and mutual referral between the sacred text (*Torah*) and the equally synchronic centrality of the reading community (Israel), in order to take advantage of the blessings that through that text and its reading God wishes to bestow on his people.[10] We have in this pair a text-reading community, the forerunner of what in our day will become the "hermeneutic circle."

It emerges very clearly in this paradigmatic biblical passage, that in this hermeneutic, despite the recognition of the relevance of the reading community, the predominant and determining dimension in the construction of meaning is given by the text. Since it is in addition a sacred text, traceable to God himself, this centrality comes out even more reinforced and consolidated. Biblical Hebrew hermeneutics is thus configured as a typical "text-centric" hermeneutic whose strength is grounded and guaranteed by God himself and the fact that he is an all-powerful God, Lord and creator of the universe. To the majesty, greatness, and lordship of God correspond the majesty, greatness, and lordship of the text. The text is as sacred as the God whom that text refers.

Post-biblical Jewish hermeneutics will maintain the validity of the two elements that foreshadow the hermeneutic circle. Their connection will be maintained and enriched. It will also be so in a creative and miraculous way because the undoubted sacredness of the Torah, reinforced even more by the territorial loss and by the emergence of Christianity, will not obscure or erase the dynamic and involved participation of the reading people. The sacred text does not stop but stimulates the creativity of the people. Jewish hermeneutics subsequent to the biblical period will confirm and reinforce this orientation in the form of the legal-moral interpretation of the Law (*Halakhah*),[11] and in the form of the religious-spiritual interpretation of Scripture (*Haggada*),[12] in the context of intense talmudic-rabbinic interpretive activity.

---

10. Keil and Delitzsch, *Ezra, Nehemiah, Esther, Job*, 143–47.

11. *Halakhah* is the religious normative tradition of Judaism, codified in a body of Scripture; it includes biblical law (the 613 *mitzvòt*) and subsequent Talmudic and rabbinic laws, as well as traditions and customs.

12. *Haggadah* is a form of narration used in the Talmud, some parts of Jewish liturgy, and the *midrash*. The term refers to homiletic and non-legalistic texts of exegesis

Thus, Jewish hermeneutics is not locked into the worship of the foundational text. In both the biblical and post-biblical periods, the sacredness of the text did not block or paralyze readers' participation. Emmanuel Levinas highlights this fact well when he states that, for the Jew, understanding the text also means understanding what is "beyond the verse." To understand the text is to transcend it.[13] Jewish hermeneutics has always ensured the connection that grounds the hermeneutic circle, between interpreted text and interpreting community. Indeed, in the *Tanakh*[14] itself, the sanctity of the Torah does not act as an impediment to further interpretive takes but, on the contrary, makes them possible. The *Tanakh* is the story of the interpretive revival of the Torah within the sacred text itself, as evidenced by the continuous reformulation of the Torah in the Prophets and other Writings; just as the formation of the *Mishna* and *Ghemara* highlights, outside the sacred text, the same widespread and recurring interpretive process.

Once again, and despite the decided involvement of the reading community, Jewish hermeneutics remains a typical "text-centric" hermeneutic even in the post-biblical period, because the reading community is regarded only as the extension of an existing sacred sense, rather than true creator of a new sense. Premodern Jewish hermeneutics is a hermeneutics of a sense that remains stable and aims to create stability. The stability of the text and its sense simply prolongs and validates the stability of life and reality in general through a faithful reading that guarantees the continuity of a sense predetermined by God himself. The sacredness of God corresponds to the sacredness of the text.

Christian Hermeneutics

The New Testament will certainly introduce a radical break. This is a perspective from which to read the Scriptures in a new way, in a revolutionary way. This new point of reference, not only theological but also hermeneutical, will be Jesus the Messiah. He is the concretization and

---

in classical rabbinic literature . In general, the *Haggadah* is a compendium of rabbinic homilies that incorporate folklore, historical anecdotes, moral exhortations and practical advice in various fields, from business to medicine.

13. Levinas, *Au-delà du verset*, 10–23.

14. The word *Tanakh* contains the three letters that make up the acronym to designate the three parts of the Hebrew Bible: Torah, Prophets, and other Writings (*Torah, Nebihim, Ketubim*).

center of the Scriptures and at the same time the one who opens new horizons of meaning. The features of this new hermeneutics are visible, for example, in the Emmaus episode:[15]

> And he said to them, 'Foolish and late in heart to believe the word of the prophets! Was it not necessary for Christ to endure these sufferings in order to enter into His glory? "." And beginning with Moses and all the prophets he explained to them in all the Scriptures what referred to him. When they were near the village where they were headed, he made as if he had to go farther. But they insisted, "Stay with us because it is getting to be evening and the day is already waning." He went in to stay with them. When he was at table with them, he took bread, said the blessing, broke it and gave it to them. Then their eyes were opened and they recognized him. But he disappeared from their sight. And they said to one another, "Did not our hearts burn in our breasts as he conversed with us on the way, when he explained the Scriptures to us?"(Luke 24:25–32).

Hermeneutics changes center. The new center is Jesus. It is the risen one himself who, beginning with Moses and all the prophets, interpreted[16] for them in all the Scriptures what referred to him, thus presenting his figure as the fulfillment of all Scripture. He establishes an interpretation of Scripture that no longer passes through the interpretation of the Law but through the understanding of faith in his person.[17]

The insertion of this new center, Jesus and his resurrection, does not give rise to a mystical religiosity, as one might expect given his high spiritual appeal and charismatic profile. His person and words will not alter the articulation of the text-reading pair, but will, on the contrary, produce a reinforcement of the two poles that conform this pair.[18] Indeed, the pole of the text will become even more central as the new reference text, the New Testament, will be built on an interpretation of the Old Testament. The founder of the new faith, who like any founder could have said completely new words, chooses instead to take up and re-propose words from the Old Testament, offering only a new interpretation of them. He quotes them, comments on them again and again, and, especially at crucial moments, reconnects with them almost obsessively. In the new covenant,

---

15. Tannehill, *Luke*, 352–58.
16. Cf. *Dierméneusen*, Luke 24:27.
17. Craddock, *Luca*, 365–74.
18. Bock, *Luke* 2:1903–1924.

the connection with the textual pole is not diluted but strengthened. The textual bond becomes twofold. On the one hand, fidelity is demanded in the face of the new text created by the apostles; on the other hand, the other text, the Old Testament, from which the apostles elaborated theirs, is confirmed.

From the perspective of the reader, a revolution arises because the reader-corporate of the Old Testament is gradually replaced by the reader-individual promoted by the New Testament. This reader is asked for the first time for allegiance only to God through his conscience. No longer the ethnic, political, or even religious mediation of the group. The increased value of the text, by virtue of the presence of Jesus' own words, does not at all obscure the dynamic role of the reader but even seems to guarantee and demand it. What emerges is a legitimized and empowered reader. No longer will the people alone legitimately read and interpret the text. This privilege will be granted to each individual believer. In the new covenant, the reader will become the load-bearing pivot in the elaboration of meaning. He is the instance on which the hold of the whole interpretive framework rests. He is given the mission to go and preach by interpreting, educating, and contextualizing the message of Jesus.[19] Every believer has become a priest by virtue of the universal priesthood introduced by Christ, which provides that between the individual believer and God there is no mediation other than that of his own conscience. Yet even this revolution will not break the text-reader pair, for that reader will continue to be qualified only as the reader of a text that precedes him and imposes itself on him with supreme authority.

In Christian hermeneutics the new centrality of Jesus reinforces the connection between text and reader in a new and innovative way. But the "text-centric" tendency of Old Testament hermeneutics not only does not disappear but is reinforced, albeit with a different sign. And it is reinforced through two new mechanisms.

1. Jesus and his words become the supreme revelation of God. Just as the apostles will ground their authority in connection with Christ, so hermeneutics will become "Christocentric" for the same reason. Every subsequent interpretation will find its validity in the affirmation and promotion of Christ.

2. The other is that the typical eschatological tension introduced by Christ between the *already* of his resurrection and the *not-yet* of his

19. Matt 28:18–20.

second coming will be resolved in favor of celebrating the *already* happened. Christian theology, in general, and Christian hermeneutics, grounded in the risen Christ and *Pantocrator*, will tend to accentuate the dimension of salvation and meaning already acquired because they are irreversibly guaranteed by Christ's victory. In New Testament hermeneutics, we are dealing with a typical "text-centric" hermeneutic guaranteed no longer by the community of faith around the Torah, as was the case in the first covenant, but by the victorious Jesus. The "text-centeredness" of the hermeneutics of the New Testament is christologically and eschatologically justified. The great attention given to the reader as an individual, introduced by the theological and hermeneutical revolution brought about by Jesus, will remain only in the state of latency. This individual consciousness will not explode in full force because the cultural context did not allow it. That context remained transversely, inside and outside the church, a corporate context whose goal was the stability of meaning guaranteed precisely by the group.

Patristic-Medieval Hermeneutics.

In the early Christian centuries, we see the emergence of important and well-differentiated schools of religious thought, both theologically and hermeneutically. Let us pause to briefly consider two of them because of their importance territorially and theologically.

School of Alexandria[20]

Especially with Origen,[21] Greek patristics elaborated a very refined dogmatic and scriptural hermeneutics, with the assumption of allegory as a distinctive hermeneutical method.[22] The difference between the "spiritual sense" and the "literal sense" of Scripture, corresponds for Origen to the difference between the soul and the body and essentially determines all

---

20. Tillich, *History of Christian Thought*, 84–88; Lane, *Concise History of Christian Thought*, 53–58; Berkhof, *History of Christian Doctrines*, 70–76; Gonzalez, *Christian Thought Revisited*, 23–28.

21. Heussi, *Kompendium der Kirchengeschichte*, 17–19.

22. Philo had previously set the school in Alexandria. His use of allegory had been central and massive.

Alexandrian hermeneutics. In Alexandria, Platonism with its dualism is imposed. It is the "spiritual sense" that matters and is decisive in interpretive logic. Alexandrian hermeneutics is, for all intents and purposes, a spiritualist hermeneutics whose very medium and guarantor is allegory. The spiritualist theology that stands out in Alexandria does so by virtue of that specific kind of hermeneutics.

Between theology and hermeneutics, there is no purely extrinsic and instrumental relationship. Hermeneutics and its typification is already a theological exercise that is articulated according to very specific presuppositions. To every theology about God corresponds a very specific hermeneutic of the same sign. Likewise, every hermeneutic is always an extension of a conception of God that precedes and grounds it. A long line of territorial churches, especially but not only in the Middle Ages, would draw on this more spiritualist approach, taking the statements of this School of Alexandria in part or in full.

Antioch School[23]

Theodore of Mopsuestia rejected Origen's allegorical Platonism, which saw all historical reality only as a symbol of a deeper and higher reality. Drawing on Aristotelian hermeneutics, he showed greater concern for an exegesis of a historical, grammatical, and philological kind. Against the spiritualist idealism of the Alexandrian school, the Antioch school will assert the validity of history, concreteness, and "literal sense." Antiochene hermeneutics is historical hermeneutics whose go-between and guarantor is the literal interpretation of the text. Once again we note, even for this theological school of Antioch, the strong solidarity that exists between hermeneutical strategy and theological orientation.

So strong is this connection that we could almost say that it is not theology that chooses its own hermeneutics, but it is hermeneutics that founds theology and typifies it in its distinctive features and main thrust. Unlike the school of Alexandria, the school of Antioch will not have many followers during the Middle Ages. In terms of its basic perspective, however, it will compensate for this diluted and sober presence with a strong and widespread presence in the early modern period.

---

23. Tillich, *History of Christian Thought*, 80–84; Lane, *Concise History of Christian Thought*, 57–60; Berkhof, *History of Christian Doctrines*, 103–8; Gonzalez, *Christian Thought Revisited*, 28–33.

The conflict between the Alexandrian and Antiochian schools had the positive effect of bringing out a plurality of possible meanings of Scripture and also gave the opportunity to formulate some criteria for reading and interpretation. The four senses of Scripture[24] and also the principle of the "rule of faith" were gradually imposed.[25] Between the *literal sense* and the *spiritual sense*, patristic hermeneutics as a whole favored the latter. In patristics, it was not only the intra-biblical relationship between the various possible senses that determined the hermeneutical orientation. The second front arose in connection with extra-biblical instances and the relationship that the biblical text had to maintain with them. The patristic hermeneutic circle composed of the "rule of faith," "tradition," and "magisterium" found its most accomplished expression in Augustine.[26] This hermeneutic will become the interpretive model throughout the Middle Ages. For Augustine, only the "rule of faith" expressed by the articles of the *Creed*, together with *Tradition* and the *Magisterium*, leads to the understanding of the *spiritual meaning* of Scripture in all its fullness.[27] Thus the typical patristic paradox is configured, where a wealth of interpretation of the Bible in its various levels of meaning is, however, subordinated to the extra-biblical instances of which the Magisterium and Tradition possess a monopoly.

The patristic principle of the dual sense of Scripture, literal or historical, spiritual or mystical, will be developed by medieval authors in all its hermeneutical subtleties, as H. De Lubac's classic study shows.[28] In contrast to patristic hermeneutics, scholasticism will privilege the *literal sense* without erasing the plurality of senses of Scripture. Thomas Aquinas will also value the literal sense, but it will not be identified or reduced to the univocal sense, and he, like the entire Middle Ages, will continue to

---

24. Jeanrond, *Ermeneutica teologica*, 27–30.

25. Jeanrond, *Ermeneutica teologica*, 19–20.

26. Jeanrond, *Ermeneutica teologica*, 41–47. See *De doctrina christiana* by Augustine of Hippo (354–430).

27. Augustine, *Confessions*, I.

28. See de Lubac, *Exégèse médiévale*. The first of the four volumes of *Medieval Exegesis* by Jesuit theologian Henri De Lubac (1896–1991) is devoted to the study of the four senses of Scripture. The best known formula is the one handed down to us by Nicholas of Lyra around 1330: "*Littera gesta docet, quid credas allegoria, moralis quid agas, quo tendas anagogia.*" The literal sense refers to the deeds or history, the allegorical sense goes in search of metaphorical meaning, the moral or tropological sense targets the transposition of the Word into concrete life, and the anagogical sense seeks mystical and spiritual meaning.

defend the principle of the multiple senses of Scripture.[29] The separation of the literal sense from the other possible senses and, above all, the identification of the spiritual sense with the literal sense, will come later, with the arrival of Protestantism. Erasmus of Rotterdam, while agreeing, at least initially, with many of the theses introduced by the Reformers, will take a more critical stance in the face of this strong emphasis on the literal sense, defending the twofold sense, literal and spiritual, of Scripture.

The impression is that medieval hermeneutics, with the abundance of meanings it creates, especially through widespread allegorical interpretation and with its privileging of parallel avenues of spiritual meaning over the Bible, has finally accomplished and realized the shift toward a reader-centered hermeneutics. Instead, even medieval hermeneutics remains to all intents and purposes a "text-centered" hermeneutic, despite its innovations. Although it moves away from the Bible as the sole source of meaning, and although it departs from literal interpretation, the basic mechanism is still the same. Meaning is stable because it is already given in the foundational text and is stable in and through the church, which claims for itself the monopoly of its reading. The meanings produced in the Middle Ages are not new meanings but mere extensions of what is already included in the text. In this case, the stability of meaning rather than from Christ (as in New Testament "text-centered" hermeneutics) will be provided by the church. It is the church that is the stabilizing element in the interpretive process. In the Middle Ages, a "text-centric" hermeneutic is configured but one that is ecclesiological in nature. It is the church that guarantees the meaning of the foundational text of the Christian faith and makes it stable.

Despite the diversity of accents and angles, premodern hermeneutics have maintained a common conception of the hermeneutic circle. The cross-cutting element that unites them is embodied in the priority given to the text rather than the reader. It is the text that appears as king. The reader has only to apply what he reads. The strength of the text is in its fullness and completeness. The meanings are already there. They are not to be invented. The reader can and must become active only in the application of the meanings discovered, but from the standpoint of meaning-making he remains passive. The text, and this is even more valid for the Bible, already has all the meanings ready. The text is sacred because it conveys stable, proven meanings. That the reader does not see

---

29. Jeanrond, *Ermeneutica teologica*, 26–30. See also Mura, *Ermeneutica e verità*, 101–22.

them because he does not know them or because he has not yet made them his own does not detract from the fact that they are already there, complete, defined, and definitive. They are enshrined in the perfection of an unchanging text. The text bases its authority precisely on this. If it did not have the stable meanings, it would not be an authoritative text. Its authority is based on the completeness and definiteness of the meaning it offers.

Not only the Bible but all premodern texts are sacred because they convey a meaning that is not to be twisted and questioned. It is already there, and it imposes itself with its own weight. They possess the stable register of what life and the life of faith must be. That is why the mechanism of reading is a highlighting of what is already there, and that it is only a matter of discovering, revealing, and bringing out through reading.

This understanding of the stability of meaning that the text guarantees is certainly not just a linguistic issue. It is part of a broader cultural vision and one that is typical of the Middle Ages.[30] The hermeneutics of a historical period cannot be dissociated from its cultural matrix. It is always, with relative innovations and shifts, an expression of the cultural model that nourishes it. The cultural model of the Middle Ages and the entire premodern period is the "holistic," not "atomistic," view of reality and the world. In this view, it is not the individual who can be the bearer of meaning but only the group. Between group, cosmos, family, church, God and text, there is a compact and unbreakable sodality. The logic of that fellowship is embodied in the belief that the individual is preceded by a sense that is greater than himself and that he cannot create. This sense is guaranteed by these transpersonal demands. The reader is called upon to be not a "creator" but merely a "ferryman" of a sense that does not belong to him and that he can only undergo, grasp, and transmit.

The stability of group life must necessarily be matched by a hermeneutic that reflects that stability. Whether the text is secular or religious, Catholic or heretical, it matters little. That is not where the foundational trait lies. All pre-modern texts, and the Bible all the more so, serve as stabilizing artifacts. A text cannot overturn the meaning and arrangement of a culture, but it is born and articulated within it. Every hermeneutic is a child of its time.

The individual, whether he reads a book or lives his life, has only to find his place in the world. This is a world that he did not create but

---

30. See Le Goff, *Dieu du Moyen Âge*, 24–32; *Pour un autre Moyen Âge*, 43–54.

that precedes him. The medieval reader, like the medieval believer, is a being preceded. Preceded by a world that already carries with it in a predetermined way the meanings of everything that exists. The text, like the world and the reality outside the text, is a stable reality ready only to be inhabited, not to be constructed.

Two realities par excellence embody this premodern stability: the group and the cosmos. The group, and only it in its backbone, offers safe haven and certainty to the individual, who by nature can only be lost, hesitant, and adrift. Only inclusion in the group saves the individual from insignificance. It saves him precisely because it does not even offer him a choice. The free choice to belong to this or that group would already be the negation of the group. The group is not chosen. In the group one is born. The individual is already born into the group, and any formal choice can only be a confirmation, not a decision whether to belong or not. The group precedes the individual as stable sense precedes reading.

The same thing happens with the cosmos. The cosmos is the primary reality from where the group takes its stability. The order of the cosmos is predetermined and does not depend on the choice of individuals. This order is hierarchical as in nature, and salvation is realized only when in that order one knows how to find one's place. Premodern communities are essentially all cosmo-centric. They recognize that there is an order that precedes them and is found in the cosmos. This is a cosmos created by God for those who are Christians. It is an eternal cosmos independent of God for those who are not Christians. In either case, the cosmos has a complete, stable, and ordered outline.

The text only prolongs, in the act of interpretation, the same structure of stability given by the cosmos and the group at the cultural level. Cosmos, group, and text are parallel expressions of the same admiration and submission to the mesmerizing charm of the world's stability.

MODERN PERIOD: "READER-CENTRIC HERMENEUTICS"[31]

What changes with modernity? It changes the emphasis of hermeneutics. The centrality from the text gives way to the new and revolutionary centrality of the reader. The hermeneutic circle is turned upside down. The variations and modulations of schools and thinkers, important

---

31. Palmer, *Hermeneutics*, 33–45.

but secondary to this epochal change, should not make us lose sight of this essential and fundamental shift in perspective. Behind this shift of emphasis from the text to the reader lies something that is even more central. This is that it is the focus no longer on "stability" but rather on the "fluidity" of meaning. Let us sketch a concise description of some moments that determine the lineaments of interpretation in modernity.

Protestant Hermeneutics and Hermeneutics in "Early Modernity"

Some particular features will characterize the arrival and establishment of modern hermeneutics, such as the innovation introduced by the Reformers in their approach to reading the Bible, which becomes a book available and accessible to all. These include emphasis on and defense of the individual believer as an articulator of meaning; enfranchisement of secular hermeneutics from biblical hermeneutics; development and enhancement of research methodologies in related fields, such as philology, history, jurisprudence; the emergence of historical sciences; and the formation of an autonomous hermeneutics of a philosophical character by Friedrich Schleiermacher.

The affirmation of philosophical hermeneutics will be a long process that cannot completely disregard the links that even in modernity it had with biblical hermeneutics, partly because of the impetus received from the Reformation.[32] Luther elaborated a hermeneutics focused on the relationship between "word and faith" in antithesis to scholastic hermeneutics. He strongly united "spiritual sense" with "literal sense." Very early, in 1517,[33] Luther rejected the doctrine of the fourfold sense of Scripture for two reasons. First, to reject the explanatory and dogmatic allegorism of scholasticism, and second, to abandon the strong partnership that Catholicism had built over time between the "rule of faith," "tradition," and the "magisterium." For Luther, faith will be the only principle underlying the interpretation of Scripture.[34] We are faced with the birth and affirmation of a concrete and existential approach in biblical reading.

---

32. Jensen, *Theological Hermeneutics*, 64–77.
33. Lane, *Concise History of Christian Thought*, 155–60.
34. Nitti, *Lutero*, 229–55.

Luther will assign primacy in the interpretation of Scripture to practical application,[35] in sharp contrast to scholastic hermeneutics, which privileged the moment of explanatory analysis.[36] The Word of God must have real, actual, and immediate efficacy in the life of the believer. The Pauline antithesis between letter and Spirit[37] is radicalized by assigning to faith the sign of the presence in the believer of the Spirit of Christ, the task of understanding the meaning of Scripture. Beyond exegetical methodologies and rational analyses, the understanding of Christ in faith will become decisive for the understanding of the historical Christ. The Council of Trent censured Luther's hermeneutical principle as subjectivistic, contrasting it with the binding principle of Catholic hermeneutics, which assigns to tradition and the magisterium the task of establishing the true meaning of Scripture.[38] With Luther, the concrete and pragmatic approach of faith in reading the Bible is affirmed.

The innovative and propulsive force of this immediate approach to Scripture introduced by Luther introduced a limitation which emerged only over time. The "spiritual sense" favored by Luther needed a more solid foundation.[39] Thus a technical interest in languages and translation work gradually developed, initiating a process of textual improvement never known before. Philip Melanchthon,[40] humanist and disciple of Luther, introduced the canons proper to literary hermeneutics into scriptural exegesis. However, we owe the first edition of the Greek text of the New Testament (1516) to Erasmus of Rotterdam[41] who, completing the work begun by Luther, carried out intensive translation and editing of classical texts.

This pragmatic orientation of faith, which emerged in Luther and was consolidated by the pragmatic linguistic interest of the philologists, had further consolidation by the non-speculative and anti-metaphysical rationalism that would take over with the Enlightenment. This rationalism

---

35. Jeanrond, *Ermeneutica teologica*, 30–34.

36. Lane, *Concise History of Christian Thought*, 103–44.

37. Cf. 2 Co 3:6.

38. Heussi, *Kompendium der Kirchengeschichte*, 337–69. The fourth session of the Council of Trent (1546).

39. Prosperi, *Lutero*, 120–31.

40. Lane, *Concise History of Christian Thought*, 160–62. See Jensen, *Theological Hermeneutics*, 64–77.

41. Lane, *Concise History of Christian Thought*, 151–54. See Jensen, *Theological Hermeneutics*, 66.

in the reading of ancient texts will be highly critical of the Bible but, paradoxically, will not change its register; rather, it will end up reinforcing the concretism and pragmatism in the reading of texts inaugurated by the Reformers. In the eighteenth century, at the height of the Enlightenment, the privilege and primacy of sacred hermeneutics will be challenged, and this will lead to the progressive and total emancipation of secular hermeneutics.[42] Already in the previous century, Baruch Spinoza,[43] starting from the principles of the new rationalism that upheld the universality of reason and its undisputed primacy over faith, had asserted that the norm of biblical exegesis can only be the light of common reason.[44]

Gotthold E. Lessing,[45] also because of the rise of the new philological disciplines, capable of ascertaining with scientific rigor the authenticity and authority of a text, will declare in his book *The Christianity of Reason* that it is solely up to reason to determine the canons and principles of interpretation, even in the field of Scripture.[46] He explicitly replaces reference to faith and the Spirit, characteristic of Protestant hermeneutics, with reference to the only hermeneutical criterion now acceptable: that of universal reason, the only element that unites the text and its interpreter. The consequence was that, in the sphere of Scripture, a rationalistic and demythicizing interpretation will develop. In the secular sphere, texts with greater rational or cultural content will be privileged. But the anti-speculative and pragmatic orientation of both is the same.

At last, after a long and troubled process, hermeneutics will assert its philosophical autonomy, clearly distinguishing itself both from sectorial hermeneutics (exegetical, philological, legal) and from those attempts to elaborate an abstract universal hermeneutics still present in the eighteenth century. The affirmation of the centrality of reason, embodied in a new and autonomous subject (reader-centrism), and the anti-speculative direction of a concrete and efficient reading strategy (hermeneutic pragmatism) by now are already fully integrated into the structure and direction of modern hermeneutics. The formal birth of philosophical hermeneutics with Schleiermacher will only take note of this situation and have the merit of making this address comprehensible

---

42. Jensen, *Theological Hermeneutics*, 78–89.

43. Kraus, *Antico testamento*, 102–8.

44. Cf. Spinoza, *Tractatus theologico-politicus* (1670).

45. Kümmel, *Nuovo testamento*, 102–7. Compare Jensen, *Theological Hermeneutics*, 78–89.

46. Cf. *Das Christentum der Vernunft* (1753).

in a philosophical program built all around the maxim "understanding the understanding." According to Paul Ricœur's historical description, this definitive affirmation of philosophical hermeneutics will take place in two related but distinct stages, in which especially four names will play a central and foundational role: on the one hand, Friedrich Schleiermacher and Wilhelm Dilthey, on the other, Martin Heidegger and Hans-Georg Gadamer.[47]

The Foundation of Philosophical Hermeneutics and the Transition from "Epistemological" to "Ontological" Hermeneutics

Friedrich Schleiermacher[48] *(1768–1834)*

Schleiermacher is credited with the foundation of modern hermeneutics. In addition to the first formulation of a philosophical hermeneutics understood as a reflection on the meaning of human understanding through language, Schleiermacher is also credited with some central hermeneutic notions, foremost among them that of the "hermeneutic circle." With this, Schleiermacher also establishes a second hermeneutic principle: the principle of intuition (*einfühlung*), by which he indicates that beyond external rules and methodological canons, hermeneutics is characterized as a process of identification with the author's interiority. To truly understand a text, it is necessary to understand all that cultural, poetic, religious, literary and spiritual world that presided over its creation. It is necessary in a sense to descend, through a process of identification and intuition, into the interiority of the author of the work, so as to inwardly relive all that spiritual process that presided over his literary creation.

Schleiermacher[49] was driven initially to elaborate his hermeneutical philosophy by a pastoral concern. He was a theologian with a strong motivation to communicate the gospel in its essence and in language persuasive to contemporary man.[50] He aimed to make nineteenth-century men

---

47. Ricœur, *Ermeneutica filosofica*, 13–52.

48. Jensen, *Theological Hermeneutics*, 90–104; Palmer, *Hermeneutics*, 84–97; Grondin, *Introduction to Philosophical Hermeneutics*, 63–75.

49. Jensen, *Theological Hermeneutics*, 90–104.

50. Schleiermacher, *On Religion*; especially important is the first of the five speeches (pp. 41–63) where Schleiermacher describes his interlocutors; in the second speech he describes the essence and nature of religion.

formed by an Enlightenment culture understand the message conveyed by ancient texts written by authors formed by a predominantly mythical culture.

Schleiermacher introduced a strong point of rupture. This rupture is articulated not so much at the level of a radical rationality, but rather in tying interpretation to the individual interpreter and not to the group. It is at this level that the criticism made of him by Catholicism resides. This is disregarding tradition. He who says "tradition" says "group." In Schleiermacher, in fact, it is no longer the group nor tradition but only the individual that guarantees the articulation of meaning in the interpretive act. It will later be Gadamer, too, from a more secular perspective, who will make the same criticism of him, recalling that tradition is an indispensable horizon in the articulation and understanding of meaning. Gadamer and the "new hermeneutics" will understand the interpretive process as an intersubjective relationship.

The most severe criticism of Schleiermacher has come from the Protestant side. This critique was articulated by Karl Barth[51] in his famous commentary on the *Epistle to the Romans*,[52] where he contests Schleiermacher[53] (and all Protestant defined liberal theology that is inspired by his hermeneutics) of turning the Word of God into human words, thus faith into culture, revelation into philosophy. Referring to the theses of Kierkegaard, Barth considers it fundamental for the theologian and the Christian to make a radical choice between the Word of God and the word of man, because faith does not come from a cultural exercise of interpretation. The Word of God is a sign of contradiction for every culture, because it contradicts every worldly and philosophical attempt to speak about God. This is why Barth aims to free theology from the "Babylonian bondage" represented by philosophy, particularly in the form of Schleiermacher's hermeneutics.

In the work *Fides quaerens intellectum*,[54] Barth argues that the absolute and unconditional starting point for speaking about God is not philosophy or the cultural categories of one's time, but God himself, whose revelation is the foundation of faith, which is pure initiative of grace. Faith is a sign of a pre-choice by God and not a human choice due to

---

51. Jeanrond, *Ermeneutica teologica*, 127–37.
52. Compare Barth, *Römerbrief*, 261–76.
53. Barth, *Protestant Theology in the Nineteenth Century*, 411–59.
54. Cf. Barth, *Anselm*.

efforts of interpretation. Schleiermacher's critique of hermeneutics,[55] and of theology as "human discourse about God," could not be more direct. His criticism is also directed at Catholic positions based on *analogia entis*, to which Barth contrasts an unconditional *analogia fidei*, with which he wants to emphasize the infinite distance between the Word of God and the human word, between the free gift of faith, the absolute starting point of theology, and all forms of culture and theological hermeneutics.

Wilhelm Dilthey[56] (1833–1911)

Dilthey will continue the foundational work of philosophical hermeneutics through the specification of its nature, beginning with the distinction between explaining and understanding, between the sciences of nature and the sciences of spirit. Together with Schleiermacher, Wilhelm Dilthey[57] equally represents the first stage of a hermeneutic philosophy, which opposes the traditional "art of interpretation" to the study and analysis of the very fact of "understanding" and indeed conceives hermeneutics primarily as a reflection on the meaning of understanding and interpreting. It is with regard to a philosophy of understanding that Dilthey sets up the distinction, which later became classical, between explaining (*erklären*) and understanding (*verstehen*), between natural sciences (*Naturwissenschaften*) and spiritual sciences (*Geisteswissenschaften*). "We explain nature, but we understand spiritual life" was Dilthey's motto.[58]

While it is the task of the natural sciences to make evident, through the protocols of scientific explanation, the laws that govern physical and natural events, the spiritual sciences have the arduous task of understanding the whole vast world of man's spiritual expressions, from art to religion, from philosophy to culture, products of the spirituality of man who is essentially a historical being, not reducible to an entity of nature and not explicable through the protocols of the natural sciences.

The notion of life (*leben*), as well as those of vital experience (*erleben*) and lived experience (*erlebnis*), will become important and fundamental concepts in the context of later developments in vitalistic and

---

55. Barth, *Der Römerbrief*, 225.

56. Jensen, *Theological Hermeneutics*, 105–14; Palmer, *Hermeneutics: Interpretation*, 98–123; Grondin, *Introduction to Philosophical Hermeneutics*, 76–90.

57. Jensen, *Theological Hermeneutics*, 105–9.

58. Ferraris, *Storia dell'ermeneutica*, 162–83. Cf. Dilthey, *Entstehung der Hermeneutik*, 144.

phenomenological hermeneutics. Lived experience takes on in Dilthey the meaning of the link between an author's work and his life, in the sense that to truly "understand" a work one must understand the "lived experience" expressed in it. This does not coincide with the author's external life but rather with his existential experience, which is the "life project" that qualifies his existence and constitutes the most valid context of reference for its interpretation and understanding.

To the various currents of historical positivism in the nineteenth century, Dilthey contrasts a hermeneutic notion of history as the creative work of subjectivity and one that cannot be understood without an understanding of the radically historical character of man. Human essence is not determined a priori, but is determined historically through the creative process of his freedom. Hermeneutic understanding, as historical understanding, is therefore temporal, historically determined. Beginning with Dilthey, the hermeneutic problem of understanding thus becomes the problem of "historical understanding," because of the historical character assigned to man, thus also to his interpreting and understanding.

For Schleiermacher and Dilthey, at the center of the interpretive process, albeit with important nuances, is the interpreter (reader) and his or her "understanding." We are faced, in essence, with two "reader-centric" hermeneutics. This determines the epistemological orientation of interpretation in their project. Here, at this level, lies the strength and limitation of their enterprise. The strength lies in this focus on understanding and in the rigor of describing it with technical and formal categories of high precision, equal to those used in the natural sciences. It is also here that their great limitation emerges, which also becomes the limitation of all modern hermeneutics in its first phase.

This hermeneutics suffers from a major ontological deficit that neither Schleiermacher nor Dilthey was able to correct. According to Ricœur's reading, only with Heidegger and Gadamer will this deficit be filled, but in a bad way. In their solution of the ontological problem both will create a new one. It is the problem of minimization and trivialization of the critical instance which every hermeneutic must always be able to integrate into its own project. Let us briefly describe the ontological corrective of the hermeneutics proposed by Heidegger and Gadamer.

Martin Heidegger[59] (1889–1976)

Martin Heidegger shifted the central problem in his philosophical hermeneutics from the interpretation of texts to ontological understanding.[60] He regarded this as a direct being-in-the-world, not mediated by texts or other symbols, thus a more authentic being and not simply as an empirical presupposition for knowledge. Hermeneutics becomes analytic of the conditions of existence, no longer as one of the possible ways of understanding or knowing through authentic interpretation. It is the essential feature of existence itself, since man is a continuous self-interpreting being.

When we read a text and interpret it, we do not accumulate important information to know better how to move and orient ourselves in life. Understanding is a sign that we are already rooted in life, before we can develop reasoning on that belonging. The typical division between the knowing subject and the known object, which presupposes any kind of cognitive approach, is preceded in Heidegger by a prior state of binding and belonging that represents his ontological extract. Hermeneutic understanding cannot be reduced to knowing more. It articulates more at the base, a presence in the world, a mode of being.

In the second Heidegger, the *Kehre* (turning point), this ontological dimension will become even more substantial. The question of being has been flawed from Plato onward because it is Plato who thinks of being as an entity. This is where the misplacement of the ontological difference between being and entities comes from. For Plato it is the subject who sees truth and goes in search of it but ends up tampering with it because he makes it an object. This is quite the opposite of what happened with the pre-Socratic philosophers, for whom truth is not grasped by the understanding gaze but is itself revealed by itself (*aletheia*). It is not the subject that reveals truth. Heidegger follows the pre-Socratics in the non-objective definition of truth. Truth is an unveiling and a hiding. This means that Heidegger decenters the focus of reflection from the subject to being.

It is not central to man, who is only a conduit of being. It is being that takes the initiative to reveal itself. In response to a text by Sartre entitled "Existentialism is a Humanism," in which he asserts that at the center of the action of a reality, in which there is no god, is man, Heidegger

---

59. Jensen, *Theological Hermeneutics*, 115–34; Palmer, *Hermeneutics*, 124–39; Palmer, *Hermeneutics*, 140–61; Grondin, *Introduction to Philosophical*, 91–105.

60. Ferraris, *Storia dell'ermeneutica*, 237–63.

responds with his *Letter on Humanism*,[61] in 1947, in which he asserts that for him at the center is not man, who is only a vehicle of being; at the center is being that self-manifests itself. Heidegger is thus one of the most important figures of anti-humanism. Heidegger's philosophy can be said to be "post-humanistic," because it places other structures of ontological character as priority and before man.

Hans-Georg Gadamer[62] (1900–2002)

Gadamer would follow in the same wake begun by Heidegger and aim, like him, to correct the risk of a cognitive drift in modern hermeneutics.[63] From the very first pages of his major work *Truth and Method*,[64] he made it clear how his hermeneutic reflection aimed, more radically, to reveal the universal and ontological character of the phenomenon of understanding. In this sense, Gadamer's attention, in the wake of Heideggerian teaching, is directed primarily to the figure of pre-comprehension (*Vorverständnis*). This is the tendency that thought shows to attribute to Being, knowing a sense to some extent preconceived. This is not entirely arbitrary, since it reflects a dimension of belonging that precedes and founds a subsequent relation of knowing.

The focus on the necessary character of pre-understanding in all forms of knowledge leads Gadamer to distance himself from the traditional Enlightenment gnoseological view, according to which knowledge consists in holding that the subject is quite distinct from the object, so that knowledge is all the more adequate the sharper the mutual autonomy of the two terms. Indeed, according to Gadamer, if every researcher begins his typical activity only from a pre-understanding of the meaning of what he proposes to know, then it must be agreed that no original separation can be given between the two terms and, ultimately, that they exist from the beginning within a single dimension.[65]

---

61. Heidegger, *Basic Writings*, 213–65.

62. Jensen, *Theological Hermeneutics*, 135–60; Palmer, *Hermeneutics*, 162–93, 194–217; Grondin, *Introduction to Philosophical Hermeneutics*, 106–23.

63. Ferraris, *Storia dell'ermeneutica*, 265–76.

64. Gadamer, *Verità e metodo*.

65. As Gianni Vattimo points out well, in reference to Gadamer, every interpretation is given within an Überlieferungsgeschehen (a historical tradition), which in Vattimo's case is that of the Catholic church, to which he explicitly refers. Vattimo, *Essere e dintorni*, 325ff.

The criticism that Ricœur makes of Heidegger and Gadamer, beyond the undoubted benefit of having given an ontological foundation to understanding, is that of skipping too easily the dimension of cognitive and analytic verification that any hermeneutics must instead always be able to protect and guarantee. Gadamer and Heidegger's position cannot be described as "reader-centric," however, the extreme, anti-critical ontological corrective they propose leaves the "reader-centrism" of modern hermeneutics intact and, by leaving it intact, paradoxically reinforces it. Even after Heidegger and Gadamer, the "reader-centeredness" of contemporary hermeneutics has not diminished. It has even increased. The only difference is that today it coexists with a parallel ontological direction inspired by, among others, Heidegger and Gadamer. This does not correct it but paradoxically keeps it alive.

What really changes with the arrival of modern hermeneutics in its various moments and manifestations compared to ancient and medieval hermeneutics? Our reading hypothesis is that modern hermeneutics produces a radical shift that essentially marks the transition from the realm of the "strong text" (text-centrism), typical of the premodern period, to the "creative reader" (reader-centrism) typical of contemporary hermeneutics. Modern hermeneutics is not only a chronological event. It represents the site of a new foundation: the foundation of the subject capable of standing rationally before the known object. Beyond Schleiermacher's specific contribution in introducing new hermeneutic categories, this new foundation is the same foundation that is also articulated in other parallel modern disciplines, such as sociology and psychology. This includes all the other modern disciplines that often retained the old name, but were in fact already taking shape as strongly rational disciplines having the subject as their center.

This centrality of the reader as a rational subject was not and is not always evident, because modern hermeneutics is also simultaneously the period in which textual criticism was born and established and thus the attention, care, and obsession with the accuracy of the text. The modern period is where scientific attention to the text is born. For the first time, there will be critical texts of ancient works, including the Bible. Yet, the implicit and primordial assumption does not decay. All modern hermeneutics, despite its enormous attention to the text, remains a "reader-centered" hermeneutic.

This fact will not leave the hermeneutic circle intact. While preserving it, the status of the text itself will undergo profound change. The definition of the text as a stable text could not survive. The text becomes fluid. This is a system that offers the reader only a set of initial ingredients and suggestions, which it will be up to the omnipotent reader to complete in a new and original project. Although we physically read the same Bible, in reality, our Bible is different from what the apostles and even the Reformers read. Our constructivist understanding of reality and the Bible leads us to see in the Bible only the inspired ingredients of a "cake" that is not given but that we must create ourselves. Even those who refuse to adapt to the current worldview in biblical interpretation are actually already widely applying a constructivist approach in all other levels of life.

This is understandable only if we analyze modern hermeneutics in the context of modern culture. Modern culture introduces a radical shift from a "cosmocentric" view, based on the stability of the world, to an "anthropocentric" view of life, based on movement and change. In this new perspective, the world, life, identities, events, and meanings do not exist as finite and fixed realities. They are merely ingredients that each individual is called upon to use in the construction of a particular chosen project. The world, the family, the state, etc., are not houses to be inhabited, but materials to be used in new constructions. The modern and its twin brother, the postmodern world, are "constructivist" in spirit and intention. Hermeneutics could not escape this fate of the culture in which it was born.

Hermeneutics in the "Second Modernity"

This new phase of modernity is sometimes called postmodernity and sometimes second modernity or late modernity. At the hermeneutic level we will use them as equivalent terms, even though they represent different understandings of this historical period. One would hope that with the arrival of postmodernity the centrality of the reader would diminish or disappear. But this is not what has happened. Postmodernity is an important phenomenon that marks and describes today a new way of standing in front of life and that, in a break with modernity, deconstructs the validity and relevance of the metanarratives foundational to the various spheres of our contemporary culture. This makes them on the one hand partial, thus no longer transversal and universal, and on the other hand, relative and thus objectively non-binding in the way they were in early modernity.

Modern culture, in its early Enlightenment period up to the first half of the twentieth century, despite its secularism, would not have changed course with respect to the explanatory and realizable confidence of human reason. It would still have believed in the possibility of explaining and, consequently, changing the world from objective, rational, and totalizing human projects. Today, however, ideology, any kind of ideology, has entered a crisis by implosion from within and not solely from external causes. This would be the logic that marks the advent of postmodernity or second modernity.

Something important has also happened in hermeneutics. We are no longer dealing with the same hermeneutics. The problem is to specify what has changed and what has remained as before. Our reading hypothesis is that the distinctive feature of modern hermeneutics has not gone away. The typical "reader-centered" character of modern hermeneutics has not changed with the arrival of postmodernity. Only its justification has changed.

Here we need to pause briefly to describe the true scope of postmodernity so that we can then connect it with hermeneutics. There is a diatribe about how much has really changed with the arrival of postmodernity. In Anglo-Saxon circles and in philosophy people more willingly speak of the arrival of a new era, postmodernity. In European circles and in the social sciences, especially in sociology, people prefer to speak of a second modernity to identify this new historical period, which took over roughly from the 1970s onward. Sociologists speak of late modernity (Giddens), second modernity (Beck, Tourraine), and hypermodernity (Sebastien Charles).

They wish to affirm two things. First, that something has indeed changed since the beginnings of modernity. What has changed is not easy to say. Some speak of the demise of the great ideologies, others of fragmentation, still others of the loss of institutionality, etc. All of these are descriptive of an undeniable change. The psychological-anthropological attitude must also be taken into account. The great confidence of early modernity seems to have been succeeded by an across-the-board distrust. One wonders, however, what came before. Have we lost confidence and as a consequence also lost confidence in the great ideas that were previously evident and imposed themselves on us with their force? Or did the great explanatory systems first collapse, and then did human self-confidence also fail?

Anthropological change is just as visible as ideological change. Yet, in the essential data, nothing has changed. If we take some specific areas and elements of modernity, we not only find that these still subsist but that they have even become radicalized. This is the thesis of Sebastien Charles[66] regarding four typical characteristics of modernity: individualism, democracy, economics, and techno-scientific development. Let us take only one of these four elements as an example: individualism. This has not only not disappeared in so-called postmodernity but has even gained more ground. Today, in postmodernity, we are even more individualistic. Only the format and perspective of its foundation has changed. The typical pragmatic and optimistic individualism of early modernity has been overlaid by the equally typical aesthetic and uncertain individualism of late modernity.

What implications does this have for hermeneutics? Basically two. First, the status of the text has changed. The text is neither definitive nor final. The text has become, in its status, even more fluid. It is only a starting point, a kind of initial ingredient that requires new elaboration. Second, the reader has reinforced his presence. This becomes decisive for the elaboration and construction of meaning that without him would remain unconcluded. All contemporary hermeneutics tends to be even more "reader-centric" than it was in Schleiermacher's time.

It is in this light that the rise of the most recent methodologies in textual analysis and exegesis must be seen. For example, the school of reader response criticism[67] has shifted the center of gravity completely to the reader's side. The reader becomes an active agent in the creation of meaning, as he or she contributes to the "real existence" of the work and completes its meaning through interpretation. This school of thought argues that literature should be viewed as a performance art in which each reader creates his or her own performance related to the text. Although literary theory has long paid some attention to the role of the reader in creating the meaning and experience of a literary work, it was not until the 1970s, and particularly in the United States and Germany, that this approach became established through the work of Norman Holland, Stanley Fish, Wolfgang Iser, Hans-Robert Jauss, Roland Barthes, and others.[68]

We must include Umberto Eco in this list of authors. He will give this new centrality of the reader its most accomplished and articulated form, speaking of the "open" text. The text in his view allows multiple interpretations in a different qualitative sense. This is the sense of creation and not just application of meanings. Here truth is never unambiguous, but is constituted by an infinite interpretative process of objects in which

---

66. Charles, *L'hypermoderne expliqué aux enfants*, 15–22.
67. Jensen, *Theological Hermeneutics*, 192–206.
68. Fry, *Theory of Literature*, 68–81.

there remains only a "shaping form" that the subject must continually interpret. The work of art itself, meaning both "high" art and mass and popular artistic productions, is never bound to a single and permanent meaning. It needs a continuous interpretive integration of both critics and the common user. The "open" work is a text that allows multiple interpretations. In contrast, a closed text leads the reader to only one interpretation. Later Eco will complete his theory by arguing that the "novel" is a "lazy machine" that must continually renew itself in its meaning through readers' interpretation. Eco says that a text requires and needs someone to help it function, since it is a product whose interpretive fate must be part of its own generative mechanism.[69] Postmodern hermeneutics has radicalized even more the "reader-centeredness" that was already present in modern hermeneutics from the time of its founding.

This fact has qualitatively introduced two new opposing phenomena that mark and condition the landscape of current biblical hermeneutics. On the one hand, there is the exponential multiplication of interpretations that are not always convergent and that create a strong hermeneutical fragmentation. On the other, there is, as a reaction to this fragmentation, a trend that aims instead to defend the compactness of the Bible and its interpretation.

We will provide from a predominantly descriptive and an non-evaluatative point of view a description of the "hermeneutic fragmentation" and "hermeneutic monolithism" that mark our present in the next section. In Part II, in chapters seven and eight, we will pause to consider instead the change of these tendencies into real hermeneutic dysfunctions or even hermeneutic pathologies. We will also explain why we choose to use strong and categorical terminology (pathologies) regarding these interpretive deformations.

HERMENEUTIC FRAGMENTATION. PLURALISM,[70] AND HERMENEUTIC POLYTHEISM[71]

Let us begin by briefly describing the first of these two phenomena. A great diversity of interpretations has always existed in Christianity.

69. Eco, *Lector in fabula*, 52–54.
70. Kärkkäinen, *Christian Theology for a Pluralistic World*, 1–8.
71. Hermeneutical pluralism, which has become structural today, is prolonged, according to Geffré, into a religious pluralism typical of our time. What has caused what? Was it religious pluralism that flexibilized the hermeneutics of sacred texts or

However, this diversity was embedded in a context of basic stability and was given by an understanding of God, reality, and the group as ordered and stable systems. Unlike the past, in addition to the increasingly radical dynamism of reference systems, the diversity of interpretations that exists among us today possess some new features that we would like to briefly highlight. We mention four of them.

1. Interpretive diversification is markedly more widespread and cross-cutting. What was the exception in the past has now become the rule. One does not have to go very far to confront an interpretation different from one's own. It is close to us, next door. It has become familiar to us and is part of the territory we inhabit. While in the past the territories were "hermeneutically" more homogeneous, today they are very fragmented and diverse. Unlike in the past, today, when there is no interpretive diversity, there is a spontaneous feeling of being in a dogmatic and totalizing system. This proves that diversity has become structural.

2. This hermeneutical diversity is widespread and structurally more tolerant and open to dialogue. There is not necessarily a sustained dialogue and a constant exchange between these differentiated hermeneutical positions, but while they were on the warpath in the past, they now coexist side by side without too much conflict. Tolerance today is demanded as a virtue for all. It is no longer only a desirable attitude as in the past. From an abstract value it has become a moral task: everyone, indifferently, is called upon to cultivate it. Without tolerance comes a lack of the familiarity with diversity that today is a prerequisite for making any aggregative system work.

3. This fragmentation occurs not only between communities or between faith systems. It occurs within the same communities and within the same religious systems. In order to confront hermeneutical diversity, one only needs to remain within one's own group and try to take note of the dynamics that occur within it on a regular basis. Interpretive diversity today, unlike in the past, does not loudly and explicitly claim its legitimacy. It simply exists and precedes the typical recognition mechanisms that were instead the norm in the past. More than

---

the flexibilization of the hermeneutics of sacred texts that opened the profile of religious communities? It is difficult to say. In any case, the final effect, hermeneutical and religious pluralism, is now a cross-cutting fact that stands out. Cf. Geffré, *Credere e interpretare*, 104–26.

a choice, it is a fact. So spontaneous is its establishment that it can be embodied by the same person who just before fought it. Not only communities but individuals themselves are traversed by different stances according to the times and levels of life involved.

4. We should note that an implicit legitimization of this fragmentation has taken over, given by a hermeneutic relativism that seems to be the most natural and appropriate response to this new situation. There is a tendency to explain this diversity according to a preferential scheme. The hermeneutic choice seems no longer to be the object of truth or falsehood but only the result of a personal sensibility and as such always legitimate. Loving blue or yellow or reading this way or that way is neither true nor false but is the product of simple subjective preference. This legitimization from below is more implicit than explicit, less compact and less overbearing. Paradoxically, it is more effective and more durable. More effective because, although slower, it spreads more transversally. More durable because, being preferential, there is no argument that can deconstruct it.

What to do in this situation? At first, one must simply take note of it as an irreversible fact and then try to adjust. We need to introduce a hermeneutic realism that recognizes not what we would like to be there but takes simply note of what is there. Several times the ideal prompts us to turn our backs on reality and live in an illusory world. This test of hermeneutic realism is not necessarily a renunciation of truth, as it might seem. On the contrary, it might be a way of welcoming a different truth that we do not yet know. It might be truth that knocks on our door from an atypical place that is unfamiliar to us. It would not be the first time that truth comes in unexpected and unusual forms. Is this not a characteristic of truth since time immemorial? This indicates to us that taking serious note of the diversification taking place is not an improper act. It is suggested by the widespread presence of this differentiation in other areas.

Such is the case, for example, in ethics. In modern-day ethics we find the same fragmentation with the corresponding widespread relativization resulting from it. Could we really say that the undoubted relativization of contemporary ethics, a product of its marked differentiation, is completely negative? Certainly not. It has freed us from bullying, false values, rigidity, obsessions, and millenarian ethical arbiter. Hasn't this ethical relativism, in certain areas, made our faith and our lives more humane?

The best way to respond to this diversification and fragmentation is not to suffer and accept it as an event of fate. Neither is it to oppose it to the bitter end and on principle. One must learn to understand what reality offers us. Understanding already implies a first degree of acceptance. At the hermeneutic level this is what Paul Ricœur suggests to us when he speaks of the inescapable fragmentation of contemporary hermeneutics of which we must take note. It is what he calls "conflict of interpretations,"[72] multiple and unassimilable, as a structural fact of our age, with which we must learn to live, because they are not only legitimate but also irreversible.

Since Ricœur wrote about the diversity of possible interpretations as a fact of our time, diversification and fragmentation have become even more radicalized, to the point that what was sporadic and sectorial has now become the rule, not only at the level of interpretation but also at the cultural level. Diversification has become a defining feature of today's societies. Today we live in multicultural societies that must learn to live together with diversified paradigms, not only between interpretations but also between different cultures, actually living together on the same territory or in the same church. Pluralism has become not only a fact but also a moral duty.

A theological element must be added to this fact of simple descriptive ascertainment. This diversity of interpretations and cultures is not yet the greatest stumbling block. This is only the manifestation and extension of a deeper diversity, of a basic theological diversity. Theological diversity, however, which is not, necessarily and always, the result of either petty quarrels or short-sighted unilateralism. That combative, quarrelsome, petty, and deeply ideologized religious diversity we are not considering here. We are talking about conscious, balanced, and respectful theological diversity.

This diversity is not the dazzle of an out-of-control theological euphoria nor the mirage of a lost conviction. This diversity, at least in part, stems from deep convictions and long and suffered spiritual journeys. It arises from a fidelity to and passion for truth itself. It arises from and in respect for it. At the same time, we note that the other before us dignifiedly and respectfully claims the same validity, the same relevance for an alternative conviction of his or her own to ours. The diversity of theologies is certainly not a new factor. Diverse theologies have always existed, but they tended to exist in different systems. Today the new fact is the existence of diverse theologies within the same faith system.

---

72. Ricœur, *Conflitto delle interpretazioni*, 10–33.

For this reason, the time has perhaps come to build a new, more inclusive theological paradigm that keeps in balance a necessary convergence of theological diversity in the same system but does not downwardly homogenize this diversity that is not and cannot always be complementary. It always creates a tension given by the non-assimilability of the parties involved. So, how are we to articulate a new theological paradigm that includes and tolerates, without becoming paranoid and obsessive, a healthy tension that this irreversible theological diversity necessarily creates?

Our response is that of the introduction of *hermeneutic polytheism.* Beyond the seemingly provocative impact of the term, let us try to look at the substance. It is not the term itself that matters. It can be this one or another. It is the underlying mechanism that seems necessary to us. "Religious pluralism," as a category so far used to describe a certain degree of diversification, while useful at certain levels, is not sufficient today to explain this theological diversity. We are facing a new phenomenon. Increasingly, different views of God are being compared within the same faith community, creating de facto "interpretive polytheism," where none of the parties involved can claim a monopoly on right understanding. At the same time, however, neither can it renounce the validity of its own position.

At stake are not assertions about secondary aspects of faith. At stake are assertions about God himself, one's own understanding of who God is, the true foundation of a faith experience. Real different understandings of God coexist without being able to assimilate them into a final synthesis. We are faced with a strong "polytheism of ideas" about God. This is a fact that one must learn to understand without automatic purist jerks. One should not proceed by cliché but by analysis of substance. Fundamentally, at the heart of this phenomenon is articulated the double claim. On one hand, it consciously claims to assimilate one's idea about God to God himself. On the other hand, it unconsciously assumes that God is reducible to the idea we have about him. In both cases there is a lack of awareness of a gap between my ideas and God. If I can think and feel God close to me through my ideas—one thinks—how can my ideas be wrong and coexist with other ideas opposite to mine? The automatic conclusion is that my ideas are true and others' ideas are necessarily false, thus unacceptable. This conclusion ignores the fact that God reveals himself to us, despite the partiality and anomalies of our ideas, and that God in himself is ineffable, thus beyond any of our ideas.

One cannot demand that one's ideas about God do not aspire to express Being or reality. At the same time, one cannot demand that one's ideas about God truly and exhaustively speak about God. Two incommensurabilities are compared here. These are the legitimacy of human incommensurability in saying "God" and the divine incommensurability that challenges that of man. "Hermeneutical polytheism" can offer an alternative in that, by working on the gap between God and the human understanding of God, on the one hand it legitimizes the human claim in saying God, and on the other hand, it challenges it by imposing a constraint of plurality on it.

The polytheist paradigm is being revived as an innovative cultural form because it enacts both the recognition of faith and the relativization of that faith itself. This is why the return of the polytheist paradigm would not be a negative thing, from a cultural point of view, comments anthropologist and philologist at the University of Siena, Maurizio Bettini in his book *In Praise of Polytheism*.[73]

That polytheism is back and has taken hold in the West is a fact. The Christian world certainly cannot accept this either as a fact or as a cultural purpose. We would be shortsighted if we did not see, as Christians, that this polytheism, as cultural pluralism, already exists even in Christian communities as "polytheism of ideas," precisely as "hermeneutical polytheism." This is what we mean when we speak of the need to create a new theological paradigm of this diversity, which is not only linguistic, ethical, interpretive, or cultural, and gives a more positive and more inclusive reading. This is an irreversible theological diversity that needs to be understood and within certain limits accepted. This is what the term "hermeneutical polytheism" tries to do.

It is therefore not a matter of "ontological polytheism"—as Christians this we cannot but deny—but of "interpretive polytheism." This is important to recognize because the terms "diversity of hermeneutics" and "religious pluralism" still do not express the intensity of these differences. We are not just dealing with different readings but with different ideas of God. It is still the same God but grasped differently, and none of these interpretations can claim to have the most correct understanding, much less the most total understanding of God. It is a true "interpretive polytheism" that must be acknowledged and handled with wisdom and tolerance.

Here the lesson of Max Weber can be helpful. In one of two well-known lectures on the *Beruf* (vocation/profession) as an attitude in times of crisis, that of "Science as a Profession," he introduces the concept of

---

73. Bettini, *Elogio del politeismo*, 5–16.

"polytheism of values."[74] Weber sees a revival of the polytheism of the ancient world in a new sense, after a centuries-long dominance of a grand rationalism sprung from messianic prophecy that is reductive of reality. Rationalism and Christian enthusiasm share the same obsession: reducing everything to the one, to explain and save the world with a unified scheme and paradigm. Especially in times of crisis, we are always called to choose among multiple and conflicting values, knowing that no value can be an absolute normative criterion and that there can be no completely rational argumentation of choice.

The introduction of this paradigm on diversity could lead us to increase the degree of uncertainty. Actually, the inclusion of a limited dimension of uncertainty, determined by a "hermeneutical polytheism," would not be new. In fact, we already find it in the Bible. This is more so in the Old Testament than in the New Testament, because with the clear diversification of God into three persons that is affirmed in the New Testament, a nominal homogenization of God also takes over. In the Old Testament, on the other hand, the affirmation of the one God is synchronic with the plurality of his denomination. To the "compact monotheism" of Islam and the "trinitarian monotheism" of Christianity, the Old Testament contrasts its "differentiated monotheism" given by a "hermeneutic polytheism" that is embodied in the plurality of its denomination.

There is no one way to name God. The Old Testament is the example of a "nominal polytheism." God cannot be named in a single way, on pain of impoverishing his nature. This nominal polytheism, visible for example in the contrast between Yahweh (Ge 2) and Elohim (Ge 1), enriched the Old Testament because the same person, God, is called and thought of in such different perspectives that at times it would seem as if we were dealing with two different persons. It is still the same person but described in his complexity from two different interpretive perspectives.

INTERPRETIVE COMPACTNESS:[75] SOLA SCRIPTURA AND HERMENEUTICAL MONOLITHISM.

Now let us go on to consider the second contemporary phenomenon alluded to in this last section: "biblical monolithism." This counter-movement

---

74. Weber, *Scienza come professione*, 5–44.

75. The hermeneutical and religious pluralism just described is paradoxically accompanied by an opposite movement, which is that of a religious fundamentalism. Again, it is not easy to understand whether religious fundamentalism has prompted the

is singular because it is certainly not new. Reactionary movements are common in history—one exaggeration is answered by another of the opposite sign. This is what happened in the sixteenth century. Although it might not seem so to us Protestants, the original Protestantism is, in fact, an exaggerated and radical movement. Radicality is often necessary; otherwise paradigm shifts would not occur. The new paradigms that Thomas Kuhn[76] would like to see more gradual and sequential actually come most often by radical rupture. Protestantism is proof of this. The reaction, however, is equally disproportionate and exaggerated; in this case it is the Counter-Reformation that is the proof. But in provocation and counter-reaction there is a mutual loss. Protestantism, in some areas easily discernible today, was born already a loser, because it was precisely exaggerated and one-sided. As did Tridentine Catholicism, precisely because it allowed itself to be excessively conditioned by the radicalism of the Reformers, it responded in a counter-reactionary and radical way, impoverishing the richness it had hitherto had within itself.

It also happened in the early 1900s, first in the US and then around the world: in reaction to the strong impetus and dynamism of a rational reading of the Bible, embodied in the "historical-critical" method, many second- and third-generation Protestant churches instead chose the opposite path of biblical literalism.[77] And this is what is still happening at the beginning of this twenty-first century: to the widespread interpretive fragmentation just described, there corresponds and follows a counter-reaction of churches and groups that instead emphasize the compact, objective, and unambiguous authority of the Bible, invoking, in a strong if one-sided and restrictive way, the noble, misinterpreted principle of *sola Scriptura*.[78]

---

adoption of a fundamentalist hermeneutic or whether the opposite has happened. In any case, the obvious fact is not only the resurgence of a religious and hermeneutical fundamentalism, but also the concomitant and parallel hermeneutical pluralism. Cf. Geffré, *Credere e interpretare*, 60–103.

76. Kuhn, *Structures of Scientific Revolutions*, 6–18.

77. They are also called revival churches and in the early 1900s, in various ways, reconnected with the Protestant tradition but introducing some elements of rupture, including a stronger adherence to the biblical text in contestation of the historical-critical method that dominated in those years among the mother Protestant churches. For a description of this biblical hardening in one of these churches, namely Adventism, see: Campbell, *1919*; Reid, *Understanding Scripture*; Cole and Petersen, *Hermeneutics, Intertextuality*.

78. This is the phenomenon that Philip Jenkins describes in this twenty-first century and which sanctions the shift of Christianity to the south, giving birth to a new Christianity characterized by a fundamentalist hermeneutic, though different from that

It would be wrong to read this new form of biblical and hermeneutical fundamentalism in the present as a reminiscence and resistance of the biblical literalism of a century ago. Here we have a hypermodern phenomenon that is not of the past but of the future and that needs to be read and understood properly.

Already in describing this counter-reaction, the existing terms seem inaccurate and limiting. Propaedeutically we assign to it the name "biblical monolithism." It does not describe, as the name might suggest, that radical band we know by the name of "biblical literalism" or even "biblical fundamentalism." We are not talking about fanatical or bigoted Christians who use the Bible as a compact instrument of truth against a world warped by sin and which must be saved by the power of the Bible. In biblical fanaticism everything is out of whack: the conception of truth, of the world, of sin, of salvation, of power. We will not stop on this.

Instead, in biblical monolithism, we have a noble, balanced, and even dynamic religiosity but one that tends to have a strong idea of the Bible. The Bible would articulate a clear and immediate message. In this tendency toward a biblical monolithism, which is present in the intermediate and non-fanatical segments of Christianity, there seem to be two leading features.

One is the intent to conceive of the Bible as a compact and homogeneous unity. Continuity is preferred to discontinuity, complementarity to tension, synthesis to fragmentation, because God and truth are identified as unitary realities. If this is so, the Bible must also bear the same traits within itself. The most recurrent phrases to affirm this first conviction are "the Bible never contradicts itself," "any contrasts are only apparent," or "the apparent contrasts belong to the human part of the Bible."

The most distinctive feature of this first belief is the thought that the Bible is structurally clear. There would be no opacity in the Bible. Its meaning would be perfectly transparent and clear. It is the reader, by the vices he automatically brings with him, who introduces these opacities that must be dismantled through interpretation.

Another is an intent to conceive of the Bible as an autonomous reality. The Bible would come into being and subsist by virtue of a purely

---

of the early 1900s. Jenkins, *Next Christendom*; Jenkins, *New Faces of Christianity*, 8–25. This new phenomenon of hermeneutical hardening corresponds to a larger sociological one, which is the bet on strong and compact reference group identity (*communitarianism*) and which Elena Pulcini describes as "endogamic communitarianism." Pulcini, *Cura del mondo*, 31–112.

internal mechanism of faith. At this second level of relationship with the external, the opposite is chosen: discontinuity over continuity, tension over complementarity, rupture over integration. The Bible would not depend on any human reality. It is the pure product of divine revelation. The mantra of this second conviction is the *sola Scriptura* principle: the Bible is sufficient unto itself. To understand faith, and the way it struggles to survive, nothing else is needed. One understands the *sola Scriptura* principle in its most exclusionary, exclusive, and self-referential dimension.

Biblical monolithism thrives on the belief that the Bible is to be protected and preserved from all manipulation and distortion. A purist view of Scripture is outlined. The longer the Bible remains in contact with realities foreign to it, the greater the risk of contamination. Anything from the outside can only contaminate the sacred Word. If the external is considered in any usefulness, it is only to the extent that this allows itself to be transformed by the pure Word of God.

The Bible therefore must be protected, guarded, and safeguarded in its compactness, for it is precisely this consistency that would represent the sign of its truth and divine inspiration. This new biblical monolithism fits into the larger context of the rediscovery of identities, which have become strong bastions of refuge and resistance against a commodification of life expressed in the implicit manifesto of globalization.

Certainly faith, together with the Bible, must resist this homogenizing and widespread tendency of the economy and a consumerist culture expressed in globalization, while being careful not to create a polarization that ends up favoring it. Faith is alternative, not escape; critique, not demonization. For this reason, biblical faith must not isolate itself but enter into critical dialogue with its own time. When this does not happen, the Bible comes out deformed. In fact, the Bible becomes monolithic when it is detached from everything else, from life itself, from the world, from culture; in other words, when it becomes abstract. Conversely, when the Bible becomes monolithic it becomes detached from everything. The more monolithic an entity is, the more abstract it becomes; similarly, the more abstract a reality is, the more monolithic it becomes.

III

The Text and Distanciation
The Value of a Slow Interpretation[1]

BIBLICAL HERMENEUTICS IS AN applied hermeneutics and, as such, it uses in its work the categories introduced and established by philosophical hermeneutics. The "text"[2] is one of them. Indeed, it is the first category of hermeneutics, the most important one. In the application of this category, after Paul Ricœur, a reversal of perspectives takes place.[3] By virtue of the originality of biblical hermeneutics, progressively the category "biblical text" from application becomes a model. The ideal text presupposed by the Bible would enrich with additional data what the text in general and as a cultural category should be. And from an applied hermeneutic it becomes a leading hermeneutic category. What this originality consists of we will try to describe in this chapter, but in the meantime we distinguish two types of texts.

---

1. Marguerat and Bourquin, *Per leggere i racconti biblici*, 130–33.

2. The text, the mainstay of hermeneutics, can be described from different angles. Jeanrond emphasizes the stability dimension of the text by speaking of "written text." We chose a more dynamic dimension by speaking of "formative text," which, in essence, emphasizes less the reader's adaptation to the text's indications than the text's investment in the reader as a creative reader. Cf. Jeanrond, *Ermeneutica teologica*, 134–56.

3. "An entirely opposite relationship between the two hermeneutics appears, on the other hand, precisely when we consider theological hermeneutics applied to a certain type of texts, the biblical ones: it reveals such original features that it causes a progressive reversal of relationship, so much so that philosophical hermeneutics remains subordinate to theological hermeneutics and becomes an organon of it" (Ricœur, *Ermeneutica filosofica*, 79–80).

WHAT IS A TEXT?[4] Not all texts have the same status and nature. Regardless of the content of which texts are the means and medium, we can distinguish two major groups. A first group of texts is marked by *precision*. These texts are characterized on the one hand by the detailed and specific description of the individual elements of the information they convey and on the other by the completeness and exhaustiveness of all that information provided. Put in another way, these texts describe well and say a lot. Their accuracy lies precisely in the attention to detail and the accuracy of the data provided. Reading them requires a parallel and corresponding diligence in assimilating that data.

In contrast, the second group of texts is marked rather by the "horizon" it opens and suggests to the reader. These texts are characterized on the one hand by the approximation and inaccuracy in the description of individual data, and on the other by the incompleteness and partiality of the total information delivered. Put in another way, these texts describe poorly and say little. These texts lack the attention to detail and comprehensiveness that characterize "precision" texts instead. This deficit does not stand as an anomaly, because this is precisely where their strength emerges. Thanks to this fragmentary and incomplete nature of the information offered, on the one hand a horizon is outlined, only suggested and sketched that requires completion through participation, and on the other hand this very incompleteness awakens the reader's imagination and creative participation.

We will call the first group "informative texts," the second "formative texts."[5] And the main difference lies not in the comprehensiveness of the material conveyed but in the attitude they generate and arouse in the reader.[6]

The group of informational texts aims to take the best possible picture of reality and convey an already complete representation of it, proving the reliability of the author and producer of that text. The result is the type of reader who is precise and accurate in the transmission of the already complete representation but not necessarily in the creation or elaboration of that same representation.

---

4. Fry, *Theory of Literature*, 53–150. For not only a literary but also a cultural definition of a text, see McLuhan, *Gutenberg Galaxy*, 5–21.

5. Rizzi, *Pensare dentro la Bibbia*, 19–27.

6. This is what Ricœur will say about texts that "prompt thinking." Ricœur, *Esprit*, 48–59.

The group of formative texts,[7] on the other hand, not aiming for completeness, merely hints at the reality it is meant to describe. In formative texts, however, partiality and incompleteness are not to be counted as laziness and carelessness. On the contrary, not saying everything is the result of arduous and careful work and not the result of chance and improvisation; it takes more wisdom and technical skills to "say less" than to "say more." It is more complicated to limit oneself to, by only suggesting something, being able to say the whole than to abound in descriptive data because one is incapable of limiting oneself to only suggest something by hints and allusions. The descriptive bulimia of informational texts so many times is mistaken as a virtue, failing to recognize that, underlying it, there may be a compulsive mechanism that aims to control reality through the exhaustiveness of description.

Every common description aspires to say everything but never really succeeds, while successful descriptions are those that find the right formula to suggest the whole without saying it. The result is the type of reader who is provoked and even compelled to actively complete the suggestions that the text and its author only sketch but refuse to complete. This incompleteness of information is transformed from a negative to a positive datum because it provides the right space for the reader to become a participant in the creation of meanings that the text wisely only suggests. Therein lies their formative dimension. They train the reader to think for himself and not to be a pure receptacle of meanings elaborated elsewhere.

To which group of these two does the Bible belong? Many Christians complain that the Bible is not clearer and more comprehensive and would gladly place it in the first group. The Bible is certainly a complex book. And as such it belongs in the two groups. But the predominant and distinguishing dimension is the "formative" one. Without neglecting the importance of certain information central to life and faith, which the Bible conveys accurately, the biblical text has chosen instead sobriety and description by tracts, not only because the themes it presents are complex and would be difficult to exhaust with precise schemes but also because it aims to make the recipients of its message not only attentive and coherent readers but above all visionary and creative.

---

7. Jeanrond calls these kinds of texts "boring" because, despite the important information they can convey, they make the reader passive from the point of view of sense-making. Cf. Jeanrond, *L'ermeneutica teologica*, 18.

That is why it is not easy for the believer himself to understand what is the status and function of the text before him, the Bible. And the proper concern that drives the Christian to focus on and attend to the content of that text must never lead him to neglect its form. In the biblical text, not only the *what* but also the *how* is central.

But this is not the end of the story; rather, reflection on the nature of the Christian reference text, the Bible, has just begun. What it entails to have a text in front of one is neither a foregone nor superfluous question. With the text one must certainly create a relationship of learning and discipline. Care, attention, rigor, and constancy seem to be the characteristics that a text requires to open its meaning to the reader. If then the text is the Bible, this will only increase the proportion and intensity of those requirements. Can, however, the relationship with a text be solely cognitive? Certainly not. When confronted with the text, a connection with life also emerges that goes beyond the text itself. Indeed, it precedes it. Even when we learn nothing new from an informational point of view, a text can still contribute to the emergence of a closer relationship with life itself to which the text is merely a witness. At this level, the attitudes needed are of a different nature. No longer discipline, constancy, and rigor but willingness, intuition, and listening are needed to grasp beyond the text the voice of life that speaks and palpitates in the text.

This is why it is important to reflect more on what it implies for us as Christians to have a text as a reference point. Does it represent a pure form that we could do without losing anything of the message? Does the fact of transcribing the message in a text such as the Bible change the message itself and orient it toward a certain kind of understanding? Does the fact that the message is conveyed through a text provoke and require a particular attitude in us? Are we Christians also transformed not only by the content of our reference text but also by its form? I believe that we have not yet given enough thought to the anthropological, ontological, and theological implications for us Christians of having to confront a text in such a close, continuous, and massive way. And especially we Protestants, who have made the appeal to Scripture a strong point, must be aware that this virtue also opens the door to side effects that can be devastating. It is neither free nor painless to erect a relationship with a text at the center of one's religious experience. There are benefits, but there are also possible drifts, which we need to monitor and manage wisely and with foresight.

For example, the mere fact of conceiving the relationship with the Bible at a tendentially cognitive level—a very common fact today—introduces a type of impoverishment not only of the experience of reading but also of the experience of faith. And the integration of a more "ontological" dimension (of human growth) to correct this formal drift many times does not solve but aggravates the problem. And it is here that we would like to briefly pause to grasp, through consideration of the "cultural" dimension of the text, the elements that intervene to condition our human relationship with the text in the reading experience.

A THEOLOGICAL-CULTURAL LOOK AT THE TEXT[8]

The acceptance of text as a communicative route has posed some problems from the very beginning. Text as a cultural form introduces the typical problem of mediation. In cultures with an oral tradition, the word made by direct contact is privileged over mediation through writing. Hence the resistance, from the very beginning, to recognize the claim of the text to be relevant not only in *what* it says, but in *how it* says what it says.[9] The text, as a particular form of communication, makes the claim and cultural provocation that it wants messages to be better on the one hand when they are mediated by writing and on the other hand when the fragility of the word is overcome by the reliability of a text that supports it.[10] Even when text was finally introduced and its validity recognized, cultures, however, remained primarily oral cultures for a long time. The text served only as a

---

8. Text as a cultural artifact has posed a specific problem from the very beginning—that of the ambivalence of mediations. For Plato (*Symposium*, 202–10) Hermes is the messenger of the gods who interprets language and texts and who, by clarifying their meaning, at the same time opacifies and tampers with it. The text is thus a source of both clarity and deception. For this reason, while initiating a revolution, the introduction of Scripture and texts arouses admiration and distrust from the outset. The dynamism of the text will not explode in premodern cultures because the communicative and social structure of the oral tradition will remain strong and transversal. This is what Carlo Bordoni calls, taking up the nomenclature introduced by Walter Ong, the strength of "primary orality." See Bordoni, *Società digitali*, 7–9; Ong, *Orality and Literacy*, 5–15. Everything will change with the arrival of modernity and the democratization of texts after the invention of the printing press. The text not only imposes itself quantitatively through its massive dissemination, but also qualitatively through the development of a new anthropological model. See Ricœur, *Dal testo all'azione*, 177–203; Ong, *Orality and Literacy*, 77–114, 115–35.

9. Plato, *Symposium*, 202–10.

10. Ferraris, *Ermeneutica*, 3–5.

support but not as a social transformer. It is with the arrival of modernity that the situation changes: from being a cognitive support, text becomes a social transformer. And this happens in two ways.

a. **From a quantitative point of view**. From elite texts, texts will become affordable to all and for all; they will become democratized. And they will do so thanks to a technological invention: typography. With typography, texts will increase their draft, decrease in price, and multiply their dissemination to the nth degree. This is what Marshall McLuhan describes in his analysis of the phenomenon created by the introduction of typography in the West. His text, *The Gutenberg Galaxy: The Birth of the Typographic Man*,[11] tells how typography, then the introduction of the book in massive form, changes European culture. Text becomes "central" and no longer peripheral and ancillary. According to McLuhan, the text imposes itself and becomes the tool for building a different culture and society.[12]

b. From a **qualitative point of view**, which is even more important than the quantitative one, it changes the status of the text itself and consequently also that of the reader. The text will no longer be an artifact of "social stability" but will become an instrument of "social change and mobility."[13] The text will become lighter and more flexible and, as such, will be conceived as the beginning of a chain whose fulfillment will no longer be in the text itself but in the reader's creative take on it.[14] Thus the text becomes a fundamental but insufficient ingredient in the creation of meaning, because the meanings it suggests cannot deliver them either as definitive or as unique. The text is only a starting point. It is the birth of a powerful new cultural conception that, by relativizing the traditional text, in some ways desacralizes it.[15] And precisely because it desacralizes it, it also makes possible the birth of a new world through the active

---

11. McLuhan, *Galassia Gütenberg*, 8–26.
12. McLuhan, *Galassia Gütenberg*, 14–34.
13. This is the conclusion of anthropologist Cavicchia Scalamonti (*Morte*, 9–58).
14. Moreover, the priority of the individual over the group or stable text is what marks the birth of true modern individualism. Marcel Gauchet says, clearly and unequivocally, what the choice of modernity has been: to privilege the anteriority (priority) of men and their creative activity (Gauchet, *Disincanto del mondo*, XIII).
15. Walter Benjamin will describe this same mechanism with regard not to the text but to the work of art, characterizing modern time not only as the time of individualism but of what he calls the rise and multiplication of "expository value" at the expense of "cultic value." See Benjamin, *Opera d'arte*, 11–14.

participation of a reader who has become creative and co-participant in the articulation and formation of meaning.[16]

The text alone is not determinative as a "literary form" (narrative, poetry). So many religious and secular authors have described this specificity and greatness of the Bible. This is the analysis, for example, of one of the great hermeneuts of our time, Paul Ricœur, who continually reiterates, as a philosopher and not a biblical scholar, the greatness of biblical "literary forms" even in the sense of a formal contribution to philosophical hermeneutics.[17] Few stop to consider the importance of the biblical text as a "cultural form." It is not the same text that is read in modernity. Regardless of the content and regardless of the literary form, there is a new cultural format that arises and will be instrumental in creating a new culture. The material text of the Bible will remain the same today than in the Middle Ages. Nor will the extraordinary development in the critical analysis and elaboration of the biblical text[18], with the scientific preparation of manuscripts, change much about the materiality of the biblical text, which will remain essentially the same. It is the cultural concept of the text instead, the new epistemological status entrusted to it with modernity, that will be revolutionary and will change the structure and rhythm of daily life and faith itself.

We have here a typical example of *cultural homonymy*. The word "text," like other pivotal words (God, family, authority, church, work, bond), will be the same for the medievals and for us moderns, but the content will be completely different. This change will not affect, for example, biblical authority, as some complain. The Bible, in modernity, is authoritative in another way. It will be authoritative not *in what it says* but in what it *suggests*. This hermeneutical shift is not only essential from a theological point of view, but also from a catechetical and pastoral point of view. It is important not only for progressive Christians but also for more traditionalist Christians because being a cultural mechanism, like all structural cultural mechanisms, it will be marked not only by its transversality, but also by its unconsciousness and ethical neutrality. Being modern or medieval precedes our choice, and ethically it is neither better nor worse, just as there is no ethical virtue to being ethnically black or white, Peruvian or Italian. It is the address chosen and the use given

---

16. Cavicchia Scalamonti, *Morte*, 87–91.
17. Ricœur, *Ermeneutica filosofica*, 79–85.
18. Metzger, *Testo del Nuovo Testamento*, 235–71.

to that cultural mode that will become important and consequently the object of moral evaluation.

The text as a modern cultural mechanism will not only become an instrument of cognitive and social mobility but will also serve, unfortunately—paradoxically—as an imprisoning mechanism of meaning. Necessity or contingency? Determinism or innovation? Which of the two is the emphasis of textuality inaugurated by the moderns? This ambivalence, moreover, does not belong only to hermeneutics. Carlo Galli identifies it also in the foundation of the modern state proclaimed by Hobbes.[19] Hobbes is the prophet of a new vision of politics, the one who inaugurates the typically modern view of the state as a social convention sealed through a contract. And this innovation also concerns anthropology and the way human groups are conceived, in a total break with the Aristotelian axiom of man as a social being.[20] With Hobbes, the typical atomism of modernity is imposed, which is the anthropological presupposition of the social contract that drives individuals to converge together artificially in the face of a common benefit to be gained. Coexistence has become contingent, so much so that it must be made necessary of a second necessity. Indeed, between contingency and necessity, Galli replies, "the Hobbessian state" is a state of order and necessity.

The same conclusion we could apply to modern textuality. It is born under the banner of fluidity of meaning versus the text guarantor of stability of the Middle Ages, but it ends up imprisoning not only meaning but all culture. Modernity, which reads, develops a one-sided way of seeing the world as it has learned it from its texts. In the texts, in fact, meaning is linear, sequential, orderly, and analytical, as will become the thinking of the moderns. It is not the moderns who created the modern texts. It is the modern texts that created the moderns and their linear, mechanical, sequential, and ultimately reductive mindset of the world.

Hobbes's political ambivalence about how much freedom or how much order should prevail in the modern state and society does not only apply as a parallelism of a historical or political dilemma in which biblical interpretation can find a correlate for its own interpretive ambivalence. Hobbes's modern ambivalence is in a direct way also a hermeneutical ambivalence. Hobbes was a diligent interpreter of the Bible. *Leviathan*,

---

19. Galli, *Contingenza e necessità*, 38–71.

20. Thomas Hobbes breaks down the classical aggregative anthropology formulated by Aristotle (*Zoon politikon*) and which had dominated the entire Middle Ages to establish an atomistic view of society. Hobbes, *De Cive*, I, 2.

his main work, but also for example *De cive*, which precedes it only by a few years, are true exegetical-theological treatises. The hermeneutical ambivalence of a modern text, which radically innovates but paradoxically imprisons the new found meaning, is perfectly visible in these two books. On the one hand Hobbes gives birth to a new Christianity based on an innovative reading of the Bible (Old and New testaments), while on the other hand that same newfound sense almost immediately becomes a prison for the overall sense expressed in the biblical text. The political contract that liberates and oppresses has its perfect parallel in the hermeneutical contract that innovates and imprisons meaning. The Bible read by Hobbes,[21] with the Christianity derived from it, are both a strange mixture of freedom and imprisonment. Hobbesian biblical hermeneutics, breaking with the deterministic logic of medieval hermeneutics, actually creates a groundbreaking interpretation regarding anthropology and the modern state, but it ends up shackling them both to the contract of a sense that can only be placed in the service of the state. Bible interpretation is doomed to pander to Leviathan and to absolutely and exclusively legitimize both its monopoly of political force and its monopoly of interpretive force. The modern hermeneutic contract liberates and imprisons meaning at the same time. And all modern texts since Hobbes have become true sense contracts. A sense free but imprisoned. Free to imprison and imprisoned because it is excessively free.

We describe, in this chapter, the biblical text in its positive function. The negative dimension of the text, as the imprisonment of meaning, we will analyze in chapter seven. We want to affirm and show that the positive function of the biblical text, which will be enhanced and liberated with modernity, lies in its "formative" capacity.

Text certainly does not limit itself to being a mnemotechnical support of the oral message. Its function is more central. Indeed, the message itself is profoundly altered when it becomes writing. Although our culture today is transversely marked by writing, there survives a nostalgia for the spoken word and a belief that the best communication is verbal. Writing, we are convinced, must still be surpassed by the warmth and immediacy of the spoken word. The word preceded writing, and it is still the word redeemed by reading that must replace writing in the process of understanding the message. Writing is cold, anonymous, and too formal. Instead, the word behind it, which needs to be resurrected, carries the

---

21. Hobbes, *Leviathan*, see third and fourth parts. See *De Cive*; compare part 3 on religion, chapters 15 to 18.

force and persuasion of a warm and immediate message. It is as if writing (text) is only a necessary evil. As soon as one can, in fact, one is called to overcome it to get to the word that is hidden in it. In this view, only the word, and not the text itself, is the bearer of meaning and significance.

It is argued that speaking face-to-face, viva voce, avoids the misunderstandings associated with mediation such as writing. The more direct the communication, the better this would be. Clearly, the advantage of oral communication lies in its freshness and real immediacy. However, this does not erase the misunderstandings. Indeed, at another level, oral communication, through speech, increases these misunderstandings. In fact, in oral communication, which necessarily takes place in real time, words and responses to words cannot be stopped. The communicative flow must be guaranteed because it is precisely that flow, in its immediacy and naturalness, that constitutes the strength of oral language. But it is precisely here, in the freshness and immediacy of this flow of orality, that spoken words find their strength—but also their limitation. That flow overwhelms them, overlaps them, jostles them, bumps them, halves them, exasperates them, accelerates them. For they are forced by this flow to become fast words, words that are less thought out, instinctive, easy and immediate, but not necessarily the best.

The undoubted greater coldness of writing and text then brings with it corrective, necessary benefits. The written word, which becomes text, can indeed become a thought-out, verified, filtered word. A balanced word that communicates better, even if more slowly, the intentions and will of those in dialogue. But the benefit of a text does not lie only in the greater precision of the written form. Writing (text) causes three kinds of "formalizations" (distanciation[22]) that in the interpretive process increase the meaning of the message.[23] This is precisely where its strength lies.

THE TEXT AND ITS AUTONOMY

To exemplify these three types of "distanciation" (distancing) and their outline within what we call the levels of textuality, we will refer to the prologue of Luke's Gospel, which we quote below to facilitate understanding of the explanation.

---

22. "Distanciation" is the technical word used by Ricoeur to describe this formalization introduced by text and writing. See Ricœur, "The Hermeneutyical Function do Distanciation," 72–85.

23. Ricœur, *Philosophical Hermeneutics*, 80–95.

Luke 1:1–4

> Since many have undertaken to order a narrative of the facts that have been fulfilled among us, as they have been handed down to us by those who from the beginning were eyewitnesses to them and who became ministers of the Word, it has seemed good to me also, after I have been thoroughly informed of everything from the origin, to write to you by order, most excellent Theophilus, so that you may recognize the certainty of the things you have been taught.

The first[24] "distanciation" is that which the text creates between the author and his initial project. It is as if at some point the text becomes autonomous and independent of its creator. The text has in its genes the articulation, reinforcement, and assertion of its otherness from the author who created it. This fact might seem anomalous and unnatural. In reality, the estrangement of a text from its author is a natural and beneficial act. And as such, it triggers a process that is inversely proportional to the presence of its author. In the beginning, in fact, the text is the text of an author. The author is everything, and his text is only a part of the author's potential. It is the author who ensures the success of the text. One knows and respects a text only because of the guarantee given by its author. Subsequently, however, it is the author who is known through his text. One knows that author only through that text; everything else he has done, most of his life, does not count. It is the text that saves its author from oblivion. The text is everything, and its author has become only an accompanying element.

This mechanism of replacing the author with his text has not only a temporal logic and historical wear and tear; underlying it is a semantic fact that grounds hermeneutics precisely. It is the fact that the meaning of a text is always greater than the meaning that intentionally prompted its author to write it. The author is never fully aware of the meanings his text carries. For this reason, once given birth to (written), a text begins to have a life of its own, and the meaning that seeks interpretation is no longer limited to the author's intention, to seeking what the author intended to say. The goal is the meaning of the text itself, a meaning that transcends and goes beyond the author's awareness. The author's intention

---

24. Ricœur writes, "Writing first of all makes the text autonomous from the author's intentions, because the text, once fixed through writing, no longer coincides with what the author intended to say" (*Philosophical Hermeneutics*, 68–70).

does not lapse but is simply embedded in a larger goal that ennobles and completes it. Opposed to this broader view of the meaning of a text are on the one hand the romantic hermeneutics, based on intuition, and on the other hand the pragmatic hermeneutics of many evangelical Christians, based on concreteness, which in opposite ways try to link interpretation only to the sometimes mythologized intentionality of the author.

Take, for example, the Gospel of Luke.[25] While it was in the process of construction, the text belonged directly and completely to the management of its author. Luke tells us this directly in the prologue (1:1–4), stating that it is he, after investigating, studying, sorting, and cataloging the material concerning the life of Jesus, who manages and determines the final configuration of that text.[26] Indeed, Luke's imprint on Jesus' biographical data is not secondary. He did not limit himself to being a transcriber or a copyist. The author's imprint in reporting objective data, concerning the life of Jesus, is very strong, even to the point of appearing selective and even distorting. It is precisely the selectivity and arbitrariness that actually ground the literary and theological style of Luke's Gospel. Had he confined himself to passing on objective data about Jesus, his Gospel would have been a copy of Mark's or John's and, as such, useless. This fact simply indicates that the author, in this case Luke, is the true father of that text, because he imparts to those narrated data an outline, an organization, and an interpretation that is a true contortion of objective meaning. Therein lies precisely his undoubted authorship and the persuasive force of his text.

Yet, the text breaks that authorship. It breaks that closeness. For gradually that text will have a life of its own, independent of Luke its author and what he intended to say. Meanwhile it will survive unscathed while the author is gone. The very meaning of that Gospel will be changed by Luke's disappearance and its autonomous permanence. The central question will no longer be "What did the author mean?" Instead, the hermeneutical question will become "What does that text mean?" And the two do not coincide, because there were from the beginning meanings in that text that even Luke was not aware of. This distancing that apparently plays against, because we can no longer ask Luke what he meant, actually plays in favor because it endlessly enhances, increases, and multiplies the meaning of that text.

25. Nolland, *Luke*, xxvii-xlvii; Fabris, *Luca*, 21–34.
26. Nolland, *Luke*, 3–12.

THE TEXT AND ITS MULTIPLE RECIPIENTS

The second "distanciation"[27] that the text creates is the disconnect between the given birth text and the initial recipient. There is no text that is born in the abstract. A text is always addressed to someone. And even when the author does not have a nominal addressee in mind, which is very rare, guiding the design and articulation of the text is always an ideal addressee. A text is not based only on the coherence of its author's reasoning; the horizon of the addressee is essential for the completion of the very architecture of a text. The consubstantial, and not merely applicative, work that the reader will further introduce in relation to the text, and which consists precisely in creating together with the text the meaning that it has masterfully only introduced, actually begins even earlier, precisely at the level of the recipient.

The addressee, nominal or ideal, is the instance between the text and the reader that is still too often read only in its passivity. Without in any way detracting from the author to whom the design, ideation, and audacity of enacting the strategy of meaning belong, the addressee, as the reader will later further do, actively contributes to the creation of meaning. Not only the extension of meaning in the text, but also its precision and nuance, would remain crude and approximate if the addressee were to be absent. The fact that in texts, more often than not, we are not delivered abundant information about the addressee the author has in mind does not mean that the author does not include it nor that we, readers, can do without it. Data about the initial addressee would weigh down the text. For this reason, the reader's active participation is articulated not only at the level of reconstructing the text's message but also at the level of imagining the addressee, which the text presupposes and which is imposed only in hints. Delineating the profile of the addressee is a primary hermeneutic obligation.

Even this essential component in the relationship of meaning breaks the text. It interrupts it by imposing a discontinuity on it. Ostensibly, this interruption seems to compromise meaning. Instead, it does not. Paradoxically, not only is the sense not tampered with, but it miraculously comes out enhanced. At some point in the process, the message for a

---

27. Ricœur writes, "The liberation of the text from the author corresponds to a parallel detachment of the text from the reader. Whereas in dialogue the very condition of discourse determines confrontation, the written text can attract an audience that includes virtually anyone who can read" (*Ermeneutica filosofica*, 69).

specific recipient becomes a message potentially for everyone. It is the text that performs this miracle. The mechanism of expanding the message through multiple recipients is not just a mechanism of dissemination. It is not "one meaning," the specific one to that message, that reaches more people. It is the plurality of added recipients that allows latent meanings in the text to be surveyed and brought out that a single recipient would not have been able to bring out. Even at this second level of the chain of meaning, the text has performed a miracle, which is the miracle of expanding meaning from the text itself and without manipulating it.

Again taking Luke's Gospel in the prologue as an example, we find that, according to the evangelist himself, the initial addressee played a predominant role in choosing, organizing, and editing the material collected about Jesus. Luke's Gospel was written for him, for that specific recipient, which in this case is a certain Theophilus (1:3,4).[28] Few words explicitly describe and name him, but these are decisive in signaling the centrality of his presence. Theophilus is just as important in structuring the message, even if mentioned only briefly, as is the subject of the story itself, Jesus. This may appear exaggerated, but literally and textually it is not. Theophilus is insignificant in the architecture of Jesus' life and teaching. Instead, he is central to Luke's account of Jesus' life. Between *life* and *life narrative* there is no equivalence. They are two close but different things.

What is binding and canonical for us Christians is the *life narrative* and not the *life of* Jesus himself. The life of Jesus is very important to us but not binding, mainly because we do not know outside the Gospels what it was like. What is instead binding for us is the canonical account that the gospels have given of Jesus. Even if we were to find a writing made by Jesus himself, this would be very important but not binding (noncanonical). The account of Jesus made by Luke, on the other hand, is unthinkable without Theophilus. The Theophilus element, insignificant in the biography of Jesus, becomes instead binding as an element of the account about Jesus that is a canonical account. The historical and objective life of Jesus is filtered, for us Christians, not only by the gaze of Luke, who is the author, but also by Theophilus as the recipient of that text. All the material has been gathered and organized according to him.

The weight of this filter, imposed by the recipient, is perfectly visible in the structuring of the genealogy[29] in chapter 3, which is even presented

---

28. Bock, *Luke*, 1:51–67; Schürmann, *Vangelo di Luca*, 1:53–67.
29. Bock, *Luke*, 1:80–91.

after the baptism, whereas in Matthew it appears before Jesus' baptism. Even the configuration of the genealogy, which in Matthew is descending (beginning with Abraham), precisely by virtue of what Theophilus represents, Luke makes it ascending (beginning with Joseph) and leads it back, unlike in Matthew, not to Abraham but to Adam. Luke's constructed genealogy, with some literary and historical license that we could not afford today, is more universal and inclusive than Matthew's precisely by virtue of its recipient being Theophilus, a non-Jew. Luke's Gospel is therefore incomprehensible in some of its essential registers without its immediate addressee, Theophilus.

Here, too, the text breaks and introduces a clear discontinuity. Theophilus does not disappear, but by virtue of the autonomy of the text, which will be increasing over time, he takes a back seat. His place will be taken by all those addressees who in the initial form of the Gospel were instead only latent addressees. The obscuring of the initial addressee should lead to an impoverishment of the text. Instead through the mechanism of distanciation or breaking, the continuity between author and addressee, this does not happen. This fact not only does not reduce meaning, but even enhances it. For, having become text, that narrative is potentially addressed to everyone. Not only Theophilus, but any human being of Theophilus's period and of our own day, becomes a legitimate eventual recipient of that narrative.

THE TEXT AND BROKEN REFERENTIALITY

The third distanciation[30] is that which the text creates between the message and the reality hinted at. The reality hinted at by the author is no longer the same reality to which the reader will connect. However, in either case, one is asserting that the truth of the event or message described does not lie in the coherence of the elements within the message, but solely in the connection of these with the external world. The message of a text is articulated on two planes, which Frege[31] called the "sense" and the "reference."[32] Sense expresses a linguistic truth that is immanent to the literary form and is essentially given by the differentiation and gap

---

30. Ricœur writes, "The world of the text to which we now refer is not that of everyday language, but constitutes a new kind of distancing that we might call distancing the real" (*Ermeneutica filosofica*, 74).

31. Ricœur, *Ermeneutica filosofica*, 70–72.

32. Frege and Bonomi, *Struttura del linguaggio*, 9–32.

between elements within a given system. This is a technical truth and, as such, a truth with a lowercase "t." We might call it a descriptive truth. It does not change life, much less the world. It merely describes and affirms what reality is at a certain point in time. It is as if the truth of sense becomes small precisely because it is possessed and contained completely in sense. The result is a domesticated truth that produces neither change nor emotion nor imagination.

Instead, reference expresses a claim to reach external reality and is articulated only as a leap from the system to what is outside of it. This going outside the system can succeed or fail. But in reference, it is no longer the linguistic system that is the factor or scenario where meaning occurs and is given. The linguistic system, in the reference, de-centers itself and accepts that truth occurs outside of it, in connection with external reality. Beyond the fact that the proposed reference may then be true or false, that path is already a path of truth. It is the "reference" and not the "sense," strictly speaking, that is the locus of truth with a capital "T." This referential truth (reference) is a truth that escapes. It cannot be contained or even possessed in language. Language alone can act as a witness to reality, alluding to it tangentially, in hints. This is precisely why referential truth sets in motion, passion, and imagination and is a promoter of change.

Between sense and reference is the distance that exists between language and discourse. Speech, like reference, has the claim to connect with external reality. Sense and language, on the other hand, do not. The "linguistics of language"[33] (structuralism, de Saussure, Hjelmslev) atemporally processes meaning without subject or intentionality and for that very reason without "reference." The "linguistics of discourse"[34] (Benveniste, Ricœur), on the other hand, temporally elaborates a meaning with subject and intentionality whose goal is given by reference. The text as distanciation does not take the side of a "linguistics of language" but on the side of a "linguistics of discourse" because the text, in this its third distanciation, cannot renounce reference. The text must not be conceived as a transcription of "language" but as the freezing of a "discourse" in which reference is present even if dormant.

Here, too, the text introduces a break. It breaks a continuity with the initial reference in order to construct a new one. This rupture of

---

33. Ricœur, *Ermeneutica filosofica*, 56–58.
34. Ricœur, *Ermeneutica filosofica*.

referentiality is the defining characteristic of the text, because through it the text does not photograph reality as it is but reconfigures it as a possible reality. Every good text, in the face of the given reality, always proposes an alternative reality. The great benefit of broken reference (third distanciation) is the enlargement and enhancement of the referential and truthful capacity of the text. Every text in this sense is a poetic text and a text of fiction because it proposes a reconstruction of reality that is never the one that is already there. Proceeding in this way affirms the possibility of thinking alternative and different realities from the present one. Poetry and fiction, as literary forms, only radicalize this artificial element found in all texts. By alluding therefore to a fictitious reality, which is not there, each text becomes critical of the present reality and, as an alternative to it, proposes possible realities through imagination. In this lies the revolutionary dimension of the text.

Taking up Luke's example, we find that the reality to which he relates[35] is a complex reality but one that can be framed in two typifying perspectives. On the one hand, from a sociopolitical point of view, the Jewish people appear in a position of weakness, while Romans and Greeks in a position of strength. On the other, from the religious point of view, the situation is reversed: the privileged are the Jews who had revelation and the disadvantaged are the Romans and Greeks who did not have access to this revelation. It is with reference to this reality that Luke's Gospel articulates its proposal. It does so by overturning the patterns and parameters of the reality of the time through this broken referentiality. Reminding us that in the face of the political-social reality or in the face of the religious reality of the present, which impose themselves with their force, Jesus introduces possible alternative realities by virtue of his messianic and interpretive power. Starting with Jesus as a new criterion, on the one hand, the religious advantage of the Jews easily becomes a disadvantage and a reason for stumbling (this is in fact what happens); on the other hand, from the sociopolitical point of view, the advantage of the Gentiles becomes a religious disadvantage, but, as such, it will become an opportunity for salvation. This is what happens: it is the pagans who nurture the ranks of the first Christian communities, not the Jews.

Here, too, the text breaks the linearity of the connection with reality. When we read Luke, we no longer see the Jewish religious context and the Roman sociopolitical context, but we see our own context. It is no longer

---

35. Tannehill, *Luke*, 33–35; Rengstorf, *Vangelo secondo Luca*, 31–36.

in connection with that referentiality that we construct the meaning we derive from reading Luke's Gospel but the connection with our modern referentiality. The focus on that initial context is purely transient, because its reading and consideration actually aims to make us more aware of our context. The initial referentiality broken down through the text actually enhances the meaning of that text and those experiences that connect back to that text in the present.

INFORMATIONAL TEXTS AND FORMATIVE TEXTS: THE WHY OF BEING "IN READING"

What is a good text? This is not always easy to figure out, despite appearances. Venturing a somewhat atypical and in some ways even provocative hypothesis, we think we can confidently state that a good text is not the one that "says all" but rather the one that does not say all. With this apparently absurd answer to a seemingly obvious question, we take up the initial difference we introduced with respect to two types of texts, to add a further clarification. "Informative" texts, we said, are those that add knowledge and data to our cultural background. Contrary to what it seems, they do not require our active participation in the creation of meaning itself. At the level of meaning creation, the reader still appears too passive. This certainly is not so at all levels. At the application level, for example, the reader here is very much involved. We could say, therefore, that "informational" texts tend to create with the reader a relationship of an epistemological type, that is, of knowledge. One reads to know more, to be more informed, and to apply assimilated knowledge.

Behind this cognitive relationship, however, an anthropology of certainty is articulated that easily becomes manipulative of meaning. The subject, as reader, does not define his essential profile by virtue of the text. He is independently of the text already a subject. As such, with a certain pre-textual identity, he chooses a text or texts to read only to learn and reinforce things he already knows. That new information does not ground his being but only enriches it. The epistemological type of interpretation that one articulates in the face of "informational" texts, but can also articulate in the face of "formative" texts. In this case deforming them through reductive reading tends to downsize the texts, making them pure objects of cognitive grasp. The separation "knowing subject"/"known object," presupposed by informational texts, carries within itself from the beginning the seed of manipulation. A subject separated from the object can approach the object—texts—only by comprehending them, by taking them in their sense, that is, by manipulating them, by appropriating their content.

In contrast, "formative" texts are sober and incomplete about information. But from the point of view of sense-making, precisely because they are incomplete, they require the reader's participation. Their limitation becomes an opportunity for the reader. If they were complete they would not be formative because they would not require his or her participation. These texts are slow texts because by articulating a deep dialogue between what they propose and the reader, the process of signification necessarily slows down. This slowing down represents their virtue, because the reader's involvement is no longer only cognitive. His whole being participates in it. A formative text forces the reader to an investment of his being and not only of his knowledge. In participating with its being, it is perfected and comes out, in this relationship, enriched. With formative texts there is an enhancement of the reader's being. The hermeneutics of formative texts is thus an ontological hermeneutics that can take place, at least partially, even in the face of informational texts, if the reader so desires. A typical example of this category of text is poetry. Poetry structurally is fragmentary, approximate, not precise, pluriform, which is precisely why in order to grasp its meaning, which is not immediate, the reader must actively participate with his being and imagination.

This allows us to say that it is not easy to understand the nature of the biblical text. The true greatness of the Bible does not lie in its exhaustiveness nor in its analytical description. The Bible's greatness must be sought by placing it in the category of those texts that we have called "formative" and that have basically two characteristics.

Partial Texts

First, "formative texts" are partial. They do not say everything and do not mean to say everything. In this order of ideas, we can say that the Bible does not say the last word, does not say everything, and does not monopolize the word. On the contrary, it requires, stimulates, and demands a human word and wants to be supplemented and enriched by it. The Bible's search for the human word is not a hidden strategy to then force and smuggle its meaning. The sense of God's Word is not a sense already made elsewhere and embodied in human history to pretend and simulate an approach and involvement of mercy. No, the sense God offers in his Word is an incomplete sense, because he cannot and will not complete it on his own. That would be irreverent toward the human. He halves his Word because every procreating Word, as in the meiotic reproduction of germ cells that must halve their genetic and chromosomal makeup to pass on life, must be a halved Word. A full Word can only create nothingness. Halving oneself is the condition for guaranteeing life. And if the Bible is the Word of life, it can only be so by becoming a halved Word. A sober, partial, and incomplete Word.

When God speaks, it is said, we humans must be silent. This is only partially true. For from a fundamental point of view it is the other way around. When God speaks, we, from being silent that we were, begin to speak, dare to articulate a thought, a prayer, a praise. God does not act as a paralyzing or castrating element but, on the contrary, as a promoting and stimulating element. As an incomplete text requiring completion, through the Bible the human word becomes a valued, welcomed, promoted, requested word. Of this God and his Word are not jealous. The Bible is not jealous if other texts say better what the Bible says only in summary, only as a draft. The Bible functions, as a text, as a collection of ingredients, which it is then up to each age to amalgamate into a final proposal, into a blueprint. The final interpretation is ours by virtue of the biblical incompleteness that has driven us to go beyond itself.

Plural Texts

Second, "formative texts" are also plural texts. They are structurally polyform. They are so not only by necessity, but also by choice. In the first instance, formative texts are plural "by necessity," because the truth is too big, too multifaceted, too much in flux to expect to embrace it from a single point of view, with the gaze of a single text. It is in the order of things that formative texts recognize their impotence and limitations in approaching truth, and that from this comes the search for a plurality that better tells life and truth. This necessary plurality is not only within one system (intra-community plurality) but also of different systems (inter-community plurality). This is why the homogenization of the Bible, that is, the denial of its internal plurality, almost automatically leads to closure "in the Bible," that is, the denial of external plurality. The Bible is not plural because it is strong, but it is strong because it is plural, with a plurality that breaks its own claims and necessarily opens to others. By opening to others, it automatically becomes vulnerable. The vulnerability of the Bible is expressed in its plurality. It is the open plurality of a vulnerable text. Plurality for the Bible is not a strategy of conquest; it is an ontological trait. The Bible, as a formative book, is plural by necessity.

On the other hand, formative texts are plural "by choice." They do not suffer plurality as a fate, because it cannot be done otherwise. On the contrary, formative texts choose to be plural out of conviction, even if many times this does not suit them. Chosen plurality opens an arduous, laborious, slow, unpredictable path of seeking difficult consensuses, of promoting laborious convergences. The plurality "by choice" of formative texts is not a plurality of strength and certainty but a plurality of vulnerability and uncertainty that presupposes the unavailability of truth and life.

Precisely because life and truth are unavailable, and even less so to the gaze of a single text, the Bible at its core gives voice to various versions of a single event but also to various events uncontained in a single version. It is incomprehensible that those who perceive plurality in the Bible then reject the plurality of bibles. Of bibles there is not just one. There are a variety of them. And this variety is not the variety of different translations and even less the quantitative variety of different specimens. Every human word is a Bible; it is sacred. Sacred not canonically (canon) in its form but certainly in its essence.

One is the canonical Bible, it must be remembered, but many are the non-canonical bibles. One must resist the temptation to overestimate the canonical Bible and underestimate the bibles of men. Every human story, with its successes and failures, with its joys and sufferings, sometimes prolonged indefinitely, is a sacred story and is configured as a bible that God reads with emotion and attention. We need to resist even more tenaciously the temptation that makes the Bible precisely that instrument that undervalues, minimizes the history of men. That is not its task. The vocation and task of the canonical Bible is to recognize and appreciate the value of men's bibles. And the biblical canon is not a boundary of bullying, of excluding other texts, but of self-limitation, of relinquishing control of others. Through the biblical canon, God renounces invading human speech and gives himself the task of dialoguing with it. The canon is not a limitation on human speech to prevent it from contaminating the divine word. The canon is a limit that God imposes on himself, on his Word, to prevent it from engulfing the human Word. The biblical canon expands the human word because it makes it possible by simply reminding him that the human word, desired and willed, is a preceded word. Preceded by God's (canon). The biblical canon[36] is a sign of openness and not closure. It is the sign that ennobles everything outside the Bible. This recognition of the value of all that is extra-canonical and extra-biblical, that is, human, becomes visible and articulated in the choice of human plurality of which the Bible is only a part. To the intra-biblical plurality is added by divine design choice the extra-biblical plurality, without which the Bible would be limited to being just a sad piece of museum and history.

The Bible, as a "formative text," says little (first characteristic) and that little it says in a plural way (second characteristic). The Bible is a collection of books not only in the sense of having various styles but especially in the sense of giving voice to various projects, not always equivalent and complementary. We do not have in the Bible the plurality within "one system" homogeneous, but the plurality "of different systems" living together in tension. This might appear as a problem for those who try to read the Bible in a unified and homogeneous way. The Bible was intended to be constructed in this way. Different versions of faith experiences find in it not only recognition but also a fine appreciation. What is even more striking is the fact that, after presenting them, the Bible does not overcome them through a final summarizing synthesis. It leaves them in tension and merely creates scaffolding mechanisms to make them convergent but not symbiotic. The purpose is to bring them together without confusing them. This is what creates that typical biblical mechanism of paradox. That is why in the Bible we can find a proposition and further on its opposite: both must and can remain in tension, without distorting the inclusive perspective of its meaning.

---

36. Metzger, *Canone del Nuovo Testamento*, 200–15.

IV

The Reader and Imagination
The Value of a Transgressive Interpretation[1]

EVERY TEXT PRESUPPOSES THE profile of an ideal reader.[2] It belongs to the logic of the interpretive process to conceive together with the text a structural correlate of it: the reader. Even the Bible, as a text, presupposes a particular kind of ideal reader. Whereas in the previous chapter we stopped to consider what grounds the reader and makes his or her reading possible—that is, the text—in this chapter we will stop to describe and defend the relevance of the reader as a correlate of the text. As stated from the very first pages of this essay, the "hermeneutic circle," which is the central category of the interpretive act, requires us to have this dual fidelity which is fidelity and respect for the text and fidelity and respect for the reader.

The defense of the ideal reader, as a correlate of the text, cannot be limited to the defense of the one who reads the text. The profile of the ideal reader has a broader scope that we find not only "downstream of the text," that is, in the process of reading that tries to understand the text and its message. It is also "upstream of the text," that is, in the very creation of the text at the time of its construction and writing. The description of

---

1. Marguerat and Bourquin, *Per leggere i racconti biblici*, 143–48.

2. Every text presupposes a certain kind of reader. There are various types of readers. We will describe two of them. What we call a "vital reader" is similarly described by Jeanrond when he speaks of a "transformative reading," meaning the vitality of a dynamic reader. Cf. Jeanrond, *Ermeneutica teologica*, 157–201.

the complete profile of the ideal reader is necessary because there is a tendency to attribute to the reader a purely subsidiary and external task. This tendency to disregard the relevance and centrality of the reader is directly proportional to the sacredness of the text in question. The more sacred the text read becomes, the stronger the tendency to consider the reader irrelevant and unnecessary in the creation of meaning. In this perspective, every discovery of the Bible as a sacred book, thus every Christian moment of spiritual awakening that is based on this discovery, carries with it the danger of distorting the hermeneutic circle. It does this by distorting and vitiating the interpretive process conceived as a primary and continuous interaction between text and reader, through the fetishization of the sacred text at the expense of the relevance of the reader.

The correlation between text and reader is neither purely applicative nor related to reading, as the term "reader" seems to suggest. The reader is not someone who emerges only later. The reader is actually present from the beginning; he is not only someone who uses the text but also someone who founds and composes the text. He founds it because at the time of writing and construction of the text the author shapes, cuts out, discards, chooses, and organizes his material, already having in mind the ideal reader. This ideal reader, a kind of original archetype, heavily participates and affects the construction of every text. Every text is always a text for someone. If the Bible is innovative with regard to the philosophical status of the text as the first hermeneutical category, according to what Ricœur stated,[3] it will also necessarily be so in the status of the reader. The Bible, more than other texts, presupposes an ideal reader with a central, substantive profile. The Bible is to all intents and purposes a text written for someone, not in the limited sense of someone who must read it but in the sense that this someone, the ideal reader, is present from the beginning, in the construction and drafting of the sacred text.

The impact of the ideal reader presupposed by the Bible does not end there. Its scope is even greater. How the biblical text is defined is the reason the Bible, as a text, is characterized not by its completeness and exhaustiveness, as is commonly believed, but by its fragmentary nature and incompleteness. It alludes and suggests rather than determines and

---

3. "An entirely opposite relationship between the two hermeneutics appears, on the other hand, precisely when one considers theological hermeneutics applied to a certain type of texts, the biblical ones: it reveals such original features that it causes a progressive reversal of relationship, so much so that philosophical hermeneutics remains subordinate to theological hermeneutics and becomes an organon of it" (Ricœur, *Ermeneutica filosofica*, 79–80).

completes. The task of the ideal reader becomes decisive not only in the reading or foundation of the Text, but in the creation of the Text "downstream." The moment of reading becomes not solely a moment of assimilation or application but of sense-making through the reader's creative action from the ingredients and perspective suggested but not completed by the Text itself.

Here is what we call in this chapter the "vital reader." The vital reader is the one who takes on three tasks: 1. The task of downstream reading of the text; 2. The task of ideal presence in the upstream creation of the text; 3. The task of sense-making in the moment of reading, from the potentialities and senses latent in the text as ingredients but not yet as completed and finalized meanings.

Not all readers are equivalent. We can delineate two reader profiles. On the one hand, there is the reader diligent[4] in applying the meanings gathered in reading but who remains neutral in creating and processing them. This reader limits his role to gathering existing meanings and then making them his own and applying them as best he can in his own life journey. If hermeneutics is the locus of the creation of meanings in the interaction between the text and the reader, then we are faced here with a passive reader. This reader undergoes a meaning that he or she did not help create and simply accepts as a gift from others. Whether these others are God, the group or one's own church, at this level it does not matter much. The sense here does not belong to the reader. It becomes so solely in a derivative and secondary sense, in that only later does he make it his own, assimilating it.

On the other hand, there is the reader who participates in the creation of the sense suggested by the text. That the reader actively participates in the creation of the sense does not mean that he alone creates all the sense. If he alone were to create all the sense then the text he reads would be completely useless, because he would not take it into account in the elaboration of the sense he tries to create. This is not what is meant, then, when it is stated that the active reader creates meaning without passively undergoing it. It is meant only that the active reader creates meaning as an ally, as a co-participant.

This is the ideal, creative, and innovative reader that the Bible presupposes, promotes, and creates.[5] It creates him through its language. It is

---

4. Jeanrond calls him an "apathetic reader," because despite the important diligence and application in the act of reading, from the perspective of sense-making this type of reader is perfectly "apathetic." See Jeanrond, *Ermeneutica teologica*, 18.

5. Eco, *Lector in fabula*, 50–66.

the narrative-symbolic language used by the Bible that converts the reader from passive to active. Since it is not a book of casuistry nor of rules to be mechanically applied, the reader of the Bible is called and compelled first to perceive, then, subsequently, to choose among the various possible meanings that the text offers him. It is the kind of language the Bible uses, a plurivocal language, that requires the reader's creative participation. Plurivocal is said of language that can mean more than one thing. Reader participation intervenes at this very level. And it occurs in two ways.

The first occurs because the active intervention of the reader becomes absolutely necessary in order to choose, among the various possible meanings, the one that best suits the situation in which he or she finds him or herself. At this level, the reader cannot be subjected to the standard meaning. Especially when the meaning claims to be the right one. That meaning is right once and in other circumstances but may no longer be right today in new circumstances. This requires discernment from the reader. The reader must be able to perceive the plurality of possible meanings latent in the text. He must also discern the meaning best suited to his own context.

Second, the reader must simultaneously be able to look outside the text into extra-textual reality. He must be able to read and understand it well. This ability to be able to read outside the text, even external reality, seems to be a non-textual task. But it is not, because understanding the external context does not serve solely as an application space where meaning, which would have been arrived at from a simple analysis of the text, can be poured out. Context also serves to choose well the best meaning that comes from the text and is in the text, to create meaning, in the sense of determining which of the possible senses is the most suitable. Understanding context is key and central even further upstream in meaning-making, and not just for the application moment.

We will call the first type of reader the "obedient reader" and the second type the "vital reader." The Bible presupposes both, but the one the Bible particularly prefers and promotes is the "vital reader." We call him vital because on the one hand he gathers from the Bible the "life" that is articulated in it through those textual forms and on the other hand because he knows how to extend this same life, through his interpretation, into the reality outside the text.

Certainly the Bible recognizes anyone who approaches it as a reader and does not discriminate against anyone. Anyone can read the Bible, possibly with any kind of attitude, and always he will get a benefit from it. However, the reader that the Bible prefers, aspires to, and pushes to form is the "vital reader" who does not suffer meaning but becomes a co-creator of it. This feature of the Bible, which is to create active readers, did not materialize to its full potential before modernity for two reasons:

1. Because the Bible was materially uncommon, it was not read assiduously or easily. It was not read widely in general. If people had been able to read massively even at other times as we read today, the mechanism perhaps would have been triggered earlier.

2. Because even when there were books, they tended to be read within stable cultures; therefore, people read the Bible as a stabilizing element. This does not mean that before modernity there were no creative and vital readers, just as it does not mean that all readers in modernity are creative and vital. In fact, it may be just the opposite, but at the structural level the historical periods before modernity did not privilege the creative reader, but the obedient reader. It is modernity that will structurally privilege the creative reader, because it will assign him or her a role in social transformation that he or she was denied before.

A THEOLOGICAL-CULTURAL LOOK AT THE READER[6]

The centrality of the creative reader and instrument of social transformation came, according to anthropologist Antonio C. Scalamonti, only with modernity, because it is she alone who will bet on a new subject: no longer the group but the individual. It is the individual who will be the mainstay

---

6. What it means to read and what status to entrust and acknowledge to the reader does not only recall a theory of communication, but an anthropology and sociology of cultural processes. See Sciolla, *Sociologia dei processi culturali*, 231–44; Robbins, *Cultural Anthropology*, 131–75. But it is not only cultural macro-passages, such as that of orality to writing, that profoundly alter the profile and functionality of the reader, but also those micro-passages within the same historical period that introduce important ruptures and orientations regarding precisely the profile and meaning of the reader. This had been the central point of Ferdinand de Saussure's reflection, according to which the transition from a linguistics of "word" to a linguistics of "language" entails a radical downsizing of the status of the reader. See De Saussure, *Corso di linguistica generale*. As well as the transition from structuralism to post-structuralism or deconstructionism implies once again and radically a major shift in the status of the reader. See Ong, *Orality and Literacy*, 136–52; Lewis, *Cultural Studies*, 109–43; Barker and Jane, *Cultural Studies*, 21–24.

of the new epoch.[7] In what sense? In the sense that the individual could not be born in a world, such as the medieval world, where the focus was on stability. To truly give place to the individual was to destabilize the world. Opening up the world and reality, consequently, involved recognizing both as incomplete. The declaration of their completeness is synonymous with the denial of the individual, just as the declaration of the birth of the individual is synonymous with the denial of the completeness of the world and reality. If the world is complete, the individual becomes essentially unnecessary and superfluous. Conversely, if the world is declared open, then the individual is declared essentially an agent[8] necessary to complete it and give it a new profile and configuration.

The birth of the individual in modernity is not the birth of its discrete presence. If the individual is there, it must be there in a strong way. This is individualism. Individualism is not born as an accompanying element but as the central element of a new historical period. Individualism is not the limited sign of an ethical and personalistic change. Individualism is modernity and modernity is individualism. Individualism is the cultural mechanism that transforms an era, the sign that guarantees the establishment of a new world. With individualism comes a new cosmology, a new politics, a new religion by virtue of a new hermeneutics. The individual is first and foremost an individual who interprets the world and reality from himself.

Hermeneutics with a performing reader, recognized as central to the elaboration of meaning, could only arise in modernity. Indeed, hermeneutics with a "strong-reader" or "reader-centric" emphasis is just the application or extension of modern individualism in the area of Bible reading. But the reader, in modern hermeneutics, not only becomes central; he also becomes a creator of meaning. All modernity is constructivist.[9] Constructivism means that reality is not given to us beforehand, but we construct and design it. These ingredients certainly existed before us, precisely as pieces to be assembled but not as a finished reality. It is the individual who assembles the new world. The world comes from our hands. We become creators of our world. "Reader-centered" hermeneutics is but the extension of this modern individualistic axiom into the realm of reading texts.

---

7. Cavicchi Scalamonti, *Morte*, 43–56.
8. Cf. Ong, *Orality and Literacy*, 31–76.
9. Fosnot, *Constructivism*, 11–21.

This constructivist soul is visible in all modern hermeneutics, as for example, in that of Umberto Eco. For him, the reader is the true creator of meaning;[10] consequently we will speak of an "open" text as a characteristic of all texts precisely because of the necessary creative intervention of the reader. The text is so because it requires multiple and continuous interpretations by virtue of the reader's innovative power. It is the creative reader who makes a text open. In contrast, a closed text reduces interpretations because it claims to offer the reader a ready-made meaning. The reader has become the agent that makes a text what a text is; an open work.[11]

Eco actually only enhances what modernity already carries in its bosom from the beginning. This centrality of the meaning-creating subject is in fact at the heart of the Kantian program. Kant elaborates a conception of knowledge that constitutes a real revolution, because at the center of the cognitive process he no longer places the object (text or reality),but the subject (reader or thinking mind) with its capacities and activities. Knowledge consists in the activity by which the subject organizes the data provided by experience, ordering them, processing them, unifying them through the intervention of certain mental functions. Therefore, knowledge is configured as the result of an activity, a human construction. The object of knowledge is not a datum but a product of its activity. Knowledge certainly does not create its own objects; Kant in this sense is very critical of Berkeley's extreme idealism. At this level the Kantian project is more modest. It merely seeks to give form to the material of knowing gathered from sensible intuition. But by organizing the material given to him by experience, which is presented as formless, disorganized, and chaotic material, it is as if the subject were creating reality. The mental organization of reality is almost equivalent to creating that reality. The change is radical: we are faced with a new perspective.

Until Descartes or Kant, the definition of truth to which Western philosophical culture had adhered was that of Aristotelian-Thomistic derivation, that is, of the adaptation of the intellect to being.[12] Now, on the other hand, it is argued that it is reality that must adapt to the ways in which the subject knows things. From this perspective, knowledge, for Kant, is configured as a synthesis between a subject of knowing and

10. Eco, *Lector in fabula*.
11. Eco, *Lector in fabula*, 52–54.
12. *Adequatio rei et intellectus* (correspondence between reality and intellect), a classic formula that goes back to Aristotle and was taken up by Thomas Aquinas. See *Somma contro i gentili*, 46.

a form by which the knower organizes it. Indeed, Kant states in a famous phrase, "Everything begins with experience, but not everything is derived from experience."[13] Kant argues that forms and structures operate in knowledge that do not come from experience and are a priori. A cognitive field is constituted common to all men, precisely because common are the criteria for organizing the material of experience. Each of us has a way of organizing sensation that rests on conditions common to all men. These conditions are the a priori forms of knowledge. It functions independent of experience and is possessed by us "before" sensory experience. It belongs to our way of perceiving and thinking.

"A priori" constitutes the conditions of possibility of experience itself. The investigation of such forms constitutes Kant's "transcendental philosophy." In this sense, the term "transcendental," referring to the a priori forms by which experience is constituted, has a different meaning from the term "transcendent," which instead concerns a sphere that lies beyond (transcends) experience itself. Only by admitting the presence of those a priori forms and structures can the existence of universal and necessary knowledge be explained. That is why it can be said that "We of things do not know a priori except what we ourselves put into them."[14] This breakthrough in the field of knowledge theory is called a "Copernican revolution" by Kant. This is the essence of the synthetic, a priori knowledge articulated by Kant, in which the central role becomes that of "the observer," that is, the man who, by investigating nature, structures and orders it through the organization of collected data.

Modern and postmodern hermeneutics is nothing but the extension in the interpretive sphere of the Kantian transcendental subject. It could not be otherwise simply because of cultural contiguity and proximity. This is why the apparent one-sidedness and exaggeration in describing contemporary hermeneutics as "reader-centric," which has been our reading hypothesis, is not ultimately as improbable as it may seem at first glance. The reader is the linchpin of the modern hermeneutic project.

The value of the reader is not solely related to the instrumental value of his or her act. If there were no readers, who would read texts? The reader's contribution is deeper and has a great impact on the text itself. The reader is an indicator of an essential characteristic of the text: its

---

13. Kant, *Prolegomeni ad ogni futura metafisica*, 95–167.
14. Kant, *Prolegomeni ad ogni futura metafisica*, 25–41.

openness to the world. Through this openness of the text, we understand that the reader is not so foreign to the text. Therefore, although there is a risk that the reader will alter the scope of meaning of the text—and distort it—structurally we can say that there is no text without a reader. The reader is the correlate of the text, the one who brings the text to its fullness. It is as if the text remains, without the reader, in the state of an unexplored latency. This latency manifests itself and becomes real only with the reader. Through the mechanism of reading and interpretation, it is the reader who unfreezes the dormant potential of the text. A text cannot unfold its full signification until it is exposed by him. The reader embodies two important attitudes in the face of the text: 1. He must submit to the text and, almost annihilating himself, allow the text to unfold its full potentiality of meanings independently of him; 2. The reader must bring to bear in the face of the text his own specificity, which, while being the least textual thing, becomes the most suitable element for bringing out the latent meaning of the text.

Even more typically, the reader represents an opportunity for the text. In this the reader is a challenge to the text, and a good text knows how to welcome this challenge. A good text does not demand from the reader its flattening or passive subordination. There are four claims of the reader to the text.[15] To better exemplify these four dimensions of the ideal reader's profile, we will refer to the prologue of Luke's Gospel, which we quote below to facilitate understanding of the explanation.

Luke 1:1–4

> Since many have undertaken to order a narrative of the facts that have been fulfilled among us, as they have been handed down to us by those who from the beginning were eyewitnesses to them and who became ministers of the Word, it has seemed good to me also, after I have been thoroughly informed of everything from the origin, to write to you by order, illustrious Theophilus, so that you may recognize the certainty of the things you have been taught.

---

15. Ricœur, *Ermeneutica filosofica*, 95–100.

THE READER AND HIS ROOTING "UPSTREAM" OF THE TEXT: PRE-UNDERSTANDING[16]

Before anything else, the reader reminds the text that it is not first but second: every text is always preceded by life. If the first human experience were a textual experience, life would be reduced to a written formula. Even when a text is well-written or the text in question is the best possible text, as might be the case with the Bible or another religious text, that written formula does not have sufficient consistency to replace and precede life. A true text recognizes its derivability and dependence on something that precedes it: life. The true reader is the one who finds, recognizes, and claims his or her "rootedness" in life upstream of the text. While it is true that the text informs the reader about things he does not know, it is also true that the reader learns from the text only details of experiences that are familiar to him, before the text and apart from it.

This is the meaning of the pre-comprehension included or presupposed in any reading of a text. The text tells me about things that are already familiar to me because I am already grounded in life. The text is only a deepening of things that are not new to me. The text is not life but a mapping of it. Useful and necessary but subsequent to a pre-textual grounding in life. A text is great not when it claims to know more about life from the fact that that life has organized it around a successful cognitive schema. A text, even when it succeeds, fails because it is never able to contain life, all of life. Life will always be more than a text, just as life is always greater than any rule about life. That is not why the text lapses and loses its relevance. The relevance of a text is not to replace life, but to bear witness to it. That persuasive testimony, if constructed well, induces the reader to be interested in the text and even to go beyond the text. A good text, therefore, is always preceded by life and, at the same time, is surpassed by life. The good reader is one who is anchored in life and who, by virtue of this anchoring, is driven toward texts as expressions of life but without becoming trapped in them.

We take up the passage from Luke's Gospel (1:1–4), which we used in the previous chapter, to describe the three types of "distanciation" that constitute the essence of the text and, in this new context, to illustrate

---

16. Ricœur writes, "The theory of knowledge must be preceded by the recognition of the situation of rootedness in the world from which the anchorage of the whole linguistic system, and therefore also of books and texts, is assured" (*Ermeneutica filosofica*, 38).

now the profile of the reader. Theophilus,[17] as Luke's friend, is not born out of reading the text Luke writes for him, just as their friendship is not born because of that text. Rather, that text will be the product of the life of which that friendship, that emotional bond, that human affinity, is an expression. Luke's text is not first but second to a life-relation and belonging that sees Theophilus and Luke already connected. Regardless of the Gospel, there is a bond between the two of them that the writing of the Gospel will come to enrich, illuminate, enhance but not create. And even when relationships arise at the root of a reading, motivated by a text, in reality the reading of that text is always preceded by an excerpt of life with which the reader is familiar before knowing the text. If we did not know love, no text about love would be understandable to us. If we did not know intuitively and from life experience what friendship is, no text on friendship could ever break through to us. In other words, there is a grammar of life that we carry within us in an immediate way that highlights the fact that we are already in life, and only after that do intentions arise to improve it through the information conveyed to us by the texts. But those texts with new information about life are already an expression of life itself.

The friendship between Luke and Theophilus, or the desire to know the truth, is not born with the text Luke writes. That text enhances that life that already exists, giving it an opportunity for growth and reinforcement. This is the meaning of belonging, which, as such, is the condition and starting point for good interpretation.

THE READER AND HIS UPROOTING "IN FRONT OF" THE TEXT: SELF-CRITICISM[18]

The second moment the reader must assume is to put himself "in front" of the text and accept that that text upsets him,[19] making sure that he feels and accepts the criticism that, starting from the text, comes directly to

---

17. Nolland, *Luke*, xxvii-xlvii; Fabris, *Luke*, 21–34.

18. Ricœur writes, "The metamorphosis of the ego just alluded to implies a moment of distancing even in the relationship with the self, as a result of which understanding is appropriation as much as expropriation. Self-understanding can, indeed must, consequently, include both a Marxist and Freudian critique of the illusions of the subject" (*Ermeneutica filosofica*, 77–78).

19. It is what L. A. Schökel calls "the primacy of the question." See Schökel and Bravo Aragon, *Appunti di ermeneutica*, 92–93.

him. Being in front of the text thus causes a double effect. In a first moment the text reminds us that we are rooted in life. In a second moment the text tries, on the other hand, to uproot us from life through a critic of that rooted life. Not to destroy that rootedness but to improve it. Improving it sometimes means deconstructing it, dismantling it, subjecting it to scrutiny in order to rebuild it as best we can. This second effect, which takes over after the primary process of rootedness in life, is a process of critique that becomes necessary because the connection with life so many times is given in an abnormal and deforming way. It easily becomes misleading ideology. Not all certainties are real and true certainties. When that rootedness in life has become symbiotic and uncritical, the text bursts in as a salvation because it produces, if there is willingness and flexibility in the reader, a radical self-criticism of that anomalous symbiosis that one wants to pass off as necessary and beneficial.

This verification exercise, starting from the text, should not be directed only at those elements that seem anomalous, arouse doubt, and whose consistency must be verified. Critical verification must be applied to all elements in play, even those seemingly healthy and beyond doubt, because ideology easily creates appearance of truth and similarity of functional path in all departments and lanes of interpretive experience. Self-criticism is always an uncomfortable and apparently an unnecessary and an inappropriate exercise. It is never in time but out of time, never programmable but extemporaneous, starting with something unexpected that the text suddenly suggests. It must be realized by virtue of the fact that unfortunately not every "grounding in life" is necessarily a grounding that promotes self-affirmation and self-realization. There are purported rootednesses that actually are not.

The critique of false "rootedness" in life, advanced by the shrewd reader, does not reverse the relationship between "rootedness" (belonging) and "text" (distanciation). Structurally, first there will always be rootedness and then later the text, which generates criticism because it is only by virtue of the positive that the negative can be revealed and criticized. If this were not the case, criticism would be the grounding and would take precedence. Instead, it is the other way around: criticism, as a derivative event, is only possible if first there has been the affirmation of life to which the text bears witness.

Anomalous entrenchments in life, unfortunately, are not only common and widespread but tend to perpetuate themselves precisely by virtue of texts that support them. Structurally anomalous texts or good texts read roughly and one-sidedly. These anomalous entrenchments are not always visible precisely because they stick to the reader like a second skin. For this reason, the critique that generates being "in front" of the text must always be a self-critique, not a critique of what is distant and peripheral; not a critique of others or of application strategies, but a critique of oneself, of the reader in his or her innermost essence. It is the reader himself who is the bearer of anomalies of which he himself is unaware. Self-criticism before the text is an exercise that partially corrects these anomalies because it at least highlights what tends to remain hidden.

Anomalous entrenchments are presented as pure evidences. But they are not. They take the form of ideologies and as such resist any critical analysis. They exist at the collective level as well as at the individual level. Criticism that arises within groups or in individuals themselves, as internal corrective mechanisms, beyond apparent effectiveness, is often unsuccessful because it tends to maintain ideologies through updating them. This is why the text, as an external element, represents a unique opportunity for critique, for self-criticism. Not to deny belonging but to correct it and, by correcting it, reinforce it. Before proceeding to the application of what I have read, I must be able to critique myself "in front" of the text. If this does not happen, diligent application of the text risks reinforcing existing ideologies in the reader. Instead of being a tool for liberation, the text becomes a justification for maintaining those anomalies.

In Theophilus's example, Luke's Gospel serves, before becoming a push toward application, as a space for self-criticism.[20] Theophilus, as his name indicates, was by nature a man sensitive to religion and God. *Theo* (God), *philo* (to love) "friend of God, lover of the things of God, inclined to religion, sensitive to faith, vulnerable to transcendence," all these meanings and paraphrases of the name Theo-philo are the spontaneous extension of what this name bears at its core. It is a theophoric name par excellence because it encloses at its center the need for God. In ancient times, and not only in Israel, the name carried a distinctive characteristic of people. People recognized themselves in their name and their name was a strong expression of who they were in reality.

Theophilus, by virtue of this natural inclination toward religion, which his name embodies, could have remained as he was, cherishing this connatural and structural attitude of his temperament and enriching it only with what Jesus offers to every human being. That is not what

---

20. Bock, *Luke*, 51–67; Schürmann, *Gospel of Luke*, 53–67.

happens. That text that his friend Luke is offering him as a gift, instead of validating that natural religious virtue in him, ends up criticizing it, dismantling it, overturning it. That text serves as a space for self-criticism. Reading that text, which Luke writes for him, Theophilus finds the best part of himself, his belief, contradicted. For that text will tell him that much of what he believes is pure superstition.

We do not have records of Theophilus's reactions; however, we can well imagine them. To a man who is very religious, Luke's Gospel says that to a great extent his religiosity is false or, at the very least, superstitious, because true religion consists only in recognizing Jesus as the Christ. This is the Christ whom Theophilus does not know and must struggle to know and accept as savior. That text thus represents a harsh critique of Theophilus's religious and human ideologies. Luke's Gospel is not condescending to Theophilus. It does not mold a Christ to his measure, for the use and consumption of his natural religiosity. That text, written by Luke, will complicate his human and religious journey, because it will introduce into the center of his life an obstacle, a stumbling block, an element of scandal. We know, however, indirectly, that Theophilus, on the other hand, is open to such criticism. And that is why Luke will dedicate a second book to him.[21]

This self-criticism "before" the text the Spirit accomplishes, at first, through the unhinging of our certainties. The text must create in us an awareness regarding our own anomalies. If the reader does not first correct his or her own anomalous and improper assumptions, which he or she often holds up even with biblical justifications (racism, machismo, speciesism), it is clear that direct application would only end up reinforcing them. In the moment of self-criticism, the reader distrusts his or her deepest beliefs and allows himself or herself to be unhinged by the text.

THE READER AND HIS PRO-ROOTING "BEYOND" THE TEXT: IMAGINATION[22]

In a third moment and before application, the text pushes us forward in an unusual way: it pushes us to go beyond it through imagination. Not

---

21. Acts 1:1.

22. Ricœur writes, "If, in other words, a fundamental dimension of the referentiality of the text is its fictional character, so too is it in regard to the subjectivity of the reader. As a reader, only when I lose myself do I find myself; from reading I am introduced into the imaginative variations of the ego; in accordance with play, the metamorphoses

to escape and run away from belonging but to create new ones and, by creating them, reinforce them through their renewal. A good text always promotes a possible beyond. The text always has a latency. It proposes meanings just by suggesting them, by introducing them as possible, indirectly, almost without mentioning them but only alluding to them. Instead, these incomplete and sketchy meanings from the text explode only through the reader's imagination. It is the reader who brings these insights to fruition and concretizes them into alternative visions, outlines, and forms to the text through imagination. With imagination, the reader, starting from the text, goes beyond it through the creation of alternative worlds, practices, and realities. The reader has a revolutionary vocation in the interpretive process.

Reading cannot become the place where the reader's passion dies. On the contrary, every good reading gives birth to passion through imagination.[23] Through the text, the reader imagines[24] worlds that do not yet exist but can exist if we begin to perceive them as possible. If application took over immediately without this explosion of meaning, which is the moment of imagination, reading would become a place of imprisonment, not only of meaning but also of the reader. We could say that imagination represents true self-criticism. In some ways, imagination comes before self-criticism and grounds it. Self-criticism is an unconcluded imagination and imagination is a fully realized self-criticism.

Reconnecting with Theophilus and Luke,[25] although we do not find an account of how the moment of imagination takes place in Theophilus, it is clear that the reading of that text prompted Theophilus to look at the world, life, and reality differently. The change in behavior was preceded, thanks to the Gospel text, by a change in vision, in mindset. This is *metanoia*. Metanoia as conversion is, before moral, a conversion in imagination. It represents a change in thinking. A different way of posing to the world, a going beyond what we perceive. Metanoia as conversion is an imaginative process at the basis of salvation, because only through it can the believer perceive a new world. In the present he does not see it; he can

---

of the world are also playful metamorphoses of the ego" (*Ermeneutica filosofica*, 77).

23. Imagination, on the other hand, is not a pure distractive and consoling mechanism but transforms reality the most concrete and leads it toward freedom and personal flourishing. Jennings, *Christian Imagination*, 21–32.

24. Imagination is that attitude that exploits the potentialities latent in the text and brings them to fruition. See Schökel and Bravo Aragon, *Appunti di ermeneutica*, 94–97.

25. Tannehill, *Luke*, 33–35; Rengstorf, *Vangelo secondo Luca*, 31–36.

only imagine it. Faith itself is a strong imaginative process, making visible what is not yet there in the present. It introduces a horizon that includes that reality which, according to the criteria of the present, is not real but becomes so through imagination. It is precisely this flight of imagination that becomes reality in the life of Theophilus, of which we have no explicit record, but which is undoubtedly there, for it is by virtue of that and the great transformations it produced that Luke dedicates a second text to him, the book of the Acts of the Apostles.

THE OBEDIENT READER AND THE VITAL READER: THE WHY OF CREATIVITY[26] "IN READING"

In a fourth moment, the reader remembers and claims before the text his "grounding" in life downstream of the text. While it is true that the text tells the reader things he does not know, it is also true that the reader, in the application of what he learns from the text, tests how much of what he has learned from the text is true or false, relevant or irrelevant, functional or illusory. In application, the reader takes note of the latent meanings of the text and extends them into concrete life.[27] Every application always goes beyond the text and adds things to the text that it does not say. The guarantor of this passage is precisely the reader. The text is not an authoritarian king who says what reality must be by decree; rather it is reality that offers and initiates a path and opens to a new reality. Of this larger reality and beyond the text, the reader is the ambassador. The true reader is the one who does not feel obliged to pay an eternal tribute to the text that has guided him for a stretch of his path. The true reader is transgressive in his essence. He is so because of the text itself. The text itself, if it is true and noble, is the element that impels the reader to go further.

This space of transcending the text, which we call the space of application, is not a subordinate stage. It represents an important place of realization for the reader and also for the text. It is as if, in application, the text itself rejoices in being transcended. Application is not the place of flattening the reader who prolongs the text in its fullness. The moment

---

26. Ricœur writes, "I rightly said imagination and not will, because the power to allow oneself to be seized by new possibilities precedes the power to make a decision and choose" (*Ermeneutica filosofica*, 99).

27. In this sense any hermeneutic application is necessarily creative. Jeanrond, *Ermeneutica teologica*, 157–201.

of application is not the pure reflection of a sense of the text applied to perfection in the reality of life.

The word "application" easily misleads, because application suggests the complete replication of the text and its pattern in real life through the diligence of the reader. Instead, diligence is not the central point in application. It is necessary and essential but at the same time insufficient. Application,[28] more than being a space of diligence, is a space of creativity. This is because a true text does not want the subjugation of reality to its mapping but rather the opposite. A true text desires to be a map that the reader uses as a point of departure, not as a point of arrival, because, if that were the case, the text and its mapping would become mechanisms of bewilderment. The map should serve to explore the territory, not to confuse it and replace it with the map. It is only the reader's creativity that allows that mapping (text) to be used well in the moment of real confrontation with the territory.

Only after the recognition of "rootedness in life," "self-criticism," and "imagination" does "application" become a corrective and constructive path because it outlines a possible process of redemption and growth. There is nothing magical about application, but it opens up possible worlds because it becomes the natural sequential stage of a prior work that takes and prolongs positive life thrusts from the text. Application structured in this sequence is transformed from repetition of the past to fidelity to the future, from validation of the already happened to the not-yet of the project. Verification changes into promise.

Reconnecting once again with Theophilus,[29] we can only imagine how the moment of application becomes the final stage of this interpretive journey. We are told nothing about how Theophilus applied what he learned from the text before him, the Gospel of Luke. Yet, much is suggested to us. That the book of the Acts of the Apostles, also dedicated to Theophilus, is a sign of the greatness of his application. Indeed, the whole missionary turn of Christianity, which from centripetal will become centrifugal, precisely by virtue of its decentralization to foreigners and pagan peoples, is placed in the perspective of what Theophilus represents. He is the pagan who became a Christian. The prototype of the new believer is not the unbeliever who begins to believe. This profile will be a profile

---

28. Application does not only have to do with an external realization. It includes a personal and internalizing dimension. See Schökel and Bravo Aragon, *Appunti di ermeneutica*, 97–102.

29. Bock, *Luke*, 51–67; Schürmann, *Gospel of Luke*, 53–67.

of modern times. The profile of all nascent Christianity, which, beginning with the obsession with purity of faith (typical of the Judaism of Jesus' time) will become a Christianity in search of new inculturation, is embodied in Theophilus and put as the incipit of the book of the Acts of the Apostles (1:1). This is the typically ancient profile of a man already a believer who corrects that belief by orienting it toward Jesus. The Christian preaching of which Theophilus is the prototype is in its essence only a reorientation of faith, not its creation. The ancient man who converts is already a believer, like Theophilus, because that is how the anthropology and culture of that time is structured. Different will be the profile of contemporary man who, being secularized to varying degrees, must, in order to recognize Jesus as his Savior, learn to believe anew.

Let us take up the initial question of this chapter: who is the real reader? Let us problematize the situation by answering it atypically in this way to give an additional but decisive step in identifying that characteristic that qualitatively distinguishes the reader. The true reader is not "the one who reads everything" but "the one who does not just read everything." This answer to a seemingly obvious question will allow us to specify further. The best reader seems to be, at first glance, the disciplined, knowledgeable, purposeful, and attentive reader of the text he or she reads. The problem is that the attention and awareness of that kind of careful reader already presupposes two anomalies.

The first consists in the fact that the text, implicitly, has already become an "object" for him. An object he needs to focus on, grasp, conquer in order to finally possess. The text seems to have become the object of an obsession with possession. This desire for possession presupposes the disenchantment of the text and its reduction to a primary source of information. The text is reduced to its informational dimension, its quantitative component, as if a text is valuable solely on the condition that it possesses new information. A typical textual reductionism is outlined in this view.

The second consists in the fact that this careful and determined reader not only embodies the greed of wanting to possess the object he lacks (the text) but, further upstream, also betrays a lack of his own, a primary emptiness. He starts already impoverished because he appears disconnected from the object he greedily seeks. That reader is orphaned and as such missing an essential connection. Here between reading subject and read object (text) there is a rupture, a detachment, a deprivation. This detachment, this initial non-attachment, creates a compensatory mechanism that is expressed in the attentive and disciplined greed of compulsive desire and conquest. The discipline and attentiveness of this attentive reader in front of the text, hides a non-binding that is intended to be corrected and is an expression of it. The noble intent to overcome that anomaly through reading, which aims precisely at the reconnection of the subject (reader) with the object (text), only adds to that rupture because it delivers to the greedy and orphaned reader a disenchanted text, a text that has become an object.

The best reader cannot be recognized in this careful and disciplined, decisive and determined reader. In this reader there is a hypertrophy of intention that translates a poverty and obsession. The true reader is more relaxed but not because he already possesses the text. On the contrary, not only does he not own it, he is aware that he will never own it. This is because the text is not an object to be owned.[30] This reader, of type two, has a desire that is the telltale sign of his incompleteness. By this desire he is driven forward. His is not an obsessive incompleteness. His is a light incompleteness that leads him not to a desire to possess but to a courtship of the text, knowing that it will never be his completely. With that text that will never be his he already feels connected and therefore desires it. He is not orphaned by what he seeks. With what he seeks there is already a connection, a memory, a belonging. This reader, by virtue of that presupposed connection with the text, can do without possessing that text because he is already unconsciously connected to what that text is about, that is, life. The true reader is the one who is already connected to the life to which the unobjectified text bears witness. And he is connected to life for two reasons.

First, precisely because he is connected to life, he has no problem reading that text without the obsession of possessing that life that is expressed in the text. His is not an obsession with the text because he does not escape from life. Obsession and escape are not opposite experiences that often create an ironclad partnership. One tends to insistently seek what one is fleeing from but is unable to take in without possessing. Too much reading easily becomes escape from life. Not escape as detachment and disinterest but escape as obsession and attachment. It is all or nothing, so why nothing, then everything. Symbiotic attachment is the most refined type of escape because there is no estrangement but its opposite.

---

30. In this sense Jeanrond speaks of "an ethics of reading" that is not one that stops at the letter of the text, but grasps its perspective and makes it its own. Cf. Jeanrond, *Ermeneutica teologica*, 196–199.

Attachment is rapprochement in form but estrangement (escape) from the substance of life. A controlled life is no longer life. The greedy subject, who seeks attachment to the object through reading, actually turns away, despite approaching life, because he seeks a controlled life, a life made object, a manipulated text. This triggers a real mechanism of addiction and, like any addiction, it drives away that which it wants to approach. That thing that one approaches and feels the need for has become a dead thing, which one possesses quantitatively but escapes qualitatively. The best reader, on the other hand, is the one who, being rooted in the life that unites subject and object, does not read in order to have life but reads because he is already connected to life. Reading does not become a sublimation but an expression of life that dismantles the gluttony of wanting life by aiming to control it. Even the apparent and legitimate pursuit of the "meaning of life" through reading actually conceals the perversion of having life by trying to control it, by controlling its meaning.

The second reason for the connection to life is explained by the fact that only this rootedness in life sparks the imagination. Imagination is what distinguishes the creative reader. The creative reader is not the one who transcends text and life to jump into the void and chaos. On the contrary, he is the one who is rooted in life and the text and, by virtue of this rootedness, flies to the beyond, to new forms of life. He is an heir who receives and transforms, listens and innovates. Rootedness and listening to the text does not stop him but nourishes him and propels him forward. The creative reader is not a loose cannon. The creative reader is the one who empowers life and this creates new spaces of expression. He gives life new forms by virtue of the very life that animates him. Only life creates life. This is the imagination.

The best reader is not the one who wants to com-prehend (take) meaning by making it his obsession through assiduous reading of texts. This kind of reader, who appears as a model to many, is actually a bad model because he or she is a reader in "withdrawal." The best reader is one who is well before reading and is well because he is rooted in life, so he does not aim to possess it. And being in life means being aware that you can lose it. Approaching life must always elicit an attitude of vulnerability. If we want to enjoy it, we must know that we cannot possess it. If we owned it, we would immediately kill it. Life embodied as an object in the sense of a text ultimately turns out to be a poor life that does not convey life. As readers in reading, we must seek not a strength but the discovery of our vulnerability. True reading of a text is the discovery of the unavailability of life and its meaning. In reading we look at a goal (life) that we cannot have, but if the desire animates us it means that that life is already in us and it is by virtue of it that we are moved by the desire to read. It is when that life is not there, because there is no rootedness in it, that paradoxically the obsession to have it is triggered, but as soon as we have reached it, it slips from our grasp and we are left with only its carcass.

Let us now briefly return to the differentiation introduced at the beginning of this chapter between the "obedient reader" and the "vital reader." The obedient reader, we said, is a reader who is very active in the application but not in the creation of meaning, while the vital reader is not obsessed with the application of the meaning of the text but is the one who seeks, desires, acts, and actually participates in the creation of meaning. Let us add a specification to this differentiation. An important specification that concerns the reader's being and not just his knowledge. For it is primarily at this level, and not only at the level of sense-making, that the most important difference between these two types of readers manifests itself.

The obedient reader is the one who receives from the text the meanings already made that he only has to apply. In this he takes no risks. He does not assume the price of freedom, so he prefers security in the paths established by what precedes him, whatever that may be: tradition, family, church, or God. We might say that his obvious activism and application efforts may well be a compensation mechanism for not being able to create new meanings. He compensates for his lack of creative capacities at the level of meaning by hyper-presence in the dissemination of that meaning he did not create. The dirigisme that requires him to apply the meanings he alone has collected extends to imposing on him who he is to be. The obedient reader accepts for himself a norm that does not feature him and which he suffers as an obligation. Interpretive obligation becomes ontological obligation. This is the dimension of ontological laziness that delineates the contours of his profile. What he owes, can do, or what he simply is, he does not derive from himself but receives from others, from elsewhere. He suffers his being, so he avoids the beneficial suffering of those who instead seek to be themselves. The obedient reader is one who bends before the text without asking the text questions that its historical grounding would require. He is incapable, in confronting the text (even more so if this text is sacred), of claiming as legitimate what he is, of expressing his anxieties, of giving space for doubts and questions. The sacredness of the text before him instills fear and paralyzes him.

Instead, the *vital reader* is a demanding reader who claims for himself the active right to question the text from the legitimacy of its historical grounding. In this new perspective, the reader is a co-creator of meaning: he assumes and understands that the world, life, identities, or events do not exist as finite and fixed realities. They are only ingredients that each individual is called upon to use in the construction of personal projects, chosen according to what the text indicates and suggests, but also according to what we perceive our world to be and should be. The world, the family, the state, etc., are not imposed entities. They are not houses and places waiting to be inhabited but materials to be used in new constructions. The *creative reader* does not allow the agenda of his actions to set the text alone. He must be a co-participant in determining what he is to do. Not only that: even in what concerns himself, his being, he is not submissive and compliant. While he is not the sole instance in determining what he is, he believes, in determining who he should be, that his own questions, anxieties, doubts, and vicissitudes count as much as the text's suggestions.

He receives life and transmits it. It is a ferryman of life because there is meaning only if there is life. A life without meaning is empty knowledge. And the two characteristics that distinguish the vital reader are the force of "individualization" and the force of "participation."

The Force of Individualization

By "individualization" we mean the capacity for autonomy and the tenacity to mark a detachment in the face of the whole. The whole can be the family, the group, the city, the nation, or the church. There is individuality when the person is able not to think of himself only in relation to a system and according to rhythms and deadlines that are not his own. Life must be able to be single life, to claim its own specificities, the ability to express and own its own registers without having to apologize for it. Life is single or it is not. In this sense, the process of achieving one's autonomy is always a transgression. Without transgression there is no life. And the first transgression is birth. Life begins with an ontological transgression. I go beyond the limit of an organ, the womb, that has nurtured and welcomed me perfectly. But that space that welcomes me perfectly can easily become my grave if I am not born into my autonomy as a singular being. The symbiotic bond that connects us to a group or entity larger than ourselves is a human and legitimate bond if it provides for its own termination, if it is expiring. If it recognizes itself as an accompanying and promoting element of singular life. At some point, however, it must yield and be valued by its capacity to give freedom to the single life. The noble single life is the one that is affirmed as specific.

There is also the parallel concept of "individuation" developed in the field of analytical psychology by Swiss psychiatrist Carl Gustav Jung[31] in the 1920s. The concept of individuation aims to emphasize the affirmation of the individual as a specific and coherent reality. It does so more on an internal level. In fact, individuation, according to Jung, is synonymous with that unique and unrepeatable psychic process of each individual that consists in the rapprochement of the ego with the self, that is, with an increasing integration and unification of the various elements that make up the personality. When this does not occur, the individual has the deconstructive experience of psychological dispersion.

"Individuation" is thus a process of integrating and harmonizing forces and instances within the individual. While "individualization" is a claim to autonomy from external forces, individualization is what Paul Tillich calls "the courage to be."[32] The courage of one's autonomy, of one's "singularity."[33]

In hermeneutics, it means that the individual capable of individualization is the reader, who through reading is able to affirm himself. Reading and interpretation nurture and create him. It is in the text itself that the vital reader is able and learns to find reasons to affirm himself, to be autonomous, to forge his individuality. Interpretation generates and regenerates him. The text ceases to be a guilt mechanism for the individual who decides to go beyond it. It is the text itself that deconstructs his sense of shame at having decided to be different from the group. The reading and interpretation liberates him and suggests reasons for him to be himself at the cost of being different from others.

The Power of Participation

Here we are dealing with the opposite path with which the individualization process must learn to live in tension. In participation the individual recognizes himself as part of a whole. Life is always a life together with

---

31. Jung, *Phychologische Typen*, 13–25.
32. Tillich, *Courage to Be*, 4–19.
33. Tillich, *Courage to Be*, 114–51.

others; it is recognizing connectedness as a guarantee of survival. In participation we can identify two perspectives. On the one hand, participation as a condition; on the other hand, participation as a choice.

Participation as a condition means recognizing that participation precedes us. We are preceded beings, we do not choose it: it is already there before we are aware of it. It is a condition of life that makes life possible. It is becoming aware that we are born and attain an autonomy of our own by virtue of and because of a grounding in being. This is the version of participation according to Paul Tillich,[34] which he calls "ontological rootedness." Every other activity undertaken by the individual in the course of his or her existence—epistemological, pragmatic, ritualistic, etc.—presupposes this rootedness in being that one must learn to recognize.

Participation as choice, on the other hand, is that which takes over after experiencing the dispersion of one's life and then arouses the need to create bonding. Bonding between the parts and centrifugal forces of one's life, but also bonding between this life and other lives. Here participation appears not as a foundation, but as a goal, as a task to be accomplished in order to guarantee the individual life a chance of survival. This is the perspective of Erich Fromm,[35] for whom the necessary autonomy of the individual, which at first enables him or her to overcome symbiotic bonds, enables him or her, at a later stage, to direct them and place them in the service of a noble and ennobling bond, without which autonomy itself would easily become destructive. Love as chosen participation, which places life in a context of bonding that guarantees it, has four characteristics: care, responsibility, respect, and knowledge. Autonomy does not disappear; on the contrary, it becomes the guarantee of possible bonding. Active love is precisely this vocation to a participation that is not suffered but freely chosen in virtue of life.

In hermeneutics, it means that the individual capable of participation is the reader who, through reading, is able to recognize a dependency. Reading helps him to think of himself as a derivative being, someone who is preceded. Reading ceases to be a sophisticated and clumsy exercise in self-foundation. In and through the text the reader finds compelling reasons to understand that his life is a response to something that precedes him. Interpretation integrates it to something. First to life itself, then to a community that precedes and welcomes it and to which the text

---

34. Tillich, *Courage to Be*, 89–113.
35. Fromm, *Arte di amare*, 29–40.

bears witness. The text ceases to be an object of study that he tries to comprehend and use to solely reinforce his own sufficiency. The text becomes the site of an epiphany of being proper and being together. In the text, life happens and is contemplated in the witness of which that text is a medium. Reading and interpretation complement him and suggest reasons for him to feel connected to and preceded by things he did not create.

Moving to a more theological realm, we can ask how far the Bible reader has preserved its revolutionary character, especially in Protestant circles, where the relevance of the individual believer was claimed by the Reformers, from the very beginning, as the primary reality of faith experience.

In fact, Protestantism has not only produced "reforms" but, after some centuries, unfortunately also some "deformations." Some anomalies, derived from the Protestant approach relating precisely to the status of the reader of the Bible, are, for example, the conformist reader, the obedient reader, the ethically reliable and morally predictable reader, which tends to impoverish and dent the profile of a curious, innovative, dreamer, transgressive reader, which is the profile of reader that the Bible presupposes and that we have called "vital reader." The reading of the Bible is not validated by a formal appeal to it, as Protestantism tends to do, but by the quality of reading and reader that that appeal produces. Protestantism was revolutionary in proposing the Bible as a criterion of faith when faith was impoverished by a scattershot appeal to secondary instances of religious experience. This same recall to that sacred book as final instance of truth risk today to become the tomb of meaning. The call to this centrality of the Bible cannot substitute for the qualitative effects that that centrality should produce, namely, a reading and a reader who flourish in the articulation of meaning-making and innovation.

V

A Sober and Inclusive Language

WE WILL CONSIDER IN this chapter what we believe the scope and nature of biblical language means and represents. For many, biblical language is simply a hindrance and an impediment to understanding the spiritual message it underlies. This is because that language, which is indirect, imprecise, approximate, confusing, and contradictory, belongs to other historical times when mankind, due to inexperience and lack of linguistic and cognitive means, was forced to work with and use a kind of language that we today, with a bit of superiority and a dash of cultural contempt, call mythical language. That mythical language, which the Bible uses with full hands, is no longer suitable for understanding God and his meaning for us in our time. Neither is it adequate for understanding our contemporary world, shaped by science and precision languages, which serves as the context for experiencing God today.

Demythologization,[1] then, understood as the correction of that inadequate language, as proposed for example by Bultmann[2] (but certainly not only by him), would be a hermeneutical obligation. It arises from the intent to update and bring within our grasp the essence of the biblical message. Left as it is, it not only fails to reach us moderns. It also deforms the essence of its own message. Bultmann's proposal will appear radical[3]

1. Cf. Jeanrond, *L'ermeneutica teologica*, 240–44.
2. Bultmann, *Foi et Compréhension*, 101–11.
3. Criticism of the Bultmannian proposal actually comes from various fronts. In

to many from the outset, but its basic logic cuts across, through the sharing of a double presupposition, even by those who oppose the Bultmannian program.[4] This double presupposition considers that the only noble and reliable languages are the languages of precision, anti-mythological languages. On the other hand, it holds that the texts that use mythological language, including the Bible, must necessarily be filtered to try to redeem what in them has a universal but hidden value.

With regard to the value and relevance of biblical language, we do not stand against the rational analysis which is present in the demythologization program. We stand against the one-sided conclusions of Bultmann and also of those who oppose him. In both positions, although for opposite reasons and with opposite mechanisms, there subsists an obsession with the univocity of languages of precision, theoretical or practical. In this we make our own, at least in part, the more measured and differentiated analysis made by Paul Ricœur[5] of the program of demythologization. He manages to grasp the Bultmannian intention and also to defend it, without, however, sparing it a harsh criticism, because, at its basis, there would be in Bultmann a double misunderstanding. On the one hand, Bultmann fails to grasp that even in the Bible there is a program of demythologization. Demythologization does not arise only with modernity but, to a certain extent, it is already an integral part of biblical

---

the "evangelical" world, the rejection is categorical. Cf. Bloesch, *Holy Scripture*, 223–54; Erickson, *Christian Theology*, 69–71. A similarly critical position, but for different reasons, is expressed, for example, by Oscar Cullmann when he challenges the Bultmannian program, not so much for the necessary linguistic updating, but for the process of "de-escatologization" that demythologization triggers. Cullmann, *Salut dans l'histoire*, 35–37. Also critical is the position of Armido Rizzi who, however, prefers to speak of "de-Hellenization." Cf. di Sante, *Dentro la Bibbia*, 17–42.

4. This is, for example, the opinion of Eugenio Trias, a Spanish philosopher and careful analyst of modernity and postmodernity, who in a fair way recognizes the uniqueness of modern thought unparalleled in its dynamism but also categorizes it as reductive thought. And the limitation of this thought lies in its inability to mythicize, which it sublimates, however, by presenting itself only as enlightened thought (*Enlightenment*). The symbolic and mythical deficit is sold by modern and postmodern thought only as a virtue. In the inability to mythicize is evidenced the chronic symbolic deficit typical of the West, which Trias describes as the "disease of the West." See Trias, *Pensar la religion*, 99–111.

5. Much more sober, fair, and relevant in this regard is Paul Ricouer's analysis of the program of demythicization, grasping its limitations on the one hand but also highlighting its relevance. Ricœur emphasizes a double level of relevance in the word "demythicization." The second level is not only positive, which even does not belong only to the modern spirit, but is already present in the Bible itself, in the Old and New Testaments. Cf. Ricœur, *Conflitto delle interpretazioni*, 400–5.

language. On the other hand, because in the biblical language, along with a demythologization thrust, we synchronically find also a mythicizing thrust of a positive sign. Myth also serves, in part, as an unparalleled tool for describing and referring to complex and paradoxical realities that could not be said well with precision languages and for that reason use the typical descriptive strategies of symbolic language of which myth is an expression.[6]

When we talk about biblical language, we are still not talking about content but about container. The Bible is important not only because of what it says but especially because of how it says it. That biblical language is important escapes almost no one. Most of the time, however, this attention is reduced to its consideration as the medium of a sacred content that we must preserve with care and attention. There is a widespread belief that biblical language is only a medium, a channel. As such, that it has a deadline. The deadline usually given to it is the attainment of meaning. Once meaning is found, biblical language would automatically become fallen and unnecessary. Instead, in our view, and according to our analysis, biblical language is a structural and timeless part of biblical truth itself.

Considering what the Bible says, stopping merely subsidiary to consideration of the language it uses, inexorably ends up distorting the profile and scope of the content itself. Without its language, biblical truth becomes progressively distorted, even when the meaning has already been achieved. It is the *how* (language) of the Bible that actually guarantees from beginning to end the nature and scope of the content of its message. Biblical content and language are certainly not identical but neither are they disjointed on pain of deforming the meaning derived.

At this level, the myopia of Christians seems to have become chronic and almost irreversible. The tendency of both Christians and non-Christians is, more often than not, to look intently, if not obsessively, at the content, considering biblical language purely as incidental. Thus one

---

6. Realities such as the ambivalence of freedom between action and passion, between voluntary and involuntary in decision-making processes, the union of necessity and contingency in the explanation of the cosmos and nature, are unspeakable outside symbolic languages. Hence Ricœur's defense of this kind of language. For a more anthropological description of the value of symbolic language regarding the paradoxes and complexity of the human, see *Volontaire et l'involontaire, vol. 1*. For an appreciation of symbolic language instead at a more cosmological level, consider some sections of the second volume, "Les mythes du commencement et de la fin," in *Finitude et culpabilité, vol. 2*, 309–477; "La simbolique du mal," in *Finitude et culpabilité, vol. 2*, 167–306.

easily arrives at a double distortion. On the one hand, the reduction of biblical language to a pure medium takes over; on the other, the parallel and symbiotic reduction of the content to a univocal sense. In reality, it is not sense, or at least it should not be sense, that usurps the totality of the content of revelation. This would be pure biblical positivism. God is not revealed in the sense of content alone. That content, at the very least, has other possible senses, so the sense is always in tension with other latent senses. The content of the message also includes nonsense. Unmeaningful nonsense is one thing, but nonsense as meaning not yet understood is for all intents and purposes part of the content of the biblical message. So many times the Word of God has appeared to its hearers as nonsense. Yet, behind that nonsense was simply hidden an alternative sense not yet understood. This is why the formula "God reveals himself in language"[7] is different from the formula "God reveals himself in sense." Certainly God reveals himself in the sense. This fact is difficult to dispute. But does God reveal himself only in the sense? In the intelligible sense? Certainly not.[8]

It is contestable to make the connection between God, or the content of the biblical message, and sense absolute. Sense is only one part of God's revelation. To say that God reveals himself in human language is not remotely reducible to saying that God reveals himself in the unambiguous sense of that language. Language is something larger, and it is in that larger container that God has decided to become incarnate. God became verb, language, and the sense we can grasp and give to that language does not exhaust either that language or God. This specific fact is preserved by "biblical language," and that is why it is just as important as the biblical content, so it needs to be preserved with care and attention.

Biblical language is not and cannot be only a temporary means. It is not and can never be surmountable, either at the beginning, during, or at the end of the interpretive process. To leave it out is to lose even the content and to distort it partially or totally. The interpretive resumption must be able to transfer, as is necessary for it to do, the content but also

---

7. Schökel makes the difference between "inspiration in the key of judgment" and "inspiration in the key of language." The former leads to abstraction, to privileging "the idea of God," thus to theological monolithism, and finally to exclusion and war over ideas. The second, on the other hand, leads to communicative relationship, thus to privileging "the Word of God" as a plural, inclusive and un-obsessed meeting place with a monolithic truth. Schökel and Bravo Aragon, *Appunti di ermeneutica*, 19–24.

8. The language in which God reveals himself is not traceable to his verbal communication, much less to the intelligible sense of that communication of his. Cf. Jeanrond, *Ermeneutica teologica*, 19–20.

the rhythm and scope of the biblical language into other contexts and linguistic forms but without omitting it along the way.

This attention to biblical language brings with it another benefit: that of also making us aware of the scope and limitation of the language of the interpreter. Failure to perceive this difference leads us to impose on the Bible, as if it were our own, while assimilating its content, a language that is instead ours. On the one hand we impose on the biblical content a language that is not its own, thus devaluing it; on the other hand we advance as biblical a language that is not biblical, thus overvaluing a language, ours, that is instead relative.

A THEOLOGICAL-CULTURAL LOOK AT BIBLICAL LANGUAGE[9]

Our reflection is mainly articulated therefore at this second level, that is, of *how* (language) the Bible says what it says. It is articulated on two dimensions, one synchronic and one diachronic. On the synchronic

---

9. *Biblical language* must be related to but also differentiated from, on the one hand, the "biblical text," and on the other hand, the "biblical interpretation." The biblical text is the mediating but not foundational element, just as biblical interpretation is the resulting but not foundational element. Cf. Funk, *Language, Hermeneutic*, 10–25. The common element is given not only by content but also by form, which is determined by narrative and discursive "plurivocity." This common element is found in different proportions in the three instances, but it is greatest in the foundational instance, that is, biblical language. Cf. Ricœur, *Interpretation Theory*, 24–37; *Hermeneutics and the Human Sciences*, 54–69; Alter, *Arte della narrativa biblica*; *Arte della poesia biblica*. The foundational element of *biblical language*, taking into account that it is biblical language that grounds the biblical text and the biblical text that grounds biblical interpretation, is given and determined by its exuberance or "plurivocity." Schökel and Bravo emphasize this exuberance of biblical language by making the distinction between "judgment" and "language." The former is more precise but less inclusive, while the latter is more general but more inclusive. They apply the second criterion to the Bible, not the first. Schökel and Bravo Aragon, *Appunti di ermeneutica*, 19–24. Ricœur will not only describe this exuberance as the structural and characterizing center of biblical language, but will expand it to all kinds of language. Loretta Dornisch, regarding what language is for Ricœur, writes: "At the same time language is distorted; it is equivocal, it has multiple meanings, it means more than it says. Since men are born in the sign of language, it is not so much spoken by men as spoken to them. Ordinary language has an incredible ambiguity, an amphibological construction and confusion inherent in idiomatic expressions and metaphor." Dornisch, "Symbolic Systems and the Interpretation of Scripture: Introduction to the Work of Paul Ricœur," in Ricœur, *Biblical Hermeneutics*, 12. On the "plurivocity" and exuberance of biblical language, see Marguerat and Bourquin, *Per leggere I racconti biblici*, 112–128. For "plurivocity" in a general sense related to narrative, see Kundera, *Arte del romanzo*.

dimension, which aims to take the Bible as it is, without investigating its historical evolution, we have privileged two themes. The theme of "textuality," in chapter three of part one, and the theme of "linguistic form" in this chapter. Textuality and linguistic form are certainly related but not identical phenomena. We will try, in this chapter, to separate the linguistic form, which in our opinion distinguishes the Bible, from the fate of its form as a text, having reserved the theological-cultural analysis of the text for a longer reflection in the aforementioned chapter.

The historical investigation of the kind of interpretations that have followed one another over time fits on the diachronic dimension of the *how* of the Bible. We, have, instead, developed a hypothesis on the uniqueness of the modern period which is presented in chapter two. Chapters seven and eight of this second part are on this dimension of diachronic analysis. This is where we will discuss hermeneutic anomalies of our time.

We come, then, to the subject of this chapter: the nature of biblical language. The characteristic feature of biblical language would consist, according to some, in the fact that it embodies a transcendence, an other Word, so as to exclude its identification with purely human mechanisms. For others, the strong point is instead the humanization of the religious message: the fact of finding in the Bible a divine Word embodied in human language. Today, for most Christians, the characteristic of biblical language lies above all in its concreteness, as opposed to the more speculative language of other books and especially philosophy. The Bible would not be interested in the gratuitous motion of either thoughts, concepts or words because it would point to the immediacy of the application of God's unambiguous will for us. The Bible articulates a language of salvation that offers itself to the reader in an immediate, concrete, and unambiguous way.

This pragmatic view, which is quite prevalent especially in the more dynamic and zealous sections of Christian communities, fails to grasp the characteristic of biblical language. It even proposes a model of it that is opposed to it and has nothing biblical about it. On the contrary, it is inspired by and stems directly from modern pragmatism. There is nothing perverse about modern pragmatism itself, provided we do not elevate it to an ideology above criticism and, above all, do not identify it with biblical language. In today's interpretive pragmatism, one merely transfers typical technical univocity, articulated as precision, from theory to spiritual practice. In divine transcendent language or divine language embodied in human language, the important thing would be its univocity and compactness. This is the opposite of what distinguishes the Bible and its language. This is its unavailability of meaning, its mystery, its polyvalence.[10]

This is the thesis Erich Auerbach expresses in his book *Mimesis: Realism in Western Literature*.[11] He was as a German Romanist of Jewish descent, a professor of romance philology at the University of Marburg. In 1936, due to Nazi racial laws, he was forced to leave Germany and take refuge in Turkey, where he was offered the same professorship at Istanbul University. Between 1942 and 1945 he wrote *Mimesis*, his masterpiece.

In the first chapter of the book, titled "The Scar of Odysseus," he makes a comparison between the Odyssey and the Old Testament, specifically between Book XIX of the Greek text and chapter 22 of the book of Genesis. The particularity of biblical language, in this case in the description of Isaac's sacrifice, becomes clearer when it is compared with an ancient text such as the Odyssey. Homeric description is characterized by precision and exactitude. Nothing is left to chance. For Homer, it is intolerable to see the scar emerging from a dark and elusive past. He abounds in specification data. His characters speak, they are circumscribable in their action, proceeding, and destiny.

No description in Homer appears incomplete or interrupted for lack of clear and orderly logical and linguistic articulation. Conjunctions, adverbs, particles, and other syntactic devices clearly delineate people, things, and events from one another, while at the same time creating a fluid and continuous connection. In this way there is a sequential and rhythmic chaining of well-defined phenomena and events into a plot with a clear and distinct outline.

In Homer we find, according to Auerbach, detailed descriptions, connections without gaps, transparent close-ups, accompanying elements with evidentiary clearness. At the same time we have, though, limitation and greater superficiality in perceiving historical development and the depth, complexity, and paradoxicality of human issues and related human characters.

In the biblical account instead, the beginning already surprises us. Abraham says, "Here I am." But where do the two dialogues stand? This is not mentioned. The reader knows that the two in dialogue are in different

---

10. Rizzi, *Pensare dentro la Bibbia*, 28–37.
11. Auerbach, *Mimesis*.

places. Where does God address Abraham from? It is not mentioned. God's reason for putting Abraham through such an extreme test is also not mentioned. The intense inner travail that such a question necessarily arouses in the heart of any parent is neither specified nor described. The God of Abraham and the Hebrews is fixed neither in a figure nor in a place. Although present and close, he remains a mysterious God. We come to him only by hints, by informative elements that even do not depend on us, but on his self-revelation, which seems to conceal more than it manifests.

God's enigmatic nature is matched by Abraham's. Where is Abraham? We do not know. His "here I am" stands only to signify his positioning in relation to a mysterious God. As such, he remains in an undecipherable, open-ended position because he is still in the making. Abraham is more describable as a function of what he may be than as a function of what he is in the present. Everything else is of no interest to the narrator. Nothing is known about his past or even about the inner baggage he carries with him.

Biblical language, according to Auerbach, elaborates a fragmentary description, proposes a broken style, offering, more often than not, only clues. The biblical narrative proceeds by summaries, sowing here and there only suggestive traces, where the implicit and the unspoken are part of the discourse that has multiple backgrounds. This gaunt, minimalist, and dried-up style becomes pretentious and exuberant in describing the historical evolution and change of characters, situations, and human interactions. Its descriptions purport to be universal and are ambitious in proposing qualitative, important, though fragmentary insights into problems and conundrums essential and central to human living in their sequentiality and historicity.

A COMPLEX AND MULTIFACETED LANGUAGE[12]

The Bible is certainly a unique book. Some of the data concerning it are quantitatively impressive and give a clear idea of its size. It consists of sixty-six books written over a period of 1,500 years on three different continents (Asia, Africa, and Europe), by more than forty authors. There

---

12. Richness and complexity of biblical language is analyzed from "formal" and "literary" perspectives, for example, by Barr. See *Semantics of Biblical Language*, 1–8. But it is also so from a different, more "theological" perspective by Childs, *Biblical Theology*, 11–29.

are to date more than five thousand manuscripts of the New Testament alone (between those with capital and lowercase letters) dating from the first four centuries after Christ. For classical antiquity the situation is much more precarious. For example, the oldest manuscript of the work of Aeschylus (525–456 B.C.) dates from around the eleventh century A.D., and the situation for Plato or Aristotle is almost identical.[13] These numbers confirm the extraordinary evidence of the integrity of the biblical text, the first known book to be translated, the first to be printed in the West, and the first to be spread so widely and in so many languages that 95 percent of the current global population is able to read it.

Can the uniqueness of the Bible and its language be traced solely to this quantitative fact? I believe not. The uniqueness of the Bible is not related to the quantitative extraordinariness of its composition and dissemination or even only to the strength of its content. Let us briefly describe some characteristics that distinguish the qualitative greatness of biblical language.

Biblical Language and Literary Form[14]

A first characteristic of biblical language is the close link it claims between form and content. The Bible claims to be relevant already in its literary form, in its language. Its literary form is already part of its message. It is message. That is why the literary form is neither incidental nor surmountable. It is not accessory because it does not represent an exchangeable form that can be replaced by other forms. It is not surmountable because when meaning is achieved this form does not decay. Biblical literary form is related to the beginning of the message, to the middle and to the conclusion of the process of articulating meaning. If we tried to transcribe the biblical "content" into other "linguistic forms," it would be deformed. It would be deformed not necessarily in the sense of its destruction but in the sense of its impoverishment and lack of power.

The validity of form is true not only for the Bible but also for any other communicative process. This close link between form and message, which biblical language claims for itself, has helped us to understand how this mechanism is widespread and actually characterizes all processes of transmitting meaning. Between content and communicative medium

---

13. Cullmann, *Nuovo testamento*, 13–20.
14. Ricœur, *Ermeneutica filosofica*, 80–85.

(form), in its various modes, the link is much closer than what we might think at first glance. This what Marshall McLuhan had in mind when he introduced his well-known phrase "the medium is the message" (the medium—the instrument, the form—is the message).[15] This means that the narrative, the poem, or the parables in the Bible, as its internal and specific linguistic forms, as much as the external forms and channels of transmission that that message uses—such as the voice, the book, the television or the telephone—expresses already, even before the content and to some extent independently of it, a truth that precedes its content. This truth forms and shapes its content by granting it its own specific validity through a formal structure.

This is what Paul Ricœur perceives and describes in the Bible, even more specifically when he reiterates the equal validity of the forms of biblical language and the content in what he calls "the profession of faith."[16] It is not possible to grasp the meanings of faith without going through the explanation of the forms of discourse it uses. Attempts to translate the contents of faith into other forms have come to a half-truth. The necessary translation of the biblical message into Greek, for example, has resulted in the deformation of the identity and profile of the biblical God. The Greek language, and the modern languages that relate to that kind of thinking and rationality, describe God as foundation, as cause or essence. This is a God who is abstract and non-interactive because he is presented as a foundational and primary element at the beginning of a chain of events that guarantees, as a first principle in its own right, uncontaminated. Biblical language instead places God in an interactive story (salvation history) by describing him through narrative. This makes him concrete and relational, to the point of being touched, influenced, and even enriched by the reaction of human beings.[17] All this is only through the use of the narrative form.

---

15. McLuhan, *Understanding Media*, 9–23.

16. Ricœur writes, "The fundamental point to focus on is the following: in the biblical documents a 'profession of faith' is expressed that is inseparable from the relevant 'forms' of discourse, i.e., for example, the narrative structure of the Pentateuch and the gospels, the oracular structure of prophecy, parable, hymn, etc. Each form of discourse provokes not only a style of profession of faith, but the comparison between these forms of discourse promotes, within the same profession of faith, tensions and contrasts not without theological significance." Ricœur, *Ermeneutica filosofica*, 80–81.

17. Ricœur, *Ermeneutica filosofica*, 83.

Biblical Language and Ambivalence[18]

A second characteristic of biblical language is its structural ambivalence. This is where a profound misunderstanding arises. The Bible's ambivalence becomes, especially in modern and contemporary Christianity, the anomaly to be demolished, the spurious element that needs to be dismantled and erased. A new paradigm, that of "clear and distinct ideas," which extends to religion and consequently also to biblical language, is the reason why Western Christianity, Catholic as well as Protestant, has focused heavily on clarity. This typical obsession of modern times has made the biblical message clear and unambiguous while deforming and impoverishing it. The greatness of biblical language, mistakenly, has been identified with its clarity. The Bible has gained in quantitative value what was functional to a certain kind of conquering religiosity; however, it has lost its qualitative value by giving up complexity and mystery.

That biblical language is structurally ambivalent means that it can mean several things at the same time. This fact does not diminish its impact or its relevance. On the contrary, it increases and augments them, because this finds correspondence with the heterogeneity of life itself, which cannot be reduced to just one of its dimensions. Just as a point of view does not exhaust the richness of life, similarly a meaning does not exhaust the richness of biblical description. This is why the linguistic form of the Bible expresses itself through ambivalence and makes this its starting point and its ending point.

This is Joachim Jeremias's[19] description of the language of the Gospels. Because it can be remembered more easily and is therefore less manipulable, the language of the parables, for example, is metaphorical, exuberant, allegorizing. It is characterized by its surplus of meaning and by its unavailability. Speaking of the art of sense intensification as the defining element of biblical language, Robert Alter proposes the same description[20] for the language of Hebrew narrative and poetics. This exuberant sense underlies ambivalence as a linguistic mechanism that refuses to consign itself to a single, monolithic meaning. Biblical language structurally creates alternative meanings.

---

18. Jeremias, *Gesù e il suo annuncio*; *Teologia del Nuovo Testamento*; *Parables of Jesus*, 23–114.

19. Jeremias, *Parables of Jesus*, 23–114.

20. Alter, *Art of Biblical Poetry*, 62–84; *Art of Biblical Narrative*, 3–22.

Biblical Language and Inclusiveness[21]

Inclusiveness is a third characteristic of biblical language. The ambivalence described above is not an end in itself. It does not only express a dimension of descriptive plurality. More fundamentally, it connects with and guarantees a radical inclusiveness. The biblical form does not aim at self-sufficiency but at interaction with the other. It aims at dialogue with the other through the search for a convergent point that does not erase difference. Difference is the basis of dialogue. Difference guarantees dialogue. Difference makes dialogue possible. For this reason the ambivalent biblical language is the specific linguistic form that corresponds to the relational theological vision of the covenant. This is a typical biblical focus and motif which recurs in both the Old and New Testaments. Biblical language gives it this dialogical and inclusive form

The theological inclusiveness of the Old and New Testaments, which is obligatory because it aspires to universality, is hooked on and preceded by this linguistic inclusiveness. It is this inclusiveness that disappears or fades when instead the Bible is reduced to its clarity. Ambivalence and linguistic inclusiveness are closely linked in the Bible and determine the degree of theological inclusiveness that churches, at some point in their journey, are forced to introduce if they do not want to become purist sects. Forgetting this simple linguistic principle leads the inordinate and unshrewd spiritual ambition and excessive pragmatism of many of today's religious communities to distort the indelible inclusiveness of the gospel. The more precise a language is, the more exclusionary it becomes. The more ambivalent a language is, the more inclusive it becomes. This is why it often happens, especially in evangelical churches, that the all-out defense of the Bible and its clarity, through, for example, a one-sided emphasis on the *sola Scriptura* principle, actually causes its impoverishment and ineffectiveness.

From a formal point of view, the Bible's inclusiveness is also founded on another trait of its language: sobriety. The Bible does not build its greatness on the ashes of other books by denigrating the goodness and wisdom expressed in other texts of humanity. The Bible is not jealous of human wisdom and does not claim exclusivity of good thoughts. The fact that the Bible is unique does not exclude that there are other valuable books, religious or secular. This inclusiveness of its form is linked to

---

21. Di Sante, *Dentro la Bibbia*, 53–56.

its linguistic sobriety, in the fact that it does not say everything. It does not want to say everything. It renounces saying everything. Its silences are as important as its statements. Only this generous sobriety is able to open a space for other books to make their statements, for men not to be ashamed of their babbling words. The greatness of the Bible is its relational greatness that leads it to rejoice not when it speaks on its own, but also when the few words it expresses, those essential words, do not dumb down others but motivate them and move them to speak. The Bible is God's motivating Word, God's inclusive Word.

Biblical Language and Biblical Authority[22]

A fourth characteristic of biblical language is its authoritativeness. Two questions are important at this point for understanding the nature of biblical language and its recovery in interpretation. The first concerns its authority and authoritativeness. The second concerns how this authority is articulated and manifested. Both are important, but they must be distinguished. Responding well to the first does not imply responding equally well to the second. On one side, there are people who answer the first question well, so they recognize the value and authority of the Bible; however, unfortunately, they do not answer the second question well. They give authority an inadequate, reductive, and approximate reading, which does a disservice to their testimony about the Bible. On the other side, there are people who do not answer the first question because they are not believers; however, they can better grasp the particular way in which the authoritativeness of the Bible is manifested.

There are objective and subjective criteria which pertain to the first question. The objective criteria that are usually listed—such as fulfillment of prophecy, age and antiquity of the texts, plurality of authors and forms, important cultural effects attached to it—are not absolute and should be used and mentioned with caution. We find the same ambivalence in other dimensions as well. The validity, regarded as objective, of the phenomena one wishes to assert, sometimes turns out to be less conclusive than it might seem. The more incontestable, objective, and absolute the authority of the principle that is advanced as certain is, the less guaranteed is the attitude of deep faith and conviction. These are ultimately the ones that

---

22. Cf. Metzger, *Canone del nuovo testamento*, 232–45. See also Child, *Biblical Theology of the Old and New Testaments*, 70–79.

count. In a context of absolute and objective authority, not faith but compulsion to believe arises which is pressed by external or internal constrictions. But faith in essence is not a compulsion but rather an unnecessary and contingent act. It presupposes relative, soft, persuasive authority. If the authority it proposes were not relative, faith would be necessary, so it would no longer be faith. It would become perfectly useless because it has become mechanical and automatic.

This is why subjective criteria, which are not relativistic and for this reason to be discarded a priori, are more decisive in establishing and recognizing the authority of a foundational entity or event. Relative criteria are such because they are structurally incomplete. Incompleteness is the element that gives rise to conviction. Provocation and listening, recall and response, are intertwined in those missing spaces. The conviction that freely recognizes an authority arises. It is affirmed not in the face of force but only in the face of persuasion.

Applied to the Bible, all this means that we Christians often err strategically because we aim to make authority necessary when it should instead remain relative. This relativity gives rise to the best affirmation mechanism, which is that of conviction. Subjective, individual, and communal criteria are the ones that arise from conviction, the ones that affect the most in the recognition of biblical authority. This is not a bad thing because it confirms for us, from another perspective, that the truth and authority of the Bible are historical and relational in nature. Only through faith do we accept the bond of the Bible's authority over us. All objective evidence, if any, is such for those who have already believed.

The second question concerns *how* the authority of the Bible is structured. This is about how the kind of linguistic form the Bible is becomes a more objective fact that can be analyzed through literary, formal, and historical investigation, even independently of faith. Here another great misunderstanding arises: people often want to answer the second question with the answer to the first. Actually, positively answering the first question about whether the Bible is an expression of God's will is not at all the same answering the second question well. It is about how one believes and thinks that authority is formally articulated and expressed in the Bible.

The misunderstanding lies in thinking that the Bible expresses its authority in an *unambiguous* form, choosing the dimension of clarity and precision. An authority that expresses itself in a dispersive or ambivalent way would lose its compactness, thus its strength. This way of answering the second question is insufficient, superficial, and irrelevant. Considering it ancillary and secondary, it fails to grasp the specificity of the form and nature of biblical language. This distorts the authority of the Bible, making it an iron, inflexible, monolithic, and intransigent authority. On pain of distorting it, the nature of biblical authority cannot be dissociated from the literary form in which it is expressed. And this literary biblical form, constructed on its ambivalent and paradoxical language, doesn't articulate a direct but rather and indirect form of authority based on persuasion.

Biblical Language and Truth[23]

A fifth characteristic of biblical language is its vocation with truth. The dissociation between biblical authority and the literary form in which it is expressed has led to making it the locus of truth. Those who care about the Bible, those who read it most assiduously, are especially likely to distort it in this way. The Bible becomes for them, par excellence, the perimeter within which God's indubitable and compact truth reigns unchallenged. They claim that the Bible is the religious book that enables us to distinguish truth from falsehood with certainty. It is the only antidote against error and heterodoxy. This belief, openly expressed, represents one of the most important misunderstandings in the history of Christianity.

The Bible "is not the place of truth."[24] Pilate's pertinent question—"what is truth?"—is not a bewilderment of either spirit or thought. It is the only possible question; it is the essence of a possible truth. Truth always adopts the form of a question. Doubt about what is truth is the central and most pertinent question of spirit and thought of all life. Doubt about truth is the pilot light that points to the true horizon of that truth. The truth of the Bible is then a truth mixed with doubt. This is both a truth as a path and a path of a searching and doubting truth. The question "what is truth," then, is not a stupid or a useless question. We cannot delegitimize it by attributing to it ambiguous psychological traits related to Pilate's careerism and moral cynicism which are often present in us as well. Our moral or human smallness does not delegitimize our question about truth; on the contrary, it guarantees it. The question about truth

---

23. Cf. Mura, *Ermeneutica e verità*, 11–27.
24. Cerasi, *Dire quasi la verità*, 11–21.

always arises, as in Pilate, on dirty ground. The ground must be dirty—otherwise what real question would there be about truth?

This question should be asked especially to those who claim to have understood the truth. It is easy to confuse truth with my own truth. We can do this by not recognizing that in its fullness truth goes beyond our understanding of it. We can also do this by identifying truth with a partial manifestation of it. Truth can only give itself in the form of a question. Truth that no longer questions itself decays from the weight of its own presumption. The true Christian, the true believer in that final scene of the Gospels, is Pilate and not the crowd. He doesn't represent the indifferent people who are elsewhere that day worried and occupied with the little material things of life and who don't not believe. Neither is he the over-believing crowd which believes in everything else except in the only believable person, Jesus. Neither of them, neither the indifferent nor the over-believing, question anything. He who flaunts the truth and has his own zeal and attachment to it already sets himself up as a prophet of the false. Ours, if we claim to believe in truth, can only be an attitude of witnessing, not possessing, much less identifying with truth.

Christian churches cannot be places of truth. They can only be places that allow themselves to be crossed here and there, tangentially and sporadically by truth. They can only aspire to be witnesses to truth. This is not renunciation. This is the path of truth. Truth is a path. We cannot tell the truth or live in the truth all the time. Our lives would be cluttered with too many certainties that would prevent us from walking. We would become unbearable as well as paranoid. A church that is always in the truth is an idolatrous church. Reductive, binary thinking, which perceives error when there is not an immediate truth, has led Bible-reading Christians to be obsessed with truth. Obsessed with truth, we have become monsters. Truth, that truth, has not saved us. It has alienated, destroyed, and deformed us. It has consumed our best energies. It has isolated us. It has made us distrustful and conceited, selfish and even cynical. It has taken away our humanity, which is one of the most distinctive features of truth. Truth, on the other hand, is connection. It is desire for the other. It is trust in the other, in the different. It is accepting the challenge of difference. Truth does not want the other to control him. Truth wants to be enriched and instructed by him. You desire the other only if you are incomplete, only if you are broken and fragmented, only if you lack something. A being who claims to be full or someone who claims a truth without fractures, a compact and homogeneous truth, becomes detached and isolated from others. He also ends up being left with a carcass of truth, with a shrunken truth.

Between truth and error there is an interstice, a median territory, an intermediate space that is essential for life. It is life itself and, as such, it is already truth. This is a different truth. It is unconscious, unchosen, flowing without obsession, even mingling sometimes with error. It is, however, the error of a seeking truth. It is not error in the perspective, although it may be in circumstantial fact, in a fraction of time. That intermediate space, of an implicit and unconscious truth, is neither true nor false; it is the space of the church. Flee from the churches, Catholic or Protestant, which worship on Saturday or Sunday, that give up living and articulating that intermediate space and destroy it by having it invaded by massive truths. It is there, in that in-between space, that life grows and faith is strengthened. That is a space beyond "truth and error." That is our amniotic fluid. There a life is neither true nor false, it simply is—and if it is, it is already in the truth. It is in the path of truth.

The Bible is, par excellence, that in-between space; it is the perfect prototype of that living space that is neither true nor false. This is so because it is neither one nor the other. It is a welcoming space for any life that grows and develops trying to find its own north. If the Bible were the space of that declarative truth, it would be an exclusionary and exclusive book, suitable only for a few, or for no one. Because it is not obsessed with truth, the Bible is the Word where anyone feels at home. This is its truth. This is not a truth that sanctions and declares. It is a truth that welcomes and includes. It is so by virtue of the language it uses even before it articulates its content. It is that space that refuses to qualify itself as true. It knows that when truth reigns massively in life, all life becomes impossible. The Bible cannot be the place of truth. It is the place of the suspension of truth. When we are really in the intermediate space of the Bible, we do not have the anguish of being in error. Consequently, we are not obsessed with the truth. This intermediate space has another kind of grounding in the truth. It is the non-conscious and unconscious grounding. We are in the truth mostly when we do not know and do not realize it. If we inhabit that intermediate space, we are more likely to be in the truth without knowing it. Truth is only partially a matter of awareness and choice. Truth is linked to an unconscious grounding in life, in God and in others. It is the truth that welcomes us, not we who choose it. It is the truth that chooses. It chooses us in that in-between space that is the

Bible. It is prolonged in the church and in life. It is where that obsession with truth has been given up.

Is the Bible, then, a place of truth? Certainly not of that truth to which the churches are accustomed. It is not that conscious, chosen, consistent, militant, missionary, clear, unambiguous, functional, immediate, decisive, diriment, and certain truth. That truth[25] seems authentic, but it is not. It is not because it is authentic for too few people. It is truth only for that person who claims it for his group, for his tribe, for his church. How could such a partial and narrow truth be the truth? That truth is actually a counter-truth. The Bible cannot be a relative or accomplice of that truth.

This is why the seemingly clear formula which describes the Bible as truth is misleading. It seems correct but it is not. It is not for several reasons: first, because the Bible is the locus not of one truth but of several truths. True truth is always plural. Second, because the Bible is the place of a truth on the way, not of a final and ultimate truth. Third, because most of the Bible is beyond "truth and error," because only there, in that interstice, in that neutral ground, can life flourish. Fourth, because the Bible does not just say what life should be but more simply describes and welcomes life as it is.

Biblical Language and Diversity[26]

A sixth characteristic of biblical language is its structural diversity. It is here that biblical language teaches us another logic. A logic that includes tension and incompleteness as part of meaning. Much religious and theological reasoning, on the other hand, is too dependent on an univocal logic that stigmatizes diversity or grasps it only to overcome it. This is the logic of the West and its religion, which at this level have assimilated, in different ways and degrees, the univocal perspective of Aristotelian logic. We owe to Aristotle the full understanding of the importance of three principles of our common reasoning: the principle of identity, non-contradiction and the excluded third.[27]

---

25. Gisel, *Verité et Histoire*, 12–35.

26. Erich Fromm compares and contrasts two positions with respect to what is truth. The first ties it to Aristotle and the development of Western rationality that is related to it, including the development of religious thought, which he believes would be overly dependent on univocal rationality. Of a different character would be what he calls the paradoxical logic typical of Eastern cultures. See Fromm, *Arte di amare*, 71–84.

27. Aristotle, *Metaphysics* IV, 1005b, 19–20.

1. **The principle of identity,** states that given A, A is A.

2. **The principle of non-contradiction** holds that we cannot affirm and deny a subject predicate at the same time and in the same sense. We cannot say that Mario is greater than John and at the same time, say that he is not. We could do so only if the temporal relation changed.

3. **The principle of the excluded third** states that a statement is either true or false; a third possibility is excluded.

These three principles are interdependent and traceable to each other and basically define things, people, ideas, or events in a compact and homogeneous way. A thing is well-understood only when it becomes clear and with well-defined contours that allow us to differentiate and separate it from everything else. This grand Aristotelian formula was great for what it aimed to describe: how things are and can be classified. Aristotle certainly used it better than we do. This is because he was a shrewd and sharp philosopher. It is also because he was not obsessed with the obsessions of us moderns.

This Aristotelian logic of clarity and unambiguousness is not only legitimate but also necessary. It is useful for understanding and organizing a part of our human experience. It is also useful for our faith experience. But its indiscriminate use has become a transversal reductive model. This creates a major theological-hermeneutical problem. Its implicit and unconscious elevation as a biblical model creates a major misunderstanding. Legitimacy (acceptance) should not be confused with legitimization (absolutization).

We read the Bible with this logic, misused and misapplied, filtered into our modern languages and reinforced by the parallel univocity of contemporary technology. The result is unequivocal: a clear, homogeneous, and compact faith is born. By this logic, with the intention of wresting more and more clarity from it, we force the Bible to tell us things that it itself does not want to tell us. The Bible, by virtue of this univocal logic, has become a typical industrial machine of sense-making. A homogeneous and compact sense, little differentiated. An overbearing sense.

There is no question of delegitimizing such human language as the conceptual language typical of our time. However, one can neither reduce biblical language to that sectional language nor elevate that partial language to general biblical language. It is not a problem of recognition and legitimacy but of extension. Any human language, representative of a culture and a community, is legitimized to receive the biblical message, but it cannot replace biblical language. How to recapture the true dimension of biblical language? Let us pause to consider three levels of relevance.

WORD AND SCRIPTURE AS A TENSION THAT GROUNDS BIBLICAL LANGUAGE

The first level of relevance and richness of biblical language is manifested in the Word-Scripture polarity. There is a tendency in all theology, but also in faith practice, to make them equivalent. They would both be perfectly super-imposable and interchangeable, structurally aligned synonyms. This is not the case because these two terms, while complementary, are different. They are opposed. They create an insuperable tension that brings out the structural richness of biblical language.

The tension that this polarity articulates is even more crucial because it actually expresses an upstream rupture, a more basic differentiation, a differentiation in God himself. This is between the God who speaks and the God who "writes."[28] We are clearly dealing here with anthropomorphic metaphors of God. That God writes may sound excessive, not least because it would derive from this image a reinforcement of the already strong tendency to sacralize the biblical text itself, thus contributing to the affirmation of biblical literalism and inerrancy and place it at a foundational level, at the level of God himself. This is not the intention here. On the contrary,[29] the intention is to distance, through this image, the biblical message from manipulation, not only from inerrantism but also from what we have called "textual positivism."

Not only the category of Scripture but also the category of Word attributed to God create criticality and raise problems and objections. We therefore take them as metaphors that help us to understand partially God's communicative intentionality. Consider also the fact that they also introduce hostile elements to thinking. The term Word, as metaphor applied to God's revelation, whose limitations and criticalities do not prevent its massive use in theology. The same can be said concerning

---

28. These are metaphors we use to talk about God. Cf. Lindbeck, *Nature of Doctrine*; Lakoff and Johnson, *Metaphors We Live By*.

29. We take Scripture (God writing) here not in the sense of a full manifestation of Being, thus absolute and final, but on the contrary as a trace that one must always take up again and that creates a "difference" that is never conclusive nor final. Derrida, *Della grammatologia*.

the term Scripture. God's revelation is only partially represented by both terms. What remains irrefutable is what the two categories underlie, and this is that the God of the Bible expresses himself, wants to communicate, and makes his will explicit. The biblical God is not neutral or silent like the God of deism. He makes his will known and expresses his ideas and plans. To say that he does so by speaking (Deut 5:4–5) or writing (Exod 24:12) is tantamount to expressing metaphors that concretize his desire to express himself and to make his will known to men. These are to be taken, one and the other, as metaphors. They are metaphors that symbolically describe attitudes, ways of being of God, and we take them as such.

The linguistic structure of the Bible, in its two forms, Word and Scripture, would be preceded by a double dimension in God himself and in his way of being. While they should appear in their convergence and complementarity, this apparent pair is not an equivalent pair. It is a polarity that introduces a linguistic and ontological tension which is central to understanding the structure of biblical language and its richness.

There has always been a tendency in the history of Christianity, which prevails to this day, to privilege the Word over Scripture. This fact is understandable but cannot be justified because it leads to a one-sided and unbalanced look at the Bible. The Word is privileged to Scripture because it conveys dynamism, life, immediacy, and warmth. Scripture, on the other hand, seems like a cold medium. It is as if it were a necessary evil, a surmountable sign. The true message cannot reside in the form of Scripture. It cannot depend on a material structure. Consequently, the message must involve overcoming and transcending Scripture. Christian theology therefore tends to articulate itself as a theology of the Word beyond Scripture. This should not be so because there is instead a dialectic between the two terms that guarantees not only a greater but also a better sense of God's revelation.

The term "Word," used to refer to the Bible, indicates the dimension of "assimilability" of God's message. As the Word, the Bible has the vocation and form of the message that we can make our own. From the human point of view, the Word of God presents itself as warm communication that penetrates our being and reaches our innermost being. It becomes part of us. It is the personalized, direct, and immediate Word that we make our own. That external Word becomes an internal Word. The divine message as Word aims at becoming part of us. There is here in perspective the experience of fusion. God becomes part of us, and we become one with him through his Word.

From God's point of view, his Word expresses something particular about God himself—about what he is; how he is; his intimacy; what he cares about; what his intentions, passions, and fears are and not just his ideas. In his Word God unbalances himself and speaks to us not in the abstract language of what he thinks but in the involved language of what he feels. He tells us that he is dialogical, well-disposed, and available. Through it he conveys to us not something external to him, but himself, that which represents him most, his essence, his love. In his Word God unbalances himself, expresses his intention, gives himself to us in what represents him most. The Word thus expresses God's uniqueness and vulnerability, his mobility and emotional dynamism in a direct, immediate, and spontaneous way. God expresses the best and most intimate part of himself and offers it to us who are able to assimilate it and make it our own.

The term Scripture, on the other hand, when used to refer to the Bible, indicates the dimension of "non-assimilability" of God's message. If the Bible were only assimilable, it would be easy to be manipulated to the point of making us gods ourselves, because God's Word, by becoming ours, would come to reinforce not God and his otherness but us and our interpretation. This is why the term "Scripture" is a specific and contrasting term if it's used as a complementary term that emphasizes the fact that the divine message represents a reality that is hostile and resists our understanding and manipulation. Scripture is God's revelation that cannot be assimilated and stands as an immovable rock. From the human point of view, this means that Scripture will always be and remain foreign and external to us. It will never be fully ours. We will never be able to feel it close and familiar. It expresses God's otherness on a linguistic level, which we must attend to continuously, not by relying on what we remember of it, but by going to it as it is expressed in that external *Scripture*.

To us humans, the Bible, as Scripture, always appears and will always appear as an external, formal, cold sign, especially since it implies and requires effort. The Bible, as Scripture, will never appear immediate and spontaneous to us. It embodies an effort that it is up to us to make. It is a challenge. To encounter it we must always move. In the Word, on the other hand, it is God who comes to us. In Scripture we toil and go toward God. We are not spared this toil. That external sign we must learn to know it and read it again and again, but it will never be ours. Although we have internalized that sign, that sign will always escape us. The memory we have of it does not represent God, but because it is our memory, it is our sign. It represents us while referring to God. The memory of that external sign, even if true, grows old and easily becomes inappropriate because it is out of date. Every memory of it is past memory that easily leads us to illusion. It is like a photo taken that ages every day even if it is true. Every photo is true and is false because it easily becomes out of date, a past memory. So it happens with Scripture. We can approach it and take a picture (an interpretation), but that picture can never exhaust the otherness of Scripture as an inassimilable external sign. That is why we need to revisit that external sign, Scripture, again and again, even when we already seem to know and have grasped and understood it in the past.

Considered instead from God's perspective, Scripture conveys to us something more, something different about who God is and how God acts. If the Word conveys to us God's immediacy and assimilability, Scripture conveys to us God's resistance to becoming ours. God as Scripture remains a distant sign, opaque and mysterious, resistant to our inquiry. As Scripture, the Bible expresses the fact that this kind of communication even to him costs effort. Scripture is not an automatic and standard communication of God. Having to write requires, even for him, an act of patience and dedication. It requires of him time, focus, differentiation, specification. It is not an automatic experience. No writing is immediate and quick. Neither is it for God. Through Scripture God agrees to toil for us, to make an effort for us. He agrees to learn how to modulate his thought and word for us, working in a specific, unique, and purposeful way. He is like a craftsman who through toil and perseverance imprints on the worked object an intention of his own. This is not spontaneous but filtered through toil, effort, and imagination. For him, for God, that effort even involves going through the Scripture of men.

Scripture demands that we stop and try to bring out the best in each other. In a sense, it is more personalized than the Word. The Word is more immediate for the other, but that is why the other does not have time to think it through and perceive it well. Scripture, on the other hand, by implying toil for God himself, guarantees that that toil will help God to think better about both the recipient of that Scripture and his own intentions. It is the fatigue of Scripture that expresses even better the fatigue of the incarnation. The true incarnation of God is the incarnation in Scripture. Jesus is the incarnate Scripture of God. He is God's excellent and noble toil for us.

"SOBRIETY" AND "PLURIVOCITY" AS DISTINGUISHING TRAITS OF BIBLICAL LANGUAGE[30]

The second level of relevance and richness of biblical language is manifested in its two primordial characteristics: "sobriety" and "plurivocity." These characteristics give the Bible its profile without which it would be a lesser book. The problem is that these characteristics are not immediately visible. They emerge slowly over time, and it is only a certain kind of reading that is able to highlight them. It is as if they appear in their fullness only gradually and after an intense and shrewd reading exercise. The hasty, zealous, and presumptuous reading of a certain religious pragmatism, unfortunately widespread today, not only disregards these two essential features but even "snubs" them. Because this way of reading the Bible is not even able to perceive them, it ends up reinforcing and articulating reductive reading strategies that flatten the scope of biblical language. Let us consider them briefly.

A "Sober" Language

A first characteristic of biblical language is sobriety. The Bible, even for the number of pages it actually has, says little about the events it narrates. It is very sober and succinct. It is essential. The sobriety of the Bible is not only related to the essentiality of its descriptions; it also relates to the number of topics it touches upon. The Bible does not say everything. It does not want to say everything. Even what it does say, it says as if it did not say it. This mode of expression is not a defect, not an abdication. It is the sign of an alternative and ancient wisdom that one must recognize and learn to appreciate. If the Bible said everything, it would leave no room for human speech.

This is why the Bible is articulated as minimal language. Most of the time, it is only circumstantial because, through the little it says, it aims to engage the human being and urges him to speak and externalize. The Bible is not a book that paralyzes the human being. On the contrary, it continuously motivates and urges him. A Bible that said everything and well in an exhaustive sense would intimidate the human and force him into silence. The best way to prompt us humans to speak is to articulate not a Word that says it all but a dialoguing, inviting Word.

30. Di Sante, *Dentro la Bibbia*, 17–42.

The Bible is a sober and incomplete Word that also wants to be instructed by its hearers. Through his sober Word, God accepts our words and takes them seriously, makes them his own and rejoices because, through their words, his creatures enrich him and make him happy. This is the essence of praise. In this the Bible is the sober and limited Word of God who says, about life and the world, only essential and initial words to make dialogue and even life possible. Because God does not want to come alone with his conclusions, many topics and themes are only sketched out. In the Bible God comes to conclusions with us. God's sober and free Word provokes and gives rise to free and spontaneous words of praise. The essence of the Bible is praise.

The complexity of the biblical text is not only given by its heterogeneity. It is also given by its intentional narrowness. First, the Bible intentionally renounces saying everything. If it said everything, it would immediately become not a better text but a plethoric and heavy text, insignificant and anonymous because it claims to say too much. Great texts are great because they renounce the obsession with comprehensiveness and completeness. A good text says more when it says less. This is the magic of poetry but also of short, powerful texts such as that of some great political constitutions.

The sobriety of the Bible is also related to the character of its readers. To engage and include the reader, a good text must remain evocative only. Only a partial description of reality, such as is typical of evocative texts, is capable of awakening the imagination in the attentive reader. Without imagination, it is impossible to guarantee any learning process, ethical or religious. The Bible is limited and partial because it aims to make the reader participate in the creation of meaning. This is what the understanding of the "hermeneutic circle" really means. Text and reader go together. A perfect and exhaustive text would actually be a bad text because it would tend to exclude the reader by making him or her inessential and superfluous. A good text, on the other hand, like the Bible, makes the reader necessary, not only as a repository of an existing meaning, but as a participant in the creation of new meaning.

This is perhaps what Gregory the Great was trying to express in the sixth century when he wrote, "The Word of God (Bible) grows along with those who read it."[31] In this he expressed an incredible understanding of the meaning of what the "hermeneutic circle" really implies.

---

31. Magno, "Scriptura crescet cum legente," 86–87. Cf. della Stella, *Sermoni*, 25.

A "Plurivocal" Language

The second characteristic of biblical language is plurivocity. The Bible says "little" (sobriety), and that little it says in the "plural" (plurivocity). In Hebrew thought, a cross-cutting and ubiquitous mechanism is that of "reformulation." These reformulations are not as usually believed—mere repetitions that confirm by hammering on the same key of thoughts already expressed. They represent the diversified, elaborated look, from various angles, of the event being described. Neither reality nor the language that captures it can be monolithic. This structural compromise with the pluralism of life is already seen upstream, in the structure of language itself. Unlike European language, the Hebrew alphabet lacks vowels, so the structure of the language allows for various shades of possible readings and interpretations that coexist together. The Bible does not choose the concept form as its linguistic form.

Whether on the side of ideas or on the side of norms, pointing to the clarity of the message, the "conceptual" reading of the Bible represents a mode of reading typical of Western Christianity, Catholic and Protestant. It does not, however, represent the biblical perspective. The distinction that is constantly made between biblical and non-biblical almost always stops at a difference in content. The real difference is seen on the side of linguistic form in which its theological specificity is best expressed. This difference results in "plurivocity" (various meanings) as a descriptive mechanism of reality. This implies that there is no single possible meaning to say what people and events are.

People and events are always ambivalent, and this expresses their complexity. This way of describing reality could have recourse only to those forms that structurally compromise most deeply in expressing the complexity of life, that is, symbolic, narrative, or poetic forms and all other forms related to them (metaphors, parables, prophecies, etc.). The Bible has a direct, non-speculative but not unambiguous language. It privileges ambivalence. It could not be otherwise. If the Bible aims to describe the concrete reality of us humans, which is a complex reality, it could only choose a complex language, such as the symbolic one in its various declinations.

This plurivocity of biblical language is structural. It never wanes, even when circumstantially we privilege one meaning over others. The biblical text is structurally heterogeneous because it is plurivocal. It necessarily has several possible meanings. Interpretation chooses one among the various possible meanings but only temporarily. At that precise interpretive moment, the text is invested with only one meaning. This is necessarily so in order to personalize the meaning and make it applicable. The other possible meanings are not abolished by this reading procedure but are only bracketed. The heterogeneity expressed in this latent plurivocity of the text remains intact throughout. The various meanings are not transient or merely preparatory to the final meaning but the opposite. The final synthetic meaning is transient and circumstantial. The various possible meanings remain because they alone express the essence of the text. This is why the literary form of the Bible is not that of the "univocal" form of mathematics or philosophy. It is the multifaceted and polymorphic form of symbolic linguistic forms, such as that of poetry, narrative, metaphor, or prophecy.

The biblical text is doubly heterogeneous because, through a literary artifact, it seeks to preserve the different and even conflicting views of the same event. Whereas in the Qur'an the various stories are succinctly told by a single narrator, the Bible preserves the various versions of the various authors that the final editor has just put together with some linking mechanisms. This fact is visible, for example, in the two creation narratives in Gen 1 and 2, but it is present throughout the Bible. That is why truth in the Bible does not become multiple and differentiated only with later interpretations. It is already multiple and differentiated from within, in the Bible itself, at its origins. Biblical truth is never monolithic or compact because it always includes alternative versions from within.

CENTRIPETAL AND CENTRIFUGAL DIMENSIONS AS A DUAL VOCATION OF BIBLICAL LANGUAGE

The third level of relevance and richness of biblical language is manifested in its dual "centripetal" and "centrifugal" dimensions, which emphasize the open, flexible, and inclusive character of its structure.

The Centripetal Dimension

The centripetal dimension of the Bible is best expressed in the concept of authority. The Bible does not give up being the authoritative Word of God. If this dimension of authority were amputated from it, it would automatically cease to be God's Word. In this sense, the Bible is not a necessary suggestion or an opportune consideration but God's commandment with the strong bond of obedience. It claims to speak God's truth and it requires everyone and everything to bend to its demands. She is the (centripetal) center toward which everything else must converge. This indelible dimension of the Bible can be said in various ways. Ways that are good in one historical period are no longer necessarily good in others. The traditional wording "supreme authority," suitable perhaps in other times, is counterproductive today because it does not express the kind of authority the Bible represents. Supreme authority today designates an authoritarian, non-dialogue, inflexible instance.

The authority of the Bible is not only one of command but also one of teaching and service. It is hardly identifiable in a total and compact way with a vertical and totalizing authority. Another term used to express the authority of the Bible is that of *sola scriptura*. The idea and intention is legitimate insofar as it expresses the sense of absolute priority and precedence that the Bible has over any other human instance. Today, unfortunately, even this formula expresses a sense of arrogance, non-dialogue, insensitivity, and arbitrariness that cannot be descriptive of what the Bible and its language are. The authority of the Bible is expressed mostly indirectly. It is not a frontal authority. Evidence of this is the kind of language it uses. The Bible is basically narrative, poetry, symbol. This kind of language is essentially authoritative, not authoritarian. It expresses a mediated, indirect, broken authority. This is even more effective because it maintains a fixed point in substance, but in form it is articulated in a less confrontational and polemical way. The Bible is authoritative without being authoritarian, motivating without becoming constraining, orienting without ever being deterministic.

The Centrifugal Dimension

The Bible has a second dimension, the "centrifugal" dimension, which is most often overlooked and forgotten. In this dimension, the center is not given by the Bible but by the word and the human reality it aims to reach and engage. Here the Bible has no problem in "decentering," in making itself subordinate, in listening to others. In this dimension, the Bible is not interested in asserting its authority but rather in making others authoritative. In order to do this, the Bible sets itself aside. It does not disappear but makes others the protagonists. This is the dialogical word that does not block the word of others but makes it possible. When the Bible is there, when the word of God is expressed in its centrifugal dimension, human beings overcome, through it, the paralyzing fear and silence and begin to speak, sing and witness. Here the Bible is a motivating word, a facilitator of others' speech because it enhances it. In this sense, the Bible gives space for human speech and, in order to truly do so, she herself is silent, silent so as not to block and intimidate the hesitant human being. Rather, she listens and learns, because the Bible is not the only source of wise and relevant words. It allows itself to be complemented by the human word. It is not a jealous word. It does not claim to have exclusive rights to what is right and good. It rejoices if others say better what is in its intentions. In this sense it does not want to say everything nor does it claim to be the last word. The Bible is not God's logorrheic word, compulsively articulated to say everything and more and to silence others.

Through the Bible, the Word of God, expressed in its centrifugal dimension, human beings overcome the paralyzing fear that frightens them. With it and in it humans learn to speak. The Bible gives space to human speech and, to achieve this, it makes silence. The Word of God is made up of silence. It is silence. This is not a self-referential silence selfishly articulated to meditate on one's own wisdom. It is a relational silence. It is silence to appreciate the gifts and witness of others who use that silence as a place of manifestation.

It is not difficult to understand that the Bible claims to be authoritative and prescriptive (centripetal force). But it refuses to become and be reduced to a purely descriptive formula of what the world and humans are. It is not difficult to understand also that the Bible has a strong vocation for updating (centrifugal force). It presents itself as a designer of perspectives rather than specific strategies. Its words and suggestions have been applied, supplemented, blended, inserted into the most diverse contexts and with incredibly heterogeneous formulas. Beyond the recognition of these two undoubted biblical characteristics, it is still difficult and obstructive today to say when one is in the presence of one and when the other. Which parts, which categories, which motives are centripetal, and which are centrifugal? How do these two dimensions interact? We will try to explore this dimension in the next chapter on hermeneutical levels.

VI

A Hermeneutics of Paradox

IN THIS CHAPTER WE will talk about interpretation (interpreting language), trying to keep it in connection and tension with the interpreted object (interpreted language). "Biblical language" is the interpreted object (previous chapter), and "biblical hermeneutics" is the interpreting act (this chapter). Between these two hermeneutical moments there is a continuity and discontinuity, but they never abandon their specific linguistic dimension, given by plurivocity and ambivalence. The foundational text, the Bible, is expressed in a linguistic event with its own characteristics and the reading of that text; the interpretation is still expressed in a linguistic act with equally typical and proper characteristics.

The difference between interpreted language (Bible) and interpreting language (Bible interpretation) is not that between language and word, as it would seem at first glance, according to the classic distinction elaborated by Ferdinand de Saussure.[1] Neither is that between "pattern" and "use," according to Louis Hjelmslev's well-known distinction.[2] "Interpreted language" and "interpreting language" are both on the side of speech and use, because they fit into an intentional and temporal linguistic

---

1. Ferdinand de Saussure defined language as an anonymous and timeless system or structure and speech as the intentional and temporal actualization of that system. See de Saussure, *Course in General Linguistics*, 12–24.

2. Hjelmslev established, like de Saussure, a basic linguistic differentiation between a structural element he called "schema" and a fluid, intentional element he called "usage" instead. Cf. *Essais linguistiques*.

pattern. The Bible and its interpretation resurrect and bet on an actualized linguistic project. They are living words. This distinctive feature of interpreted language and interpreting language prompts Paul Ricœur[3] to choose an even better, more inclusive, and larger category to express the actuality and intentionality of the biblical project. This is the category of "discourse," which he borrows from the linguist Emile Benveniste.[4] He is the one who, perhaps more than other linguists, has worked in this direction. It takes as its linguistic unit of reference not the phonological or lexical sign (system language) but the "sentence" (living and actualized discourse). The sentence is a set of words which expresses, even better than the word itself, what distinguishes an actualized language, namely, intentionality and design. And the three characteristics that distinguish discourse,[5] thus interpreted language (Bible) and interpreting language (interpretation of the Bible), are spatio-temporal specification (referentiality), source intention (author) and target intention (recipients). Speech is a historical event as opposed to language, which instead remains a virtual reality, anonymous and outside of time.[6]

Besides the sacred and canonical value, in the case of the Bible, from a purely linguistic point of view, the only difference between interpreted language and interpreting language is that the former is delivered to us as text. It is as if we have in the Bible an actualized "discourse," frozen in a textual structure, but that frozen text is on the side of discourse, not language. Instead, the interpreting language (interpretation of the Bible) can be written or oral.

This common element (actualized living word) and differentiation (eventual written text) conceals an even more important feature which is that of the inexorable ambivalence typical of actualized languages. The word or speech, as actualized language, would seem to overcome the

---

3. Paul Ricœur starts from a linguistics that presupposes an actualized language instead. See *Ermeneutica filosofica*, 56–61.

4. Benveniste, *Problemi di linguistica generale*, 21–32.

5. Referring to Plato's Theaetetus and Sophist, Ricœur says that for Plato the word itself is neither true nor false. The bearer of meaning is the "sentence" (discourse), not the words. Ricœur writes, "Error or Truth are 'affections' of discourse, and discourse requires two basic signs—a noun and a verb—, which are connected in a synthesis which goes beyond words." Ricouer, *Interpretations Theory*, 1–2.

6. Ricœur also attributes to Aristotle the same connection of meaning with the phrase. Ricœur writes, "Aristotle says the same thing in his treatise on Interpretations. A noun has a meaning and a verb has, in addition to its meaning, an indication of time. Only their conjunction bring forth a predicative link, which can be called logos." Ricouer, *Interpretations Theory*, 2.

typical neutrality of the language system that possesses, because it is not actualized in multiple possible meanings. It would therefore belong to the word and discourse a greater precision, thus a natural aspiration, to univocity. It is in fact the opposite because non-actualized systems (such as language, while possessing in latency various possible uses given by their differentiated but immanent coupling to the system) tend to obliterate ambivalence, thus to behave as programmable and predictable signs.

The behavior of actualized linguistic realities such as speech and discourse is quite different. They reduce the possibilities of linguistic use because they introduce intentionality, which by nature is a restrictive and specifying mechanism but at the same time are also, by nature, typical ambivalent instances. The more language is actualized through speech or discourse, the more ambivalence grows. And if this datum is present in all actualized languages, it is even more so in the biblical interpretive chain, both on the side of interpreted language (Bible) and on the side of interpreting language (interpretation). The most characterizing element of interpreting language (the theme of this chapter) is not orality or textuality per se. It is rather its strong and marked ambivalence, which interpretation derives and gathers from the language it interprets, that is, from the Bible, which by its very nature is articulated and structured as ambivalent language.

Therein lies the greatest misunderstanding. If it is conceded, still with great difficulty, that the Bible carries with it various possible meanings, that it is ambivalent in a structural way, it is nevertheless asserted with great conviction that the interpretation of the Bible must be characterized by overcoming this ambivalence.

The interpretation of the Bible must be clear, must be able to decisively and possibly definitively settle the knots of human and spiritual reality, which in the Bible still appear intertwined and confused. Our thesis moves in the opposite direction because we consider that, if interpretation is to remain biblical or biblically inspired, it must necessarily prolong, albeit in other terms and with different strategies, that primary ambivalence. Good interpretation certainly orients better but by not surrendering to clarity, much less idolizing it as a fetish. It keeps standing that distinctive feature of the Bible, which is ambivalence. It is the ambivalence of biblical language, dutifully preserved in interpretation, that is the true center of revelation itself and the language that describes it, and the only category suitable for preserving the mystery, complexity and pluralism of complex realities such as faith, love, relationship, community, God, or the world.

This strong constraint of fidelity to ambivalence, which the Bible imposes on all interpretations that refer to it, does not invalidate the creative, experimental, and innovative vocation that every interpretation is called to have. On the contrary, it makes it possible. The right of every interpretation to add things that the Bible does not say is preserved to all intents and purposes by this fidelity to ambivalence. The structural ambivalence of the Bible represents a limitation for the Bible itself, as for any kind of sacred discourse, bulimic with power and a desire to perpetuate itself. At the same time, it represents the most obvious guarantee for making possible ever new interpretations.

In this sense, the Hellenization of the reading of the Bible that took place in the first centuries of Christianity, often criticized by biblical purists as undue, is not only legitimate but also necessary, by virtue of the fact that it is biblical ambivalence that requires and grounds it. Had this not been the case, the situation would be even worse, for what was instead a hellenizing interpretation would have been described as biblical. In this sense modern demythologization is also legitimate because it is still the structural biblical ambivalence that allows and necessitates it. All modern interpretations of the Bible, not just the Bultmannian program, are demythologizing in essence. The Bible and its ambivalence impose on new interpretations only three constraints. First, that those new interpretations not be canonized as Bible, but solely biblically inspired. Second, that while legitimate, they should not become final and definitive. Third, that they must remain as ambivalent and plural as the model from which they are inspired.

The innovative and experimental interpretation of the Bible is thus guaranteed by the Bible itself. The Bible puts constraints on all interpretation, not to stop it but to make it always possible. And the basic constraint is the maintenance of plurality. Interpretation can go beyond, experiment, add, but it is its primary task to preserve plurality and ambivalence.

What is the continuing temptation of legitimate and necessary modern interpretation? That of underestimating the biblical text and with it its structural ambivalence. This is arrived at through two errors to be avoided. On the one hand, it is the overlapping of Bible and interpretation. On the other hand, it is their disjunction. The first error, their overlapping, leads to making binding (sacred) what is only relative, that is, the interpreter's interpretation. The second error, their disjunction, leads one to making binding (sacred) only the reference text (the Bible). Yet this is nevertheless filtered by the interpreter's reading, so the interpreter and his interpretation is imposed on him, even if indirectly and covertly. We can say that the one who comes out reinforced tends to be, at least in the current economy of sense-making, always the reader's interpretation, that is, the interpreting language. On the other hand, if we did not interpret the message of a text, in this case the Bible, it would never come to us. To what extent then is interpretation legitimate? To what extent is this even an obligation, a necessity? To what extent does this instead become illegitimate, anomalous, and misleading?

This imbalance in favor of the reader and his or her interpretation begins very early. It begins before the reading itself, already in the reductive understanding of biblical language and its status. Reducing, implicitly, biblical language to our current language of faith represents the first overestimation of the reader. Then this overestimation of the reader and his language is further reinforced in the first interpretive take. For even when one differentiates one's interpretation from the Bible per se, if that interpretation, beyond the content, does not maintain in form the complexity of the biblical text, overvaluation of the reader's language at the expense of the biblical language again occurs. The most suitable interpretation, at the level of content, often becomes the one that denies and kills the richness and distinctiveness of biblical language. This is because it does not prolong its structure of meaning by deeming it surmountable.

The task of biblical hermeneutics is not only to grasp the content of faith but also to maintain the essentials of its linguistic form and never make it fallacious. This is what the "hermeneutics of paradox" that we are trying to articulate in this reflection tries to do. The "hermeneutics of paradox," marked by its "plurivocity" (complexity), is merely the extension of biblical language and its corresponding plurivocity at the level of the interpreter. It is the plurivocity (complexity) that characterizes the two terms of the "hermeneutic circle." The plurivocity of the text must also remain as plurivocity of the reader who reads that text called the Bible. The plurivocity of the text cannot be resolved in the univocity of the reader and the interpretation he or she elaborates. The reader is not the locus of the ultimate epiphany of meaning. The legitimate transport that each reader experiences in discovering a sense of the text, but certainly not of the totality of possible senses, is and must remain a partial and transitory transport. Hermeneutic messianism is not a reality that is consummated in the present but always postpones forward and describes a sense that is always on the way.

The reader is not an endpoint of the text but a continuation of it and as such must prolong the essential datum of the text, which is its plurivocity. For this reason, hermeneutics as an interpretive act must necessarily be as paradoxical as the text it reads is. Interpretive resumption cannot limit itself to resuming only the content. Along with it, it must also take up and prolong the form in which that content is expressed in the text. That is, its plurivocal form.

It is true that every interpretive revival must add a clarification that the text does not have; otherwise that interpretation would remain a tautology of the text. That clarification legitimately added by the interpreter, however, cannot liquidate and make caducous the formal plurivocity of the text. This is the challenge. The plurivocity of the read text must be able to be transcribed into the new language that the interpreter uses to express what he has taken from the read text. In other words, the interpreter must be able to ensure the transcription of the content in a new context but at the same time also be able to prolong the plurivocal linguistic form of the biblical text into the new languages in which the interpreter transcribes the collected message.

That plurivocity in interpretation is given and guaranteed by certain elements. The first is the impermanence of the found sense. The sense found cannot be a definitive sense; otherwise the interpretation becomes more important than the text it interprets. The second is the plurality of meanings worked out by the interpreter himself. The interpreter's interpretation should never be monolithic, not only out of constraint to the subjective openness of the reader but especially out of obligation to objective fidelity to the interpreted text (Bible). Every good interpretation creates its own alternatives. And finally, the plurality of interpreters. The interpreter and his or her system of reference (church, community, ideology) must recognize and coexist with other systems and the different senses that those differentiated systems have worked out.

The biblical hermeneutics of paradox does not aim at the answer but at the extension and enrichment of the question. Biblical hermeneutics is not and cannot be a synthetic and resolving instance of meaning. It is not a hermeneutic of clarity but of complexity. Indeed, of dynamic complexity, that is, of paradox.[7] It is so in the two linguistic levels described. The first, at the intra-textual level, or of what we have called the interpreted language (Bible), bringing out in the text itself the articulation of paradox

---

7. Galimberti, *Orme del sacro*, 35–61. See also, *Corpo*, 11–27.

as the center of all meaning. The second, at the extra-textual level, in what we have called interpreting language, that is, in the extension and superimposition of the biblical paradox with the paradoxes of life, outside the text, through the reader.

A THEOLOGICAL-CULTURAL LOOK AT RELIGIOUS LANGUAGE[8]

Has Christianity succeeded in expressing in history, along with the content of biblical revelation, the characteristics of its language? The answer is not encouraging, as it concerns our specific historical period: the verdict by some scholars is very harsh and drastic. Eugen Drewermann,[9] for example, speaks of the exegesis of our time, referring especially to the historical critical method, as a structurally atheistic enterprise even when it speaks of God. Because the rationalistic imprint, which permeates Bible study in its various fields, would be bewitched by obsession with *objective facts*, completely leaving out the true spiritual dimension, which for him is essentially an inner, psychic reality. Biblical interpretation would be irreligious because, with the language it uses, it restricts itself to objectively describing "the Word" and is no longer able to "let speak" the world of

---

8. Religious language is in Christianity an interpreting language, because it arises from a reprise of the biblical text. But at the same time it is something more, because it tries to articulate the experience of faith from other stimuli and contexts. Is biblical language marked by "plurivocity" while religious language "by univocity"? Or must religious language also remain "plurivocal," both in fidelity to the Bible and in fidelity to the complexity of life? Ricœur attributes to "religious language" the same poetic and plurivocal vocation with which he characterized "biblical language." He writes: "It is on the basis of poetics that religious language reveals its specific character . . . Religious language modifies (enriches) poetic language by various procedures such as intensification, overstepping or transgression, pushing to the limit, which make it, according to Ian Ramsey's expression, an original, singular language," (Ricœur, *Biblical Hermeneutics*, 117). Cerasi, like Ricœur, considers that religious (theological) language is not characterized by univocity; not only because the object of religion is a complex object both as it relates to God and as it relates to life, but in addition, because the language of precision is necessarily exclusive and exclusionary, while religion has the opposite vocation. Cerasi, *Dire quasi la verità*, 23–120; Cerasi, *Mito del cristianesimo*, 165–220, 221–49. This had also been Lindbeck's innovative contribution to a more inclusive description of religious language. Lindbeck, *Nature of Doctrine*, 30–45. In a similar vein, Umberto Galimberti expresses himself by describing ambivalence as an essential and irrevocable feature of all religious language, in *Orme del sacro*, 37–43. See also Hillman, *Re-visione della psicologia*, 117–21.

9. Drewermann, "Verità delle forme," 27–120; Drewermann, *Wozu Religion?*, 203–13; Drewermann, *Heilende Religion*, 8–21.

images, dreams, and metaphors, which represents the true place where every truly religious word is born. The "univocity" of the objective word has taken over from the "plurivocity" typical of biblical language.[10]

Beyond the somewhat one-sided solution proposed by Drewermann, which may or may not be shared, his diagnosis, which is not the only one, seems to us, on the other hand, pertinent. It captures a trait that is not only distinctive but also constant and widespread throughout a historical period such as ours, which reads the Bible only in this way. Drewermann is still too soft and generous. He essentially includes the specialized work of exegetes and one school of thought: the historical-critical method. It is not only the exegetes. It is the great mass of the faithful who have collapsed before the allure of biblical objectivism in its various forms and degrees. The paradox is that the same Christian conservatives, avowed enemies of the historical-critical method, prolong and promote, unbeknownst to them and better than others, the same agenda of biblical objectivism typical of liberals. Their opposition is an opposition of form not substance. Liberals and conservatives remain, complementarily and with different strategies and purposes, prisoners of the fascination with the univocity of religious objectivism.

The even greater paradox is that the typical rational "reductionism" of moderns, of which biblical objectivism is only one expression, is no better in anything than the much-criticized superstitious religiosity of the Middle Ages. Both express hermeneutical anomalies. The medieval one "by excess" and the modern one "by deficit" of religious sense. Rational objectivism and fascination with univocity is not only a problem of biblical reading, but a broader cultural problem. On the one hand, it synchronically involves the whole of a historical period such as ours; on the other, diachronically, it highlights a structural limitation in the face of other epochs. The undoubted gain in precision of moderns, compared to Bible readings in earlier historical periods, would be ominously accompanied by a structural contraction of meaning. This realization should prompt us to historical humility.

If all historical periods, in this case the pre-modern and modern periods, have structural limitations and anomalies, how do we ensure the possibility of appropriate and relevant meanings? From the Christian perspective, we answer by saying that life and God are generous and wise. They do not wait for the correctness of either religious ideas or practices

---

10. Drewermann, *Psicologia del profondo e esegesi*, 12–25.

to pour out gifts and blessings on humans. This does not imply that life and God consider the superstition of premoderns or the reductionism of moderns right and proper. It only means that, despite them, life and God are generous to humans. Put more hermeneutically, God did not fail the premoderns, just as he does not fail us modern or postmoderns, of his presence and mercy despite the countless hermeneutical anomalies that they and we entertain and cultivate. Hermeneutical correction must not become hermeneutical purism. The attainment of meaning is not a mechanical matter. Like any qualitative experience, it can never be guaranteed at the outset by the precision of the interpretive tools put in place. The attainment of meaning is always an unknown because all true meaning, by definition, is unavailable and does not depend on the interpreter's efforts, discipline, and reading strategies.

At this level, the interpreter's hermeneutical monolithism, unfortunately, is reinforced or is conditioned at the outset by the monolithism of contemporary religious language. The reductive hermeneutics of the Bible is already the effect and cause of a religious language that resembles it. Religious language is not that which speaks of God but that which makes God possible. Today's religious language, of which hermeneutics is only one manifestation, tends to be non-religious, irreligious, or even atheistic. More than others, those who would kill religious language or compromise it in its essence would be Christianity itself.

Christianity has demystified not only religious language but also practices, rituals, symbols, and God himself. Initially, Christianity applied this strong demystifying, iconoclastic, and demythologizing thrust to other religions, and with great success, without realizing that it was preparing its own demise. The same tools that Christianity used to neutralize other religions were then used internally, to neutralize Christianity itself. Indeed, not others, but Christians themselves were the mediators of this hollowing out of their own religion.[11]

---

11. This reductionism, which has found a home within religious language itself, is part of a more transversal tendency that Graham Ward identifies in the cultural logocentrism typical of the West. Graham in the face of this drift proposes a renewal of religious language that he finds possible to do from an Augustinian perspective that links knowledge and faith, reason, and culture, with the intention of uniting what has been excessively fragmented by a structurally nominalist culture. Together with John Milbank and Catherine Pickstock, they have shaped a "radical orthodoxy" movement that aims to recast religious language from this perspective. Graham sees in Karl Barth and Jacques Derrida the extremes for proceeding in this direction. Ward, *Barth, Derrida*, 53–78.

The slaughter of meaning that the univocity of objectifying language, typical of modern Christianity, has caused in today's religiosity, however, would not be an accident of the way, but would be inscribed, according to Slavoj Žižek, in the very genes of Christianity from its birth.[12] This would represent the "perverse heart" of Christianity. Certainly Žižek is not the only one who thinks this way. Hermeneutical iconoclasm and the desacralization of myth would be part of the Christian project all along. And this is why we Christians must be even more careful today in dealing with this iconoclastic genetics of ours for two reasons. First, for an "immunological" reason. That is, to prevent the destruction of what is still religious in Christian churches from happening through the use of our own uncontrolled and drifting Christian mechanisms. Second, for an external "contagion" reason. This is that parallel reigning cultural reductionism, which offers undoubted functional benefit in some areas because of the clarity and dynamism it creates, does not become a model that religions uncritically follow and use full-handedly in an effort to compete with highly productive sociocultural and techno-political systems that are at the forefront of data and event management and organization.

The interpretation of the Bible today must be able to perceive this drift and try to stem the damage. It must maintain, along with the validity of the biblical content, the perspective and nature of its language that finds in exuberance and sobriety its main characteristics. What is at stake here is not only the validity of biblical language but the validity and specificity of religious language in general.

What distinguishes the religious language of which every biblical interpretation is a part? According to Slavoj Žižek, it is the obsession with orthodoxy that has led Christianity to destroy the sense of the religious. For Umberto Gallimberti it is the loss of ambivalence,[13] as a distinctive feature of all sacred discourse, that has caused this nihilistic drift. Galimberti describes this reductive drive not only at the level of religious language. He transversally attributes it to the entire Christian culture. The whole West, as a cultural-historical phenomenon, would be impregnated at its roots with this reductive virus, because, again according to Galimberti, everything in the West is Christian, including atheism. Christianity had the great merit of having given life and form to the West.

---

12. Žižek, *Cuore perverso del cristianesimo*, 7–17.
13. Galimberti, *Cristianesimo*, 139–208.

At the same time, the West would rip the authentically religious heart out of Christianity by particularly affecting its language.

Talking about the essence of religious language, of which Bible interpretation is a part, is not easy because two needs must be taken into account: 1. The need for clarity. If religious language did not bring greater clarification of what God, life, and the world are, this language would be superfluous and useless to many. 2. This language cannot be reduced to clarity alone because it would immediately lose its ability to speak of realities that are by nature ineffable, i.e., unclear, such as God, life, and the world. The added problem is that the undeniable need for clarity has often led not only to distort the object of faith. It has also made religions belligerent and aggressive. Reductionism and belligerence are the devastating side effects of a religious language identified with clarity. These are the two deformations that Slavoj Žižek has in mind when he speaks of the "perverse heart of Christianity."

Strategies for flexibilizing religious language have been proposed to limit these two side effects. One of them is that proposed by George A. Lindbeck.[14] He rails against religious language that is intended to be non-negotiable. He divides religious (doctrinal) language models into three groups. The first is what he calls "informational propositional" language. The advantage of this type of language lies in clarity. The disadvantage is that if the truth of religious statements is propositional or cognitive, the only possible outcome is the spirit and compact conviction that sets out on crusade against all those who take value away from those propositions. If this is the starting point, religious communities can hardly come to an agreement. This kind of language underscores what differentiates religions.

The second model is what he calls "experiential-expressivist." This type of language is a non-informative symbolic language that emphasizes the similarities between religions. This type of language is typical of liberal theologies and can be traced back to, for example, Schleiermacher. The advantage of this type of language lies in offering ample space for religious negotiation and convergence. Its disadvantage lies in its limitation in explaining differences between religions and especially in not recognizing religious claims as substantive.

The third model tries to bring together both the propositional and symbolic dimensions of religious languages and takes the form of

---

14. Lindbeck, *Nature of the Doctrine*.

a hybrid model. This type of language is, for example, preferred by some Catholic theologians with an ecumenical vocation, such as Karl Rahner or Bernard Lonergan.

Lindbeck essentially disagrees with these approaches and regards religions as languages and doctrines as grammatical rules. He writes:

> Put in more technical terms, a religion can be seen as a kind of cultural and/or linguistic scheme or medium that shapes the totality of life and thought. It functions somewhat like a Kantian "a priori," although in this case the "a priori" consists of a set of acquired capacities that could also be different. Religion is not primarily an unfolding of beliefs about truth and good (although it may include them) or a symbolism that expresses basic attitudes, sensations or feelings (although it creates them). Rather, it resembles a language system that makes possible the description of realities, the formulation of beliefs and the experience of inner attitudes, sensations and feelings. Like a civilization or a language, a religion is a communal phenomenon that forms the subjectivities of individuals rather than being a manifestation of them. It comprises a vocabulary of discursive and non-discursive symbols and a distinctive logic or grammar that makes this vocabulary work by giving it meaning. Finally, just as a language (or "language game," to borrow an expression from Wittgenstein) is correlated with a form of life, and just as a culture has a range of both cognitive and behavioral dimensions, so it is also with religious tradition.[15]

Doctrines, for Lindbeck, as opposed to the liberals, are authoritative. At the same time, against the traditionalists, they are neither eternal nor unchangeable. The reference to Wittgenstein is certainly not accidental. Wittgenstein's philosophy has certainly also had a great impact in our time for religion but more generally for the understanding of language itself, its nature and function.

Wittgenstein's contribution cannot be limited to the concept of "language games." Wittgenstein is also the author of the *Tractatus Logico-philosophicus*,[16] one of the most influential books in twentieth-century philosophy. He wrote much more at the level of notebooks and notes. To these other writings belongs the text *Philosophical Investigations*,[17] published in 1953, two years after his death. This posthumous book probably

15. Lindbeck, *Nature of the Doctrine*, 51.
16. Wittgenstein, *Tractatus Logico-Philosophicus*.
17. Wittgenstein, *Ricerche filosofiche*.

exerted an even greater influence than the *Tractatus*, outlining an entirely different philosophy. In the *Philosophical Investigations*, the notion of a plurality of languages emerges, each with its own relevance and validity within its own specific life context. It is as if the idea of a single universal essence, valid for all, is to decay, and with it the idea of a single foundation of language and the world.

In the *Tractatus* it was as if, with language, only one game was being played: the fundamental game of representing the world. No, language instead possesses various other features and possibilities. Its most specific value lies in its use. It can certainly have a use through representation, but that does not exclude other uses. The uses of language can be as varied and contrasting as that of religion, art, or politics. In each of these areas a specific use will impose itself that cannot be confused or compared with other uses in different areas. One will even be able to give a metaphysical or spiritual use to language. The important thing is not to make incorrect uses of the different language games. Do not apply the language of one domain to another.

In Wittgenstein we actually find a double reflection on language,[18] valid for the tension it creates. On the one hand, there is the need to share a unique linguistic space through which mutual, clear, and specific dialogue and understanding is made possible (*Tractatus*). On the other, Wittgenstein outlines the need to grant particular areas the possibility of saying their own specificity, which is essentially unspeakable in the languages of others (*Philosophical Investigations*).

Wittgenstein's most innovative contribution, with the concept of "language games," lies in the fact that he broke the monopoly of an abstract universalism, which Europe in particular has used not only to stigmatize and minimize the language of other peoples, but also to impose its own rationality as the sole measure of what is true and real. This contribution should not hide though the problem it has created, which is that of the limit of all linguistic and cultural incommensurability. If incommensurability, which Wittgenstein defends, is absolute, then not only dialogue becomes impossible but also criticism and correction of the anomalies that each system brings with it. If, on the other hand, incommensurability is understood in a relative sense, then the dual possibility exists: to allow each system its own internal coherence and at the same

---

18. Massarenti, *Filosofo tascabile*, 227–32.

time to leave the possibility of interaction, dialogue, and comparison between different systems.

The West has nevertheless persisted in the reductivist tendency of its cultural framework.[19] This has happened even at the level of religious language. This religious reductionism can be seen, for example, in the reduction of religion to ethics. Having misplaced the last traces of the sacred, Christianity, oblivious to Kierkegaard's reminder that the religious[20] stage transcends the ethical stage, has reduced the religious dimension to a moral issue. If there is a possibility for Christianity to recover a relationship with the sacred, this possibility comes through Christianity's renunciation of *legislating morality*. There is no commensurability between human knowledge and divine knowledge, so God's judgment cannot be forced into the rules by which humans have organized their reason and packaged their morals. God is beyond true and false, just as he is beyond good and evil.

The historicization and embodiment of faith itself triggers, according to Galimberti, this reductive process. Christianity is the religion of the empty sky, the religion that desacralized the sacred. Dealing fully with the world, it would be transformed into a "diurnal event," an event of conscious and chosen meaning. We would be faced with unambiguous meaning, a religion of clarity. By producing itself in discourses that any civilized society can safely make for itself, Christianity would abandon the management of the "undifferentiated night of the sacred" to the solitude of individuals or the madness of groups.

Man has always felt, as superior to himself, powers that he has placed in another region, called sacredness. Sacredness is an ambivalent word that means, at the same time, blessing and curse. All words that transcend the human are ambivalent words. On the one hand, man fears the sacred,[21] as one can fear that which one considers superior and is unable to master. On the other hand, he is attracted to it as one is attracted to the origin from which one is one day emancipated. The sacred is an enduring dimension in the human condition. Although it can be removed, invoked, feared, even forgotten, it operates nonetheless. If we want to define this sacred dimension, we must give it a definition by default, a definition in the negative because with definitions we are already

---

19. Galimberti, *Decline of the West*, 451–59.

20. Kierkegaard defends the specificity of the religious dimension, which in no way can be reduced to ethics. See *Timore e tremore*, 9–24.

21. Otto, *Sacro*.

in the human sphere. Man tries to define, specify, and delimit, while the sacred is the undifferentiated, and the undifferentiated is that scenario within which it is not possible to find differences, distinctions.

To defend us from the sacred, religions were born, which are not dimensions that relate us to the sacred but rather defend us from it. The word "religion" means to relegate, to enclose, to contain, and religions have done a great operation of containing the sacred dimension, because contact with the sacred is a contagion; it is something extremely dangerous, with basically unpredictable effects. Christianity has carried out this project of religions to perfection. It has become the model religion. It has created a dynamic and performing religiosity, introducing a strong element of control over the sacred. It has done so especially at the level of language, reducing the typical "ambivalence" of the sacred to the "clarity" of faith. Difference, distinction, is what allows us to name things and treat them according to an unambiguous meaning. This allowed Christianity to introduce a stabilizing dimension from this neutralization of ambivalence, and extend it to all religious experience. Indeed, this linguistic order reduced distress but made behaviors predictable.

One may well disagree with this radical description by Galimberti, but in its essence it captures the complaint we have been trying to articulate from the beginning. This concerns the profoundly reductive character not only of Christian hermeneutics interpreting the Bible but also of Christians' own conception of their Bible. One of the limitations of Galimberti's analysis is that he does not differentiate between Christian interpretation and the Christian text, which he seems to know little about and poorly. But pressed by his examination, which in essence seems pertinent to us, we might say that it is not ancient paganism, the polytheistic and mythicizing paganism, that threatens us most today. It is the new univocal paganism of technology, material or linguistic it matters little, that is destroying Christianity, its language, and its basic text. We Christians do not see the effects modern paganism of the univocal, of equivalence, of precision, of efficiency is producing today. We have even made it an ally of the faith. We have substituted it for the God of the Bible. The Bible itself has become a spreading instrument of this modern idolatry. Although it might seem paradoxical and extreme, the complexity of the Bible and its multifarious language have more in common with classical paganism than with today's orthodox Christianity. We cannot dialogue with paganism—it would seem surreal—and it need not come to that. We can be challenged by the problems that paganism raises and faces and that it is perhaps facing better than Christianity. After several centuries of intemperance, counter-senses, idolatries, one-sidedness, perversions, we cannot think that Christianity has remained untouched. It is not certain that paganism cannot partially regenerate itself and make itself persuasive again. Marc Augé, along with others, believes that this is happening. In his book *The Genius of Paganism*[22] he describes the cultural strength of the new paganism of which the relevance of its more inclusive and more concrete language is a part. Christianity does not have a monopoly on truth as much as paganism is not compactly a set of perversions. Today we must analyze theme by theme, according to the relevance of each individual register, and not automatically consider a system in its totality as true or false, good or bad, correct or incorrect.

HERMENEUTIC LEVELS: SOME CHARACTERISTICS

The Bible is a generous book. It does not presuppose or establish preconditions to its reading. Anyone can approach it and find benefit in it. In this sense it is an immediate and democratic book. This does not mean that those who benefit from it always get the best or all possible benefit from it. Every reading of the Bible leaves us with something, but it does not disclose the fullness of its design. Every reading of the Bible is legitimate, but it is not representative of what the Bible embodies and wants to communicate. For this reason, we want to list briefly in this section some characteristics of the six hermeneutical levels that we will describe more specifically in the next section. These features are the articulation of the plurivocity and complexity already present at the level of biblical language, but which we now find at the level of the interpretation of that language.

Intensity

Hermeneutic levels are in the first instance an instrument of sense intensification. They are so in a twofold perspective. On the one hand, they are in a quantitative perspective in that they re-propose, through repetition, a re-articulation of meaning with the integration of an added element. A repetition is never a tautology. That added element, though minimal, sometimes given only by a synonym, expands the sense by reconfiguring it in a new perspective. On the other, they are at the qualitative level,

22. Augé, *Genio del paganesimo*, 9–14.

because the repetition of a specific element, even without adding anything more, taken up simply at a higher level, automatically changes the whole articulation of meaning. The element in question could remain the same. Nothing has been added. But it is the new placement that doubles the intensity of meaning through new contextualization.

Sequentiality

The hermeneutic levels mark not only a layering of meaning that properly determines an enrichment of it. This differentiation of them also creates a progression, which does not necessarily imply the annulment or overcoming of the previous levels. All levels are necessary and are necessary because of the complementarity they create but also because of the tension they introduce. These various hermeneutic levels are not always immediate. That is what interpretation is for: to highlight them. To census the various levels in the offered text and make them manifest is the task of hermeneutics. Hermeneutics does not aim to capture only the most immediate sense or the most convergent sense; its task is also to illuminate the mechanisms, the extracts, the differentiations, the knots that are articulated in the processes and progressions of meaning. This is sequentiality: it does not only create continuity and complementarity of meaning. Often sequentiality is a guarantor of ruptures and discontinuities that at first seem to destabilize meaning but, in the long run, enrich it.

Complementarity

These various levels brought to light by hermeneutics in their diversity create a convergence. This convergence acts as a multiplier of meaning. One thing is an element with its particular meaning in isolation, another is that same element together with other meanings. The result is not a sum but a multiplication. At the level of meanings, one plus one does not make two; it can make four, five, or ten. The combination of hermeneutic levels enhances the meaning of words and events, expanding them into unsuspected horizons through interaction and convergence. Any lucid hermeneutics must aim to build bridges between the various elements that at first glance may appear distant from each other. This convergence is not always visible; this is why the complementarity of levels is not automatic. It must be sought and sometimes imagined. It is the nature of biblical language that pushes toward this. Thus, one only needs to be drawn by the impulse of the text itself to create links and convergences that intensify the scope of the meaning being worked out in the interpretation.

Complexity

These hermeneutic levels that intensify meaning and give it sequentiality and complementarity are not to be understood in a linear or evolutionary sense. Their differentiation and progression does not intensify meaning in the sense of greater precision, thus greater effectiveness. The richness of meaning is of a different nature. It is also given by the slowing down or complication of a meaning that gets stuck, by the emergence of an alternative meaning or even a counter-sense. Not every obstacle of meaning is nonsense. Sense, in order to become noble, must always confront one of its paradoxes or opposites. This alternative element to sense, which is now contrasted, serves as a stimulating and reinforcing element because it pushes sense. On the one hand, this brings out its potentialities in an effort to tick it off. On the other hand, it coexists with other different senses. This is the complexity presupposed by hermeneutic levels.

Tensionality

These hermeneutic levels do not always create convergence and complementarity but stand before each other in a tense relationship. When this happens, the temptation to harmonization is strong. But it must not happen, on pain of dismantling and neutralizing one of the most important hermeneutic mechanisms in the creation of meaning: hermeneutic tension. It is not given by a text that is clear and a reader who, being external and unrelated to that text, tries to approach it, inevitably creating an interpretive tension. No, the hermeneutic tension is internal to one's text and remains there even when the reader is not there. The reader reproduces and maintains in his or her interpretation this tension internal to the text. Interpretation in this sense does not represent an unambiguous final synthesis that breaks down the tension. In some ways, it is the opposite. This is because interpretation prolongs and enriches this tension, introducing an added and supplementary component that does not resolve the prior alternatives but takes them up. It strengthens them and makes them dialogue with a new interpretation, a product of the singularity of the interpreter on duty. The complexity given by different hermeneutic levels should not be conceived as surmountable. Meaning is not situated beyond. It occurs within the tension that creates that complexity. It is within that complexity that convergence must be sought, not the other way around. That complexity is the guarantee of both the functioning of meaning and the opening of the text forward to other possible meanings.

Circularity

These hermeneutical levels create a sequentiality and progression and, in a sense, even a hierarchy. The third intra-textual level, characterized by "paradox"—and which we will describe next—is undoubtedly a culmination of meaning and, as such, represents the goal of any reading of the biblical text. To stop earlier is to fail to understand the meaning in its fullness. The same thing happens at the extra-textual levels. It is the articulation of the paradox in the paradoxes that represents the pinnacle in the articulation of meaning. Yet, the previous levels can never be surpassed. In a "circular" configuration of hermeneutic levels, not only are the pre-vial and initial levels not erased. They can serve, in the interpretive process, as additional spaces where the fullness of meaning occurs in an inverted and nonlinear way. Sometimes meaning is evinced in the text itself and its paradoxes, and sometimes in the reader and his paradoxes.

These six hermeneutical levels that embody and articulate the complexity of the biblical text are nothing more than the specification of the hermeneutical circle. The first three relate back to the text pole and the last three to the reader pole.

THREE INTRA-TEXTUAL HERMENEUTIC LEVELS: FROM EVENT TO PARADOX

In addition to demarcating and defining each of these hermeneutical levels from a descriptive and sequential point of view, in this section we will briefly give an application example from Ps 23, which we then quote below to facilitate understanding of the explanation.

PSALM 23

Psalm of David.
1 The Lord is my shepherd: nothing I lack.
2 He maketh me to lie down in green pastures, He leadeth me beside the still waters.
3 He restores my soul, He leads me by paths of righteousness for His name's sake.
4 Even when I walk through the valley of the shadow of death, I will fear no evil, for you are with me; your rod and staff give me security.
5 For me you set the table, before the eyes of my enemies; you sprinkle my head with oil; my cup overflows.
   6 Surely, goods and goodness shall accompany me all the days of my life; and I will dwell in the house of the Lord for long days.

Hermeneutics of the Event (Literal, Intra-biblical Interpretation)

This hermeneutic is characterized by its immediacy. I read what is written and apply it directly. This immediacy presupposes a continuity between biblical times and our times. The Bible is perceived as a unified document and the reader as a purely supporting component in the articulation of meaning.

Here the meaning is already given. It is only necessary to unveil it. This kind of hermeneutics represents an essential moment. It gives immediacy and concreteness to the meanings contained in the Bible. Interpretation, by the interpreter, gathers only the already full and total meaning contained in the biblical text. This does not mean that the interpreter is passive. On the contrary, the interpreter, with the collected interpretation, can be very active, not at the level of the creation of meaning but at the level of its application.

This level cannot be skipped. It will always remain valid. We are faced here with a literal and immediate hermeneutic. Literal does not mean literalist. The difference lies in the fact that the former is a concrete but open hermeneutic, while the latter lacks this openness and this leads it to reduce it to the dimension of the letter. The Bible must be able to offer itself immediately to those who read it, and those who read it will always find a first meaning at hand. This first meaning is true because it is offered by the text itself. That this first level is necessary does not mean that it is sufficient. It is not sufficient because it does not grasp the knot of the text that is always expressed in a paradox and depth not visible to an immediate and superficial glance. Until one grasps that paradox that grounds every text and expresses its structural complexity, interpretation remains incomplete and insufficient. Incomplete and insufficient does not mean false. It means that it is an important first step but that it cannot become final and definitive.

Taking Ps 23, "The Good Shepherd," as an example, we can say that the literal hermeneutics of this psalm puts us in immediate connection with the central message of this passage, which is articulated in God's top-down heroic guidance of us as "shepherd."[23] The figure of the shepherd who is secure and firmly at the helm by virtue of his knowledge and skill in leading the sheep immediately conveys and instills a sense of trust and confidence. Even for someone who does not grasp other crucial nodes of the psalm or grasps only part of it, this first message of confidence comes through smoothly and immediately. This interpretation of the good shepherd protecting us is true, legitimate, and captures an essential address of the psalm. It certainly does not exhaust the total meaning of the psalm expressed in the other hermeneutical levels. Even beyond its undoubted relevance, this first meaning falls short of the perception of that "paradox" that we believe is the constitutive and central element of this text.

Hermeneutics of the Principle (Ideal, Intra-biblical Interpretation)

This hermeneutic is characterized by its clarity. It is no longer an immediate hermeneutic like the previous one because, behind the events, rules, and narratives, we are called to grasp the universal principle that does not wane and transcends the circumstantial forms it takes in that passage. This hermeneutic is characterized by the perception of an inevitable difference between biblical times and our time, but it continues to regard both as homogeneous and transparent times. The perception of biblical unity prevails over the perception of its diversity and pluralism. The reader emerges only as the circumstantial custodian of universal and eternal principles. Interpretation and the interpreter here emphasize a

---

23. The classical reading of this psalm stops at this first metaphor and captures it in its literalness. This is the approach of Luther, who emphasizes the power of this clear and direct scripture that proclaims God's uncontested sovereignty. Indeed, the reformer links this psalm to the third commandment. Luther, *Reading the Psalms*, 59–60; Ravasi, *Libro dei Salmi*, 425–46; Schökel and Carniti, *Salmos*, 396–407.

greater grip on the text given by the ability to go beyond the primary and immediate, formal, and theological forms to a more hidden but nevertheless evident meaning in the text.

This hermeneutic marks an important step because it opens the text to a universal constant that is not necessarily immediate and visible but is nonetheless present. The universal constant, embodied in the universal principles, is hidden. It is the nobility of the hermeneutic of the principle that brings them out and affirms them as central. This hermeneutic level introduces an important qualitative shift in the understanding of both the text and the role of the reader. This element lies in the positive distance that the reader introduces with respect to both the text and himself. The goal of interpretation is neither the first glimpse of the text nor what the text provokes in the reader. It is the universal constant that is always hidden and must be sought with insistence, perseverance, and intelligence.

This hermeneutical level, while legitimate and necessary, and while representing an advance over the previous hermeneutical level, still does not discern, in the found meaning, any asymmetry, rupture, or tension that expresses the complexity that every biblical text has. The meaning found and linked to a universal principle that does not coincide with an immediate reading of the text appears as a compact, homogeneous, and absolute meaning. The compactness of meaning has only transferred from the primary and initial event to the hidden universal principle. For this reason, in this second hermeneutic level, we do not yet find the confrontation with what Ricœur calls "the thing of the text,"[24] which is given by the figure of paradox. We have not yet arrived at the central and foundational knot of every text that is expressed in a paradox. This is why the hermeneutics of the "principle" is necessary but still insufficient.

Connecting to Ps 23,[25] we might say that the reasoning within this second hermeneutical level prompts us to consider important not the country and peasant form that care and guidance take in this psalm,

---

24. Ricœur actually uses various expressions to describe the center of a text. One of these expressions is "the thing of the text." Only after perceiving "the thing of the text" can one say that one has understood a text. Ricœur, *Ermeneutica filosofica*, 89–95. We are more of a guarantor because we grant that even when the interpretation lies on this side of this discovery, that is, of the "thing of the text," the interpretation is not only legitimate but also true. To this concession we add only one condition: that a legitimate and also true reading of a text does not yet mean having understood the text in its centrality.

25. This is what Calvin captures in Ps 23. The principle of guidance from God even when this is expressed in different ways today. See Calvin, *Commentary on the Psalms*, 125–28; Ravasi, *Libro dei salmi*; Schökel and Carniti, *Salmos*, 396–407.

but the principle of care and guidance itself, which in our time will be expressed in other forms. The peasant and country form was essential for the primary recipients of that text, but that form to us moderns no longer says anything or says too little, because we have all become urban individuals, bound to cities, to the rhythms and deadlines that the city imposes on us. Instead, the principle of care and guidance expressed in the psalm is still valid; however, it will be embodied in other forms that correspond better to our new urban context. And this is what the hermeneutics of the principle does: it tries to grasp the mechanism behind it, which has not changed, but from the ancient forms in which it was expressed, it tries to embody it in forms that are appropriate to the reality of today's readers.

Hermeneutics of Paradox (Pluralistic, Intra-biblical Interpretation)

This hermeneutic is even less immediate. It notes the existence of a knot that is not external to the text but at its center. Meaning then is given only at the center of this knot and by the tension it creates. This hermeneutic is characterized by the perception of an inevitable difference between biblical times and our own and considers them both heterogeneous and opaque. The Bible is perceived in the tension of its different, heterogeneous patterns, categories, and narratives. The perception of the Bible's internal "complexity" mirrors the parallel "complexity" of external reality. At this level, the interpretation and the interpreter no longer function only as immediate collectors and applicators because the perception of this paradox creates in them a pause, a surprise, an unexpected contrariety that allows and requires reflection as a necessary complement in understanding that asymmetry of meaning.

This attitude of surprise and even perplexity, because the clarity of meaning appears broken in the text itself, leads not only to reflection on the text but also triggers a second mechanism that will be to push to go beyond the text. This third hermeneutical level of paradox is central to understanding the vocation of the text, which is always a vocation to point beyond it, toward external reality. Every good text highlights this inherent limitation that de-emphasizes it and forces it to look at reality. Every good text is a referential text that does not exhaust its vocation within a purely intra-linguistic and immanent sense. Every good text, by virtue of this third hermeneutical level based on paradox, is and necessarily becomes a transgressive text, a text that always goes beyond a linguistic form to land in reality itself.

This is why the perception of the intra-biblical paradox is essential for hooking up with extra-textual reality. Without this paradox, the connection with extra-textual reality would become more difficult, perhaps not impossible, but certainly flatter and more linear, more orphaned of that complexity to which paradox is flame, driver, and witness. It is only at this hermeneutic level, and by virtue of the perception of the paradox foundational and present in every text, that we can speak of successful interpretation. This is the minimum goal. Before this level, interpretations can help, guide, orient but they do not do so from the centrality of the text but from its periphery. Without grasping this center, which is expressed in the paradox, interpretations, while true, remain insufficient without being false for that reason. The perception of paradox is not immediate. One must search for it and exercise, in addition to patience and perseverance, a good dose of curiosity, imagination, and relational analysis.

The main paradox, the one around which the central perspective of a passage is articulated, is also always hidden behind a more immediate and more superficial paradox. The paradox is sometimes given in the same verse, sometimes in a chapter itself, other times only within a section or book, sometimes only outside the text. In the case of Ps 23 it is given not in one verse but in the logic and within the whole chapter.

There is a fundamental paradox in Ps 23: only in case one grasps it does the psalm disclose its fullness.[26] Only when this level is reached can it be said to grasp the full meaning of the biblical text. Its true horizon Ricœur will describe as "the thing of the text."[27] Here the text expresses and unveils its essence, its purpose through a paradox, a rupture. In this text the pastor's metaphor is only one part. The other part is more hidden and is given by a second metaphor, that of God as a housewife preparing a table for her guests. That of the shepherd is a "theocentric" metaphor; that of the housewife is "anthropocentric." In the first metaphor God leads and is the protagonist. In the second God follows and indulges, but

---

26. Ravasi captures this paradox in Ps 23, which is given essentially by not one but two metaphors; the metaphor of the "shepherd" and the metaphor of the "house," creating a sense-creating tension. Ravasi, *Libro dei salmi*, 434–38; Schökel and Carniti, *Salmos*, 396–407.

27. He also calls it "the World of the Text." Cf. Ricœur, *Ermeneutica filosofica*, 89–95.

the protagonists are the guests, the humans whom God, as the housewife, serves by enriching them.

Psalm 23, like any other biblical text, changes after grasping its paradox, its central fracture. This is why we can say that this third hermeneutical level is the one that represents the pinnacle of biblical hermeneutics. How to grasp it, however? We will see that, surprisingly, this center, this paradox that grounds every text, is best grasped by relating the text to the extra-textual element, to the reader and his world. The extra-textual reality is not secondary to the creation of meaning and should not be taken only as an applicative realm of the meaning found in the text. The extra-textual sphere (reader) is functional and essential to the creation of meaning itself, hence the need to consider the other three hermeneutic levels, which are extra-textual but not extra-hermeneutic levels, since the hermeneutic is given not only by the presence of the text but also by its correlate, which is the reader as an extra-textual instance, but nevertheless connected to the text, not only because he reads it, but because he is anchored in life itself, of which that text he reads is an important, though not unique, register and witness.

THREE EXTRA-TEXTUAL HERMENEUTIC LEVELS: FROM PARADOX TO PARADOXES

In profiling each of these three extra-textual hermeneutical levels, we will again refer to Ps 23 as a starting application example and to facilitate understanding of the explanation.

Reader's Hermeneutics (Biographical Interpretation, Extra-biblical)

The reader becomes, at this level, the protagonist in deciphering the interplay, overlap, and tension of the various biblical levels and in making the decision as to which of these is more significant. Here the hermeneutic proceeds through the subjectivity of the reader, who becomes the filter for better looking at the text. The reader is not an intruder, someone who asks the uncomfortable and impertinent questions. On the contrary, it is the reader with his questions, anxieties, perplexities, doubts, who gives the text the opportunity to express itself and bring out the best of its latent meanings.

Without the reader provoking the text, it would remain unexplored, locked in its latent meanings and semantic potential without topicality.

The reader is not the one who undergoes the text by passively receiving meanings that are already complete and ready for their application. Without the reader there are no relevant meanings, for it is in connection with the situation in which he finds himself, and it is in relation to his mediation that the meaning of a text completes its configuration as such. However, the reader does not create meaning by himself but articulates it from the ingredients that come to him from the text and its context: he is the one who does this mediation. Thus, the reader's mediation is twofold because on the one hand, through his existential and historical position, he provides the text with extra-textual outlets for connection and application; on the other hand, he highlights in the text itself the various possible meanings that often emerge only from the text's confrontation with the extra-textual element and forces the interpretive gaze to review the text not only to survey those hidden latent meanings, but to evaluate and choose them in accordance with not only intra-textual but also extra-textual relevance.

Reconnecting with Ps 23[28] we find that taking seriously the status of the reader not only illuminates this psalm differently but also introduces a new reading of the reader himself. The intent to understand the reader's situation and profile leads us to see, behind this typically theocentric psalm (because it speaks primarily of God and his guidance), a profound and relevant description of the human being as well. We discover that this is not only a psalm about God but also about the reader-man. So behind the two foundational metaphors of this psalm, those of the "shepherd" and the "housewife," which the hermeneutics of the third level has helped us to discover and focus on, lie two implicit images of man. The first is the image of man as a "sheep," related to the first metaphor of the shepherd; the second is the image of man as a "diner," related to the second metaphor of the "housewife." Thus, reflecting on himself, the reader discovers that his ideal profile is not monolithic but that he, like God, has a differentiated and heterogeneous profile. He is asked not only for "obedience" as a sheep but also for "freedom and creativity" as a diner invited around the table by the housewife. Final destiny of the believer's vocation is thus not only obedience but becoming free people. And this complexity, found at the

---

28. This sense of connection with the situation of the present reader is emphasized, for example, by Bonhoeffer. Bonhoeffer, *Pregare i salmi con Cristo*, 29–32; Schökel and Carniti, *Salmos*.

level of the reader, prompts him or her to reread the text differently, later finding ingredients and stimuli that already orient toward a diversified understanding of human beings in the horizon of their complexity.

Hermeneutics of Reality (Contextual Interpretation, Extra-biblical)

The reader is only a part of this reality external to the text, not all of reality. This hermeneutic is characterized by the tension created not by an internal diversity but by an external one, introduced by reality itself, without which it is impossible to perceive and understand the Bible. The serious consideration of "external reality" does not intervene to diminish the value of biblical meaning but to amplify and enhance it, because the main feature in the Bible is to describe the external complexity of life and reality. The Bible is amplified in its meaning and scope by external reality, and the mediator of the interaction between the text and reality is the reader, who has become an active interpreter. But the interpreter-reader does not exhaust that external reality. It is only a first dimension. That reader enters into a network of relationships, human and non-human, of events and places, which represent the historical world on which the biblical text aims to say something.

But as in the previous hermeneutic level, there is a double referral between reality and text in this fifth level. On the one hand, understanding our present historical reality prompts us to reread the text in a different way, highlighting details that previously escaped us; on the other hand, the text itself prompts us to read the external reality in a way that is destabilizing because it is new. This new reading of the text, starting from our historical and not just individual reality, is not immediate. It is not reducible to the first impression. Just as the appropriation of the biblical message requires years of attendance, learning new linguistic tools, care in gathering data, organizing the categories surveyed—rhythm, familiarity, and intuition in the handling of meanings—in the same way knowledge of external reality is not immediate. It is not reducible to slogans. It requires the same effort and time, perhaps even more. But there is no alternative. Non-knowledge of extra-biblical reality condemns one to fail to grasp the stimuli latent in the biblical text.

Reconnecting with Ps 23, we can say that to understand it well, it is necessary to know well the present time in which we live.[29] Every histori-

---

29. This is the dimension that Bernd Janowski emphasizes. The psalms would not

cal time wrests new meaning from the Bible. But knowledge of our present is not immediate. Understanding our present requires significant reflective effort. Is our time a time of moral, anthropological, and institutional rigidity, or is it rather a time of ethical dispersion and social disintegration? It could be one and the other, and more. Depending on the answer we give to this question, the psalm will be read and applied differently. And neither of the resulting readings from the "shepherd" or "housewife" metaphor will be true or false. At a more essential level, the biblical meaning is more relevant, not very relevant, or not relevant but not necessarily false. One must be careful about labeling as false what is actually only a latent sense of the text, which at some point is not the most corresponding and appropriate sense for a given situation. The alternative views of reality given by the metaphor of "pastor" or "housewife" can be matched, overlapped, contrasted, ordered in various ways. And it corresponds to the reader to innovatively choose, without betraying the essence of the text but going beyond it, the most meaningful combination. The openness of the text and the nature of its language do not allow establishing a single combination. The reader will be able to emphasize the firmness of the pastor's interventionist leadership or the soft, subdued, purposeful leadership of the housewife. He or she may focus on the obedience of the sheep or the freedom and creativity of the diners. The text offers all these various possibilities, but it will be up to the reader to semantically exploit them and apply them according to the relevant context.

Hermeneutics of Imagination (De-contextual, Extra-biblical Interpretation)

This sixth hermeneutical level introduces an uncomfortable question. What is the true reality? Is it the one that is there now or the one that could be there? A good text is never validating of what is there. It is not merely descriptive. Certainly a fictional text is more creative than a historical text. But all texts, if they are such, are partially fiction texts because they implicitly critique what is there from what could be there. Present reality is always shorter than possible reality.

---

only be texts of spirituality but would refer to an anthropology of which those texts would be just one component. Janowski, *Konfliktgespräche mit Gott*, 1–35; Schökel and Carniti, *Psalmos*.

In other words, hermeneutics cannot be used to validate the world and reality that is in the present even though they, being the object of reflection in the previous hermeneutic level, are essential steps in the interpretive process. Hermeneutics, with the interpretations it gives birth to, tries to open new realities through imagination. The true reality is always the one that is being created. And it is interpretation that has to create this opening process. It represents the art of exploring, intuiting, creating new trails of meaning from a text that propels us forward through the imagination that categories, forms, and paradoxes create in us. This is why we could also say that the legitimate intent of contextualization, which breaks and opens up a hermeneutic that would like to stop only at the reader and his or her self-referential search for meaning, is in itself insufficient, because it is part of the hermeneutic process of de-contextualizing our present perception of reality in order to imagine a context that is not yet there but is possible. This further step is fostered by the text itself and the reader's present imagination. If the biblical text has from the beginning fostered a beyond-itself, opening to the extra-contextual element, it is still the text that pushes toward a beyond-present context and points to an extra-contextual reality that is not yet there but can be there by virtue of the power of interpretive imagination.

In connection with Ps 23, the imagination[30] can find marginal elements that, however, with its exercise then become central. The theme of guidance, of trust, is strong and recurrent in the psalm. The motif of inclusiveness is almost absent. The sense of the flock in the metaphor of the shepherd, or of the family in the metaphor of the housewife, emphasize the sense of the exclusiveness of the group, which is best articulated in the exclusive circle of their intimacy. Yet, this psalm, through imagery that exploits, in and out of the text, seemingly secondary elements, has great potential for inclusiveness. And this can start with the exploitation of the "enemies" motif. That enemies are also seated at a table[31] is suggestive. So the home, quintessentially a sign of intimacy, can actually become a place of welcome and inclusion not only for one's own group but for anyone. That table is actually the place where anyone can find a place.

---

30. This component of imagination is very present in Brueggemann's interpretive takes with respect to the Psalms in general and Psalm 23 in particular. Brueggemann and Bellinger, Jr., *Psalms*, 122–126; Schökel and Carniti, *Psalmos*.

31. The reference to enemies is an explicit one and we find it in verse 5: "For me you set the table before the eyes of my enemies."

If interpretation is only there when there is interaction between "text" and "reader" (hermeneutic circle), only levels 4, 5, and 6 deserve to be called hermeneutic in the strict sense. Levels 1 and 2 still remain sophisticated forms of readings without yet configuring themselves as true hermeneutics. Levels 1 and 2 tend to neglect, underestimate, and disregard the structural necessity of true interaction between the Bible and the believer's historicity. The central hermeneutical level remains level 3 because it is the one that signals, through paradox, both the incompleteness of the text without reality and the partiality of a reality without a text.

FOR A BIBLICAL HERMENEUTICS OF AMBIVALENCE AND PARADOX

In the previous chapter, we considered some load-bearing features of biblical language: sobriety and exuberance. This creates a double movement of contraction and expansion of meaning within which any interpretive revival must fit. Interpretation is not the repetition of biblical language and its message as the reader found them. That would be pure tautology and, as an interpretive event, perfectly useless. No, interpretation adds specification to the Bible read. The interpreter does not stand there before the biblical message as a purely decorative element, as an ornamental hermeneutical element with no real impact on the process of meaning formation.

The interpreter is required to leave his or her own imprint on the biblical language. Indeed, to add to that language something it does not have. Through his intervention, the interpreter ennobles the Bible because he converts its latency of meaning into something specific. The interpreter is not only a potential deformer from which to protect the sacred text, he is also a necessary enhancer of the sacred text. And he does so as a ferryman of a sense that, from latent, becomes explicit by virtue of extra-textual events that allow one to look at the Bible from new perspectives. In this sense, it is as if the Bible awaits the creative hand of the interpreter to deliver to the world meanings that, without this hand, would remain purely potential and in a state of latency.

This is what we mean by a hermeneutics of ambivalence and paradox. Among ambivalence and paradox, the common element is given by the synchronic existence of various possible meanings. Both are thus declensions in the plural. In ambivalence and paradox, plurality does not wane but becomes the hallmark of the interpretive act in all its stages. The interpreter is required to maintain and reproduce in his interpretation the plurality he has found in the Bible and which is not to be overcome in the newfound meaning.

The sense derived does not mark the demise or exhaustion of biblical language and its plurality. How then to maintain the biblical message and language without being tautological and without denying the necessary addition of the interpreter and his creative intervention? The challenge is therefore daunting and can be summed up in this maxim: the exuberance and sobriety of biblical language must be prolonged in the interpretation that the interpreter constructs from the Bible.

Ambivalence and paradox, while similar, are not completely identical. Ambivalence refers to a plurality of senses that coexist together and may eventually converge until they overlap. In paradox, on the other hand, there is a plurality that does not assimilate but remains in tension. In paradox the senses present remain asymmetrical and unassimilable, but it is this structural tension that provides the space where the senses occur and confront each other, thus opening up a horizon of meaning. Ambivalence and paradox are thus two looks at the plurality of meaning, similar but different.

New meaning, thanks to this preserved or repurposed plurality with equivalent strategies, remains mysterious. A statement by clues and fragments. There is never complete epiphany of meaning. The sense derived can never be definitive. True interpretation is prohibited from totalizing synthesis and clarification. It is testimony, not explanation. That is why it offers not only answers but increases questions. It refuses to convert into a doctrinal casuistry of confessional orthodoxy, to become meditation and prayer.

The Bible truly becomes a guide when the characteristics of its language are preserved in the interpretations it gives birth to. Interpretation is successful when the exuberance and sobriety of biblical language are prolonged and survive in new faith formulations that draw on the Bible.

What does it mean to preserve, in interpretation, the sobriety and exuberance of biblical language?

1. They must not become totalizing or definitive. They must remain like the Bible, indicative and circumstantial. They must elaborate prospective and guiding indications. They must remain sober, for if they were full, they would not tolerate alternative interpretations or even further updates. They would present themselves as concise

and definitive definitions. The Bible and its language, as indeed any religious language, necessarily expresses an inclusive intent, not of a synthetic but a tensional inclusiveness. This means that the accepted meanings will never be surmountable in an unambiguous synthesis but will always coexist in a creative tension.

2. They are and must always remain "exuberant," that is, "multiple" as is the Bible they interpret. The fact that interpretations are also multiple means that they cannot create a final synthesis, thus claiming to close the rushing stream of meanings that biblical language typically provokes. Each interpretation must create possible alternatives. If an interpretation instead becomes compact and monolithic, it is not good because it has not taken from the Bible the openness of its language. Good interpretations are those that always create alternatives.

This is the essence of a hermeneutics of paradox. A hermeneutics that aims at prolonging questions rather than closing them with final, resolving answers. The biblical hermeneutics of paradox does not aim at a final and resolving synthesis of meaning. It does not identify with a hermeneutic of transparent clarity. It remains, from the beginning to the end of the interpretive process, linked to the complexity and productive tension it can create.

This dynamic complexity, i.e., of paradox,[32] is expressed at three levels.

1. At the intra-textual level, bringing out in the text itself a tension of meaning that is the birthplace of all meaning.
2. At the extra-textual level, highlighting that even in the life of the one reading the text there are paradoxes that create existential tensions parallel to those found in the text.
3. At the level of linkage, the non-synthetic comparison and juxtaposition between paradoxes inside and paradoxes outside the text; it is in the tensional space between inside and outside the text that meaning occurs and is given.

Biblical hermeneutics is not only complex in the sense of its plurality. That plurality is not always complementary. Sometimes it presents itself as irreducible. It does not integrate but resists synthesis. Paradox is thus a guarantee of truth. The Bible works with a structural tension

---

32. Galimberti, *Orme del sacro*, 35–61. See also, *Corpo*, 11–27.

that does not wear it down but makes it possible. This is in essence a hermeneutic of paradox.

But paradox is not easily identified. Therefore, a hermeneutics of paradox cannot be immediate. It presupposes legitimate prior levels of interpretation that cannot claim to express the main perspective of the text. Only when one discovers the paradox that grounds a text can one claim not to exhaust the text but to follow its horizon. A text unveils its message and offers itself to the reader only from its central paradox. This is why all texts of the Bible are difficult, because the paradox that grounds them cannot be traced immediately. We list below four levels where paradoxes can emerge.

Proximal-immediate Paradox

The proximal-immediate paradox is given when it emerges in proximity, in the same verse, but it does not mean that its understanding is instantaneous. It just means that the paradox is closer spatially than we might imagine. It is found in the same verse. An example is Ps 119:105:

> Your word is a lamp to my foot and a light to my path.[33]

The message of this verse is that when we take God and his Word seriously, we immediately experience clarity and certainty in our life journey through the illumination of his Word. In this first interpretation, however, the proximal-immediate paradox, because in the same verse, has not yet been grasped. The paradox here is twofold. The first paradox is given by the light of the lamp that goes, not, as we might naturally expect, to illuminate the path but the foot. Almost suggesting that the light, initially at least, is not to be applied to the path but to the walker, that is, the one who walks, so it is an introspective light.

The second paradox, on the other hand, is invisible if we limit ourselves to modern translations. This only emerges when reading the original, because the word used for light, in the second part of the verse, in Hebrew *ohr*, means "little light." Thus suggesting that we do not have here an illumination of the whole path, of the whole of life as we would like, but a circumscribed illumination, more problematic than decisive, because it is small in scope. A limited enlightenment that constantly needs to be refocused, readjusted and only according to the next step that is to

---

33. Version NR.

be taken. It does not allow a planning, a filing, a synopsis of the path as a whole. The paradox lies in the fact that this light of God illuminates by hiding and hides by illuminating. That is why it is not on the light itself that one must rely, but only on the God of light.

Proximal-deferred Paradox

The proximal-deferred paradox is given when this emerges not in the same verse but within the entire passage or entire chapter of reference. This means that reading, much less hasty application, is not enough to grasp the central address of the passage. Because it is deferred, this paradox is grasped only later, after much reading and reflection, which, however, must not create habit or habituation. The challenge is to maintain a repeated and recurring reading without erasing the imagination. An example of this kind of paradox is found in Ps 23.

Psalm of David.

> The Lord is my shepherd; nothing I lack. He maketh me rest in verdant pastures, He leadeth me along still waters. He restores my soul, He leads me by paths of righteousness, for His name's sake. Even when I walk through the valley of the shadow of death, I will fear no evil, for you are with me; your rod and staff give me security. For me you set the table, before the eyes of my enemies; you sprinkle my head with oil; my cup overflows. Surely, goods and goodness shall accompany me all the days of my life; and I will dwell in the house of the Lord for long days.

The immediate message of this psalm is the shepherd's skill, care, and attention in guiding his children. When we choose God as our shepherd, we immediately experience the confidence, consolation, and assurance that his guidance communicates to us. This message is immediate and perceptible in the first reading and runs throughout the psalm from beginning to end. But the paradox is not so obvious: it emerges only when we grasp the second metaphor, that of the "table" with which the first metaphor of the "shepherd" is in structural tension, because the shepherd is a metaphor external to the house, while the table is a metaphor internal to the house.

It is as if this psalm describes two modes of being: not only ours as humans but of God himself as the supreme Being. We do not behave outside the home as we behave inside the home. Attitudes, emotions, strategies are different. The believer, consequently, is not monolithic in his attitudes but has structurally diverse ways of being; therefore, flexibility is required of him as an essential characteristic of a shrewd and wise faith. He needs to know how to live wisely inside the church but also outside in the world. This double emphasis on the complexity of the believer's profile and his actions emerges only when we grasp this proximal-deferred paradox and the tension it introduces into the reading through these two metaphors.

Distal Intra-textual Paradox

The intra-textual distal paradox occurs when it does not emerge in the same verse nor in the same chapter but at a distance (distal), either in other chapters of the same book or in a different book of the Bible. This means that reading, much less hasty application, is not enough to grasp the central address of the passage being read. Because it is distal one grasps it only later, after several readings not only of the passage in question but of the whole book in which the passage is found. Reading the whole of a book should be neither scattershot nor monolithic, because it is a matter, through familiarity with style, typifying themes and imagination, of finding connections and highlighting them. An example of this kind of paradox is found in the thematic parallelism of these two verses:

> If anyone comes to me and does not hate his father, mother, wife, children, brothers, sisters and even his own life, he cannot be my disciple (Luke 14:26).

> Children, obey in the Lord your parents, for this is right. Honor your father and mother (this is the first commandment with promise (Eph 6:1–2).

The immediate message of Luke's passage is that when one chooses Jesus, one must be willing to leave everything behind, including such fundamental ties as family. This renunciation, difficult in the immediate moment, turns out to be compelling later, because we see that, despite this loss, life with God gratifies us in other ways, and eventually it is possible that the family itself, over time, will understand the goodness of our choice of faith. Immediately we see, however, that there is a difficulty in this interpretation and also the danger of a drift in our faith. We note that this passage can easily be interpreted one-sidedly, thus misinterpreted. For if someone is already in dispute with his or her family, he or she finds in this gospel request the perfect alibi to break with it permanently.

Therefore, this passage should not be read alone. One must read other passages in other books of the Bible (distal) that give a different look at the same topic. The Ephesians passage suggests a completely different attitude, introducing a tension that is difficult to resolve. There we are asked to adopt a less radical, more guarantor-like, more sober attitude, reminding ourselves that faith and faithfulness to Jesus is not played out, most of the time, in breaking with the family but remaining there, as the text suggests, because if there is one place where it is possible to test the consistency and validity of our faith, it is the family. Only by knowing how to live the family, with the family, in the family, do we show that our faith is mature. Breaking with the family, even for reasons of spiritual choice, many times is an escape from reality and true faith. The way to live faith and family is not given only by the verse in Luke, but in the comparison of the verses detached and inserted in different (distal) passages that we have to tie together through the Spirit's guidance.

Distal Extra-textual Paradox

The extra-textual distal paradox arises when this emerges not in the same verse nor in the same chapter or even in the Bible, but at a distance (distal) and in connection with a non-biblical fact or event that occurs in reality itself. This requires us to make a different kind of effort. A different reading of the Bible. A knowing how to read not only the Bible but also reality and everyday common life. This extra-textual distal paradox reminds us that the Bible cannot be read alone. We must, along with it, know how to read reality and the world. Because it is distal, this paradox is grasped only later after various readings, which include non-Biblical readings.

The Bible is not the whole of reality but only an important part of it, so in order to grasp its message, we cannot escape but must confront the reality to which the Bible is a witness, guide, and reflection. It is the Bible itself that pushes us toward reality. If this does not happen, it is a clear sign that we are reading it wrongly. The Bible is a map of reality, not reality itself. And this extra-textual distal paradox reminds us of this very essential fact. To read the Bible well we need to read it together with, and not instead of,

A HERMENEUTICS OF PARADOX

reality. An example of this kind of paradox is found in the thematic parallelism of the passage in 1 Cor 14:34–35 with the world today.

> As is done in all the churches of the saints, let the women be silent in the assemblies, for they are not permitted to speak; let them be submissive, as the law also says. If they want to learn anything, let them question their husbands at home; for it is shameful for a woman to speak in the assembly.

The immediate message of this passage is clear for premodern, hierarchical, patriarchal communities that did not know what individual freedom and the right to self-determination was, much less that referring to women. This is not to say that their social and cultural configuration did not have merits and did not express guarantees that today, for example, we do not have and are unable to offer people. It was simply a different historical configuration. The immediate message is clear. It is to be favored, even with the support of faith, order, authority, stability, continuity, and verticality of relationships, because those are what guarantee the balance of a faith community.

We note at once that there is a difficulty in this interpretation and also the danger of a drift in our faith. We note that this passage can easily be interpreted one-sidedly, thus misinterpreted. We cannot find verses in the Bible that say otherwise. We can find individual verses that allude to certain minority experiences where the woman showed initiative and resourcefulness even then. But, on the whole, we will not find in the Bible, as some would have it, either the defense of the individual as such and detached from the value of the group, or even less consideration of the woman herself, even beyond and outside the group or her family.

The Bible could not anticipate the times, nor was it necessary. Not only for the family but also for the conception of politics or science: the Bible, while correcting some excesses and individual elements, is a child of its time. But its greatness is in introducing, not completing, reflections valid for all times. Then again, this is true not only for the Bible, but also for the so-called great classical texts, which have a timeless and current value because they only suggest, introduce, and outline universal perspectives, not specific recipes. So this passage from 1 Corinthians, though harsh and provocative for us contemporaries, should be read and grasped in its perspective, which is still valid and not taken as a recipe for dealing with women today. The extra-textual distal paradox is not created by the Bible but by comparing the Bible with the external world of today's reality.

VII

Neutralizing the Paradox by an "Excess of Text"

Textual Positivism

IN THIS CHAPTER AND the next, we deal with some interpretive dysfunctionalities. These anomalies are perfectly possible and more common than we think. They emerge and are chronically present where they are least expected. Reading the Bible, unfortunately, does not cause only benefits and blessings, as we would like. It also causes anomalies and sometimes real hermeneutical pathologies.

Most believers think that it is only failure to read the Bible causes spiritual anomalies. This belief is vitiated by two assumptions. First, that reading the Bible, because it is the product of an authentic and personal search, always produces a benefit. Second, that the Bible itself is transparent and immediate and that it is enough to read it to understand its various propositions. The first is an anthropological error that overestimates the value of personal conviction. The second is a theological-cultural error that disregards and downplays the complexity and difficulty of every communicative process, including the religious one.

The problem of hermeneutics, that is, of reading and assimilating meaning, is faced by those who read the Bible, that is, believers. It is not faced by those who do not read it, that is, non-believers, as most Christians believe. Those who do not read the Bible have other kinds of problems, including possible spiritual problems, but not hermeneutical ones. This is because they do not make attending and reading the Bible their priority or their life commitment. Hermeneutical problems arise within that segment of Christians who are more committed and more involved in faith experience and Bible-reading. It is this spiritually militant, majority, noble, and committed band of people in the various Christian communities, only a fraction of whom meet the criterion of fanaticism and radicalism, that we will be concerned with in these two chapters. It represents the reservoir where these various hermeneutical dysfunctionalities are cultivated and articulated.

With a synoptic intent, we will say that this group of committed Christians basically incur two kinds of hermeneutical dysfunctions. We will call the first anomaly "by deficit" and the second anomaly "by excess." The anomalies are not all of the same sign, they do not enact the same dysfunctional mechanism, and, consequently, they do not all require the same kind of corrective intervention. It is not the quantitative differentiation that is most important but rather the qualitative one. This double differentiation between anomalies by deficit and anomalies by excess is, in its essence, a qualitative differentiation. We will define them both by qualitative relation to the text, which is the basic hermeneutic category. Hermeneutical anomalies by deficit are those that neglect or underestimate, theoretically or practically, the importance of the biblical text. Those by excess emphasize and affirm the centrality and foundational priority of the biblical text in any interpretive process.

Although this simple division into two groups seems clear and fairly obvious, it actually implies a series of stances, assumptions, relationships, and effects. In their intersection and interaction, they well exemplify the nature of the relationship with the Bible. They also exemplify some more hidden cultural assumptions that heavily determine the interpretive act. The theoretical and practical implications arising from this differentiation are of vital importance in properly directing the interpretive process

Hermeneutical anomalies due to a deficit of biblical reading will require a certain kind of pastoral and theological intervention. The corrective hermeneutic intervention must here focus on the mechanism of "stimulation" at both the level of supply (biblical persuasion) and demand (personal motivation). Hermeneutical anomalies due to a excess of biblical reading, on the other hand, will require another kind of intervention. The valid mechanism here is no longer that of "stimulus" but that of "cooling" (tempering) the supply or demand, or at least proposing a different and alternative configuration of them.

Two important descriptive-diagnostic confusions emerge at this level. First, churches seem to possess and offer only one kind of hermeneutical strategy. It aims to push everyone to read the Bible, because it is naively believed that the most widespread anomaly consists in not reading the Bible and that, as a result, everything is solved by reading it. Unfortunately, this is not the case: sometimes reading the Bible can make the situation even worse. If someone does not read the Bible, it is good that he reads it. But if someone reads it badly, we make the situation worse if we stimulate more assiduous (abnormal) reading.

Second, churches seem to think that the most damaging anomaly is that by a deficit of biblical reading. This possibly is the most widespread anomaly but not necessarily the worst. We might say that those who read the Bible little at least know that their problem lies in not reading it enough. The more insidious, more hidden hermeneutical problem lies with those who read the Bible assiduously. The Christian who is most committed and involved in the faith is the most susceptible to developing a hermeneutical anomaly that is difficult to correct. Reading the Bible has become for this Christian complicit in a mechanism that reinforces the anomaly one wants to correct.

In this chapter, we will consider anomalies by excess and in the next chapter those by textual deficit. The first group we will also call "textual positivism" or "biblical positivism." Textual positivism thrives on a double affirmation. On the one hand, the importance and absolute priority of the biblical text is affirmed. On the other hand, and as an automatic correlate, there is a tendency to minimize and neglect the reader's questions, situation, and anxieties. They are considered inappropriate or even unnecessary. From this perspective, the text is king, and the reader has only to comply and submit to the absolute directions coming from the text. We use the word "positivism" because like scientific or social positivism, typical modern cultural forms, "biblical positivism" also lives by the same basic assumption. This is that the reality in question, in this case the biblical text, is completely transparent, measurable, organizable, and reproducible.

This emphasis on the sacred and absolute character of the text would seem to contradict the overriding tendency of the hermeneutics of our time that we have described as "reader-centric." On a second level, however, this paradox is perfectly possible. It is so because the text presupposed and defended by those who incur this anomaly by excess of text is certainly not the premodern text characterized by its stable meaning. It is an all-modern text. The premodern text was not only characterized by its stability but also by its mystery. It was an enchanted text.

The text that is defended and elevated here is a fluid text, made artificially stable by modern biblical positivism and, above all, without mystery. It is a disenchanted text, characterized only by the functionality and correctness of shared information, typical form, and configuration of modern texts. Those who defend the sacredness of the biblical text today think or are under the illusion that they are defending an ancient text when they are defending a clearly modern and "positivist" understanding of that text. It is firm only at a point of modernity elevated to a sacred schema through the disguised, albeit unconscious, recourse to the authority of the biblical text.

The text defended from this perspective is actually an indirect defense of the individual and the typically modern individualism that underlies it. It is a kind of referred symptom. In medicine, pain cannot always be directly linked to the place of its manifestation. Referred pain is pain shifted to a territory derived from the place where it originates and which only a trained clinical eye can decipher well in its genesis and manifestation. A headache does not always originate in the head but could be caused by a metabolic and functional problem residing elsewhere. This is our hypothesis about biblical positivism, consisting of a radical defense of the biblical text. It is a mediated defense, a "referred symptom" of the centrality of the reader that one wants to affirm and maintain even through indirect mechanisms.

It is as if a typical dissimulation mechanism occurs in biblical positivism such as, for example, occurs in the "reactive formation"[1] described by Freud. In this secondary defense mechanism, an unmentionable thought is sublimated through the creation of a virtuous thought. It is hidden, unknowingly, behind extreme purism and moral rigor, a marked unmentionable sexual weakness. Similarly, the unmentionable modern individualism that has reinterpreted the Bible for the individual's use seems sublimated, in biblical positivism, behind a great respect for the Bible. It is not very complicated to show that many biblical ideas, passionately defended by many biblical fundamentalists in the present day, rather than being biblical are typically modern ideas, sclerotized and stationary at one point in modern history.

---

1. See McWilliams, *Psychoanalytic Diagnosis*, 140–42.

With respect to hermeneutic anomalies, another specification must be introduced. This one concerns the word "anomaly." What kind of dysfunctions do anomalous readings of the Bible embody? Are they just alternative looks? Fallacious techniques? Simple misreadings? Interpretive asymmetries? Or are they real hermeneutical pathologies? Two brief considerations can help us to understand the dimension of the problem.

1. All reading, including biblical reading, presupposes the existence of errors, but these do not compromise either the reading effort or the final result of the reading. In some ways these errors are necessary, perhaps even beneficial, and one should guard against stigmatizing them. That would be like expecting a child to grow up well and healthy without ever disobeying a rule. Perhaps the attitude of a child who always obeys would be more abnormal, just as a reader who always reads well and arrives at the meaning without any peripatetic reading would become suspect. No, errors in reading and interpretation should not be demonized but should be welcomed as natural stages in the long and winding process of interpretation.

2. There are, however, reading errors that not only undermine the result of reading but also warp the reader's motivation and interpretive attitude at the outset. If we are vouchers for the first type of errors, we are instead critical of this second type, for which we will use a strong term: "hermeneutic pathology." Yes, there are and frequently exist real hermeneutic pathologies.

Although this may seem excessive, we defend this terminology for two reasons. On the one hand, it is because these errors contaminate not only the reading, but also the resulting theology and its communal, ethical, and cultural extensions. On the other, it is because some hermeneutical anomalies unfortunately become chronic and, becoming so, also resistant to corrective strategies. There is no way to correct them, also because the biblical dimension is itself sensitive and of first importance. It is what is good from the point of view of religious mobility and functionality, but not from the curative and therapeutic point of view. Those who think they read God's Word out of conviction and obedience are unlikely to be corrected in the hermeneutical anomaly they embody. They perceive the correction as a sacrilegious intent to destroy their faith. This fact determines that these anomalies take the form of true hermeneutical pathologies.

A THEOLOGICAL-CULTURAL LOOK AT TEXTUAL REDUCTIONISM[2]

The description of these hermeneutic anomalies is not done on neutral territory. We do so within a historically precise world: the contemporary world. This first type of hermeneutical anomalies, which we group under the name "biblical positivism," needs to be specified in two senses. One is an "intensive" sense, in that this anomaly is much deeper and more deeply rooted in the Christian sphere than we think, and cannot be circumscribed only to so-called biblical literalism. A second is in an "extensive" sense, in that biblical positivism, beyond its deep hold in all strata of Christianity, is actually the extension and Christian form of a much more widespread cultural phenomenon that precedes it and that Christianity perfects with its own categories.

This cultural phenomenon, which Christianity presupposes and perfects, we could call "textual reductionism." It is a typical phenomenon of the contemporary world. Textual reductionism is that cultural configuration, born in the West, which tends to enclose complex and polyform reality in books and in the knowledge and concepts that books contain and pass on. It positively causes a great dynamism in and of the reference system, depending on the order it introduces at the level of the reading of reality. At the same time, it falsifies reality itself because it reduces it only to what the reference books say about it. We are faced with the reduction of reality to the description of reality, of the world to the representation of the world, of life to the concept of life. In the reality-writing (written thought) pair, everything is to the advantage of writing. Writing, of which

---

2. Textual reductionism, which is the phenomenon that claims to reduce the complexity of reality and life to the reduced dimensions of a piece of writing (text), is certainly not only a linguistic or literary phenomenon. See Zoja, *Contro Ismene*, 99–116. More underlying is a cultural phenomenon that Heidegger describes as the obsession to rationally control being, confusing it with beingness. Galimberti writes, "The West is the time of the epoché of being ... Underlying all the initiatives of Western man is indeed the overt or covert attempt to dominate being, to lord it over." *Tramonto dell'Occidente*, 282–83. However, this cultural and not just textual reductionism is not negative. On the contrary, it underlies modern efficientism and is part of its DNA and conscious project. Cf. Toulmin, *Cosmopolis*, 89–137. If this had not brought undoubted benefit, modernity, greedy for results, would not have chosen and maintained it at all. But what modernity had not calculated are the adverse side effects of this reduction, which essentially occur in the ambivalence of reason and its undoubted vocation to nihilism. See Adorno and Horkheimer, *Dialectic of Enlightenment*, 3–42; Galimberti, *Tramonto dell'Occidente*, 411–16.

modern books and texts are the form and medium, replaces true reality. From reality is considered only that which is thinkable and writable.

This textual reductionism as a typical deformation of the West has three characteristics: 1. It tends to confuse the representation of reality with reality itself; 2. It has become an across-the-board and widespread phenomenon in our time to the extent that it is implicitly enacted by all of us automatically and without questing it, in everything we know and undertake. 3. It seems difficult if not impossible to stop. Any intent to correct and to balance it merely updates and reaffirms it in an even more sophisticated way.

Cultural anomalies have a long genesis. This positively allows them to protect themselves against untimely and abrupt mechanisms and changes. Unfortunately, they also have the disadvantage of requiring long periods of time in the application of corrective mechanisms. This manifests itself in their chronic resistance to change. Cultural anomalies tend to become chronic and difficult to correct. Many times cultural anomalies, as in this case textual reductionism, are not dysfunctions that take over later at a later period of a group's historical journey. They are co-present, in an incipient form, since the birth of cultural phenomena. This anomaly of "textual reductionism" is congenital and synchronous to Western cultural greatness, hence the difficulty of its containment.

This is the diagnosis of Luigi Zoja, who speaks of pervasive and persistent cognitive patterns arising from apparently decentered or marginal cultural sectors, as could be for instance psychoanalysis. Zoja, and before him Jung himself, and with Zoja a large cohort of analyst as James Hillman for instance, all of them raise to modern culture, of which contemporary biblical hermeneutics is a part, not only a psychological question about the state of inner being but above all an epistemological question. This question and critique concern the pervasive presence of a reductive way of knowing and of approaching life and reality. Their question and contestation focus on this point. The undoubted inner decay and the clear emotional and psychological fragility of our time, which, as Philip Rieff well reminds us in his book *The Triumph of Therapy*,[3] occurs and results in the massive spread of psychotherapies, is rooted and conditioned, in a deeper level, by a epistemological problem. Not only existential and inner disruptions, which have always existed, cause the psychological withering that exists today. The cause is a type of knowledge that, having

---

3. Rieff, *Triumph of the Therapeutic*, 23–45.

become excessively rational and objectifying to the bitter end, can no longer nurture people's inner selves.

This substantive problem is not psychological but epistemological. James Hillman speaks of a radical linguistic and psychological nominalism that underlies contemporary culture and its malaises.[4] This is a distortion not at the level of inner being but at the level of the way of knowing the real. It underlies the inner attrition of modern and postmodern man. Jungian psychoanalysis, through the massive use of images, metaphors, and archetypes, proposes, before psychological therapy, an epistemological reconversion.[5]

Zoja calls this reductivist orientation and drift of all Western culture, of which biblical hermeneutics is a part, the "disease of the West."[6] This reductionism emerges not only in modern technology. It is a strong idea throughout the history of the West, and it is widespread in all levels of cultural expression. Reductionism is a cognitive experience that replaces multifaceted experiences and diverse and complex points of view with one. The result is not immediately negative. On the contrary, it results in great functionality and efficiency. Everything becomes mobile and the quantitative grows. The obvious loss in this process is the known object, that is, reality.

In this process the object is "objectified." It is made a thing, an inert and immobile reality, therefore manipulable. One knows a depowered, essentially dead reality. The depowered object of knowledge, because it is rendered a "thing," automatically takes over the depowering of the knowing "subject." The subject's strength and vitality depend on the kind of knowledge it has of the external world. Contemporary man myopically and short-sightedly traded the life-giving force of images and metaphors that nourish the inner life for depowered images (concepts) that cannot nourish him. They can give him only the fleeting impression of knowing and powering more. The modern subject finds in his hands a depotentiated (disenchanted) world that is a perfect copy of his own depotentiated being. The subject itself comes out depowered because what nourishes it and makes it alive (powerful) cannot be self-nourishment and pure self-care. It must be life that comes from outside, from others and from otherness. The modern subject is a subject that has shut itself in. It has

---

4. Hillman traces this reductionism to the nominalism that has corroded the strength of our language for centuries. *Re-visione della psicologia*, 117–31.

5. Cf. Hillman, *Re-visione della psicologia*.

6. Zoja, *Contro Ismene*.

erased the idea and actual reality of the other. It moves solely in the world of the equal and the same.

This is the diagnosis of several authors. Among others is that of Byung-Chul Han, who writes:

> The time when there was the Other is gone. The Other as mystery, the Other as seduction, the Other as Eros, the Other as desire, the Other as hell, the Other as pain disappears.[7]

Still on textual positivism related to calculus as one of its most direct manifestations, Byun-Chul Han writes further:

> Thought has access to the totally Other. It has the power to interrupt the Equal. In this consists its character as an event. Calculus, on the other hand, is an endless repetition of the Same. Unlike thought, it cannot give rise to a new state of affairs. It is blind to the event. Instead, a true thought possesses the nature of an event.[8]

Zoja, in this regard, argues that Jungian psychoanalysis was born in opposition to this tendency. It was born in opposition to Descartes and his rationalism that wants to reduce psychic existence to the ego of clear and distinct ideas. It was also born also in opposition to Freud, who wanted to reduce the unconscious to a layer of confused and contradictory existential and linguistic anomalies and blocks, which must be resolved and overcome by clarity of thought. Jungian psychoanalysis shares this corrective element and resistance to reigning reductionism with other cultural forms that resist this reigning thinking. At this point in the description, the question is also about hermeneutics. Is hermeneutics part of the resistance or the empowering group of this cultural reductionism?

How does "textual reductionism" settle and form at the level of biblical interpretation? Beyond the fact that cultural processes are multifactorial, slow, and unconscious and therefore difficult to diagnose, certain attitudes help to reinforce it. We mention three of them: unilateralism, compact conviction, and lack of counterbalancing instances.

Let us start with unilateralism. The indelible selectivity of every faith experience carries from the beginning the seed of reading unilateralism. Every choice presupposes the necessary narrowing in one's perspective in order to choose and identify with one option and leave out the others.

---

7. Han, *Espulsione dell'altro*, 7.
8. Han, *Espulsione dell'altro*, 11.

There is no choice without this narrowing. Choice is narrowing. Every reading of the Bible must wear by moral obligation the cloak of humility. It enables us to be aware of the benefits of this narrowing but also of the anomalies that this almost automatically creates. Every reading of the Bible, especially the most involved ones, is inexorably joined to a parallel process of stiffening and one-sidedness. They necessarily articulate this process of focusing. They do it by virtue of the misrecognition of other possible senses that are legitimately present in the text and that cannot be erased completely but only bracketed transiently.

Anyone who reads the Bible actually reads it badly because he or she abandons the totality of possible senses. This seemingly drastic opinion has relevance. In a more general sense, we can say that every reading, by introducing a focusing mechanism, introduces an element of arbitrariness. Thus, unilateralism settles very early in the reading and does so mainly under a guise of legitimacy. Reading the Bible reductively does not necessarily mean reading it wrongly. Unilateralism is not lacking in the best readings. Yet, reading the Bible unilaterally is enough to misread it. It is to elevate a partial reading to a total reading. One-sided reading of the Bible is that reading which reads well but does not read the whole. By not reading the whole, it automatically reads the whole badly. This is the essence of the unilateralism that leads to textual reductionism.

The second attitude is compact conviction. When humility is lacking, unilateralism is not only not perceived but even reinforced by compact and overly certain conviction. Conviction is always necessary to begin a reading. This is a sign of commitment and involvement. An excess of conviction is, though, not necessary. Asking conviction to self-limit is like asking someone who has been fasting for a few days to stop only at the first forkful of an inviting and appetizing dish. This is very unlikely to happen. Because this does not happen, unbalanced conviction changes from being an ally to becoming an enemy that does not allow us to see well. The convinced reader, almost automatically, loses clarity about the whole. He can no longer read well the overall situations and the interconnection of the various latent senses.

When God, therefore, blesses us in spite of our unilateralism, the compact conviction leads us to presumption. For in that undeserved blessing, and only granted by grace, we sometimes find inappropriate validation of our unilateralism. If God has blessed us, we conclude, then our reading is correct. Not only do we fail to see our limitation, we even legitimize it. It is by virtue of that limitation of reading, we think, that God has blessed us.

It is easy to cultivate and maintain prejudices and misconceptions about things. We know this from human experience. But the same thing happens with the Bible. Prejudices and crooked ideas about the world, life, and ourselves not only do not go away with Bible reading; they are often entrenched by it. In order to maintain and perpetuate some sloppy and unhealthy preconceptions, it is enough to read the Bible with a consistency and conviction that avoids enacting the critical instance that the Bible wants to introduce both at the level of the content of ideas and at the level of attitudes and ways of thinking. Consistency and conviction in reading the Bible, without wisdom, whose main characteristic is the pursuit of interpretation as a place of questioning, easily become destructive virtues.

Our history shows how diligently consistent, good, and well-prepared Christians with the help of the Bible and a firm conviction have supported in the past, and continue to support in the present, the current exploitation of labor, racial discrimination, gender stigma, asymmetrical occupational recognition, hierarchical authoritarianism, and self-destructive religious attitudes. Just as food is not only a pleasure but also includes a long list of eating disorders, so, too, biblical reading is not only a blessing but also includes a long list of dysfunctions and real hermeneutical pathologies.

It is not enough to claim to be biblical in order to be truly biblical. Those who claim to be biblical, because of the inevitable unilateralisms we have briefly described, easily become today hermeneutically dangerous. There is a need to temper scriptural zeal. It is not zeal that we lack today but the moderation that can dampen overly compact and monolithic attitudes. We need wise and less zealous readers. Just being "moderately biblical" would be enough to give a better testimony on behalf of the Bible. This formula is not very convincing to many. It seems renunciatory, accommodating, and minimalist. Yet it is a wise as well as realistic suggestion. In medicine, anomalies are not only those "by deficit" but also those "by excess" of functionality. While those by deficit tend to be the most prevalent, it is also true that those by excess, which may be the least prevalent, turn out to be the most complicated. A call for "biblical restraint" is never out of place.

This is the call of psychoanalyst Bruno Bettelheim in another sensitive area, as parenting can be. He says, and this is the title of one of his books, that the best goal for parents is not to be perfect but only *A Good*

Enough Parent.[9] One must aim more soberly to be only "good enough." That is not completely perfect. Total perfection, from apparent advantage, turns into nightmare. So also with the Bible. It would be sufficient to be "good enough Bible readers" or "moderate Bible readers." This would be a guarantee. On the other hand, those who want to be very biblical, zealously biblical, do not realize that within that "very biblical" are unknowingly hiding many unbiblical things. In addition to being unbiblical, they are improperly smuggled in as though they were.

"Being biblical enough" is not a status but a pilgrimage. Having been biblical in the past does not ensure being biblical in the present and future. Claiming to be biblical can be the most sophisticated way to be idolatrous and religiously static. Being biblical or appealing to the principle of *sola scriptura* is only tangentially and peripherally related to reading the Bible on a daily basis. The Bible is more concerned with our becoming than with what we are or read in the present. The goal is to connect with the vitalizing perspective of the Bible so as to give it the space to correct and reorient our lives. This is only possible if we fit properly within the interpretive arc in all its stages, as these are articulated in the "hermeneutic circle." If our biblical reading only confirms our existing deep convictions and structural spiritual orientation, whether personal or communal, this is a sufficient sign to start worrying. This beneficial spirit of iconoclastic renewal can only exist within the interpretive experience, not in the mere reading of the Bible.

We come to the third point: the lack of balancing instances. If unilateralism had, from the outset, balancing instances, it simply would not be unilateralism. Here it is important to distinguish between two levels: the functional and the structural. If unilateralism is only at a functional level, the interpretive enterprise as a whole is not necessarily compromised. On the other hand, when unilateralism is situated instead at the structural level, it drifts and becomes more irrepressible. It is the tracks themselves and no longer just the train that have an anomaly.

The element that best guarantees structural harmony and most averts the threat of textual reductionism is the hermeneutic circle. It almost automatically brings in not one but two criteria in every process of reading and interpretation. Only this double confrontation, which the hermeneutic circle imposes by obligation on every reading, actually halves the risk of any kind of unilateralism and textual reductionism.

---

9. Bettelheim, *Genitore quasi perfetto*, 5–16.

Let us now turn to consider some forms of textual reductionism as they take shape at the level of Bible reading. We will choose the term "biblical positivism" to designate these dysfunctions. At a first level, biblical positivism, in the form of "inerrantism," will be a problem related to a limited group of Christians. At a second level, biblical positivism will instead, through a central concept of theology such as *sola scriptura*, invest a more substantial swath of Christianity. At a third level, biblical positivism will remain limited to a small band of Christians, although intellectually very active and refined. And at a fourth level, biblical positivism will be reinforced through a cultural form, thus becoming a mass cultural phenomenon.[10]

BIBLICAL LITERALISM: FORMAL INERRANCY[11]

The first form of biblical positivism comes from the proponents of biblical inerrancy. To better understand its scope and nature, we compare it with the classical view of most Christians. Christians, across all the spectrum, assert that the Bible is inspired by God. They believe that those who materially wrote its text acted under divine influence. Most Christians believe that what it states is completely reliable, useful, and true. At the same time, the vast majority of Christians maintain that the historical or scientific data and details of the Bible are less important or even irrelevant to faith and conduct, and that it may contain formal errors of varying degrees that do not affect the essence of the message.

The inerrantists or literalists, on the other hand, claim that even the scientific, geographical, and historical details of the Bible are completely true and free from error. They also believe that the apparent contradictions or errors that we seem to find depend on our subjective perception or knowledge, which is inadequate or distorted. The Protestant churches and even the Catholic church, which teach the total absence of doctrinal errors from Holy Scripture, nevertheless reject any literalist interpretation of it.

To this first form of biblical positivism we add the qualification of "formal inerrantism." Let us specify the two terms more. "Biblical positivism" is that orientation, we said, which tends to make the Bible unambiguous, transparent, and clear. "Formal inerrantism" is that attitude

---

10. Zoja, *Contro Ismene*, 99–116.
11. Cf. Position of Erickson, *Christian Theology*, 188–209.

that tends to see the literary grammatical form and historical-scientific content of the Bible as free from any kind of error. Formal inerrantism is the most extreme form of biblical positivism because it places clarity, transparency, and unambiguousness of the Bible at the most visible, immediate, and material level of the interpretive chain, that is, at the formal level.

Formal or literal inerrantism represents a minority part of Christianity, although it is the most targeted by criticism and stigma. It represents in the spectrum of biblical positivism the most extreme position but not necessarily the most harmful one, despite appearances. In this band of Christianity there subsists a tendency to regard the Bible as a compact instrument of truth against a world warped by sin, which must be saved by the power of the Bible. The two distinguishing elements are an extreme emphasis on biblical clarity and a belief in the structural self-sufficiency of the Bible.

Regarding the first element, we can say that for the inerrantist the Bible appears as a unified and compact reality. In the Bible everything is important, which is why everything must be true. There are no secondary parts, negotiable sections, negligible elements. Everything in the Bible is central, and consequently, everything is imbued with truth. It is not the idea of perfection that necessarily leads the inerrantist to read the Bible compactly. On the contrary, it is the compact view of the Bible and of reality in general that, by preventing him from introducing differentiations of levels, channels, and layers, forces the inerrantist to regard everything in the Bible as true and without error. If there is truth, it must be everywhere. It is the theorem of the indivisibility of reality and the Bible that compels the literalist to give a status of truth even to secondary elements.

This textual compactness is matched by a psychological compactness. At first glance the reader seems to be forgotten completely, by virtue of this hyper-attention given to the perfection of the text. At a second glance it becomes clear that the compactness given to the text is only an extension of the reader's own psychological compactness to the text. It is the mind of the literalist that is totalizing and compact. Its compactness is transferred to the text.

The inerrantist carries with him the limitation that he cannot distinguish between what is primary and what is secondary. For him there are no minor battles. All battles are final and decisive. This unnecessarily leads to extreme consumption of energy, triggering radical battles in defense of the Bible over completely trivial issues. The inerrantist lacks discernment. In the end, this costs him a high price, because he loses his strength in futile and secondary points.

Regarding the second element, the inerrantist sincerely believes in the absolute autonomy of the Bible. It depends only on divine revelation. No contextual element, historical or moral, and even less religious, can condition its birth and development. It is autonomous from any historical conditioning. It even gives true meaning and significance to all historical events clearly and directly. It is not reality that has to say what is true or what is false. It is the Bible that says what is true or false in the outside reality.

The map (Bible) has completely replaced the territory. The map is the territory. The Bible is the reality. The emphasis on the perfection of the Bible, perfection without error, is heavily conditioned by this detachment from reality. Because the Bible is detached from reality, all the weight and presence of truth falls on the Bible and invests it massively. Having disappeared from the territory, all truth will have to reside only in the map.

In the biblical fanaticism of the literalist, everything is out of whack: the conception of truth, of the world, of sin, of salvation, of the church. The "formal" inerrantist lives completely in a parallel world.

BIBLICAL CONFESSIONALISM: CONFESSIONAL INERRANCY[12]

A larger part, indeed, the numerically largest part of Christianity, disassociates itself from "formal inerrantism," but continues to attribute to the

---

12. Adventism is a typical example of what we mean by "denominational inerrancy." Formal, literalist inerrancy has been overcome on an exegetical and biblical level, but it survives on a denominational and communal level. However, the overcoming of biblical literalism is not synonymous, in Adventists as in many other non-fundamentalist religious denominations, with a balanced hermeneutic. There remains a tendency toward a hermeneutic that is closed, ecclesiocentric, and especially for specific themes (Sabbath, lifestyle, eschatology) also highly ideologized. Cf. Hasel and Hasel, *How to Interpret Scripture*; Campbell, *1919*. The characteristics of Adventist hermeneutics can be summarized in four statements recurring in all official documents, including even the most recent ones:
   1. Scripture arises independently of its context through its own, internal logic.
   2. The Bible has no contradictions and presents a unified outline.
   3. Scripture interprets itself.
   4. The meaning of Scripture is clear and immediate.

Cf. R. M. Davidson, "Biblical Interpretation," in Dederen, *Handbook of Seventh-day Adventist Theology*, 58–104; Crocombe, *Hermeneutics, Intertextuality*, 234–37: Reid,

Bible a dimension of infallibility at the doctrinal level. Trust in the Bible as a source of truth remains intact, although it has changed in form.

A strong emphasis on biblical exclusivity, through, for example, the determined and all-out defense of the principle of *sola Scriptura*, characterizes this stance. The Bible would be self-explanatory, essentially understandable and transparent in itself. Most importantly, it would require no substantive connection or interaction either with the outside world or with society or culture to fully articulate its message. It would connect to society and culture only within the circle of a historical-temporal framing.

To this second form of biblical positivism we add the qualification of "confessional inerrantism." The "positivist" tendency to identify the meaning of faith in an unambiguous, clear, and transparent way has not disappeared; faith and the Bible are reduced to sense. Only sense gives meaning to faith. Faith cannot have a double sense, a broken, seemingly senseless, mysterious sense.

Faith must be clear by nature. The desire for clarity and the obsession with unambiguousness have not disappeared. They are always there. The tendency to erase the possibility of error (inerrancy) from faith has not disappeared either. Inerrancy is still there. Clarity and inerrancy have simply been transferred from the form of the text (letter) to one's "confession" of belonging, to communal faith. We are here in face of a biblical confessionalism. The community, to legitimize its authority, resorts to the Bible, through the principle of *sola scriptura*. It is not Scripture itself that is taken into consideration. It is *sola scriptura* as interpreted by that church. That Bible is made completely dependent on the community that reads it, and the community implicitly claims to have the only legitimate reading of the Bible. Thus a strong partnership arises between church certainty and biblical certainty. A strong fusion is created between them that prevents one from seeing and evaluating the truth claim of the other independently.

"Confessional inerrantism" represents a substantial part of Christianity and it has a greater religious impact. This is the part that contributes most to the establishment of the biblical positivism we are describing as anomalous. It is anomalous for two basic reasons.

One is its intent to conceive of the Bible as a compact and homogeneous unity. Continuity is preferred to discontinuity, complementarity to

---

Understanding Scripture; see also the more recent volume that takes up and reinforces the same claims and primordial axes of Adventist hermeneutics. See Hasel, *Biblical Hermeneutics*, vol. 3.

tension, synthesis to fragmentation, because God and truth are identified as unitary realities. If this is so, the Bible must also bear the same traits within itself. The most common phrases to affirm this first conviction are "the Bible never contradicts itself," "any contrasts are only apparent," or "apparent contrasts belong to the human part of the Bible." The most distinctive feature of this first belief is the thought that the Bible is structurally clear. There would be no opacity in the Bible. Its meaning would be perfectly transparent and clear. It is the reader, by the vices he automatically brings with him, who introduces these opacities that must be broken down.

A second is the intent to conceive of the Bible as an autonomous reality. One prefers and chooses in the relationship of the Bible with the external element—discontinuity over continuity, tension over complementarity, rupture over integration. The Bible is not dependent on any human reality. The mantra of this conviction is the principle of *sola scriptura*. One understands this sound principle in its most exclusionary, exclusive, and self-referential dimension.

"Biblical confessionalism" lives on the conviction that we must protect the Bible, preserve it from all manipulation and distortion, starting from the assumption of a supposed purity. The longer the Bible remains in contact with realities foreign to it, the greater the risk of contamination. The Bible must be protected, guarded, safeguarded in its compactness, because it is this that represents the sign of its truth and divine inspiration.

The Bible appears in this view monolithic and homogeneous because it has been detached from everything else, from life itself. But also vice versa: the Bible is detached from everything else because it has become monolithic, compact, and inflexible. The more monolithic an entity is, the more abstract it becomes. The more abstract a reality is, the more monolithic it becomes.

BIBLICAL-THEOLOGICAL RATIONALISM: IDEOLOGICAL INERRANCY[13]

Another part of Christianity disassociates itself from "formal inerrantism" and from "confessional inerrantism," arguing that these forms of

---

13. An example of this type of more sophisticated positivism are the representatives of the liberal Protestant movement who lived at the turn of the nineteenth and early

"religious positivism" are excessively schematic and reductive. Here it is important to grasp, beyond biblical and confessional forms, the universal principles that ground not only faith but life as such. Those historical forms, biblical texts, or faith communities are not the truth. They cannot be the truth. They are only a concretization, an application, an intent to embody universal principles in structures close to us so that they give us a sense of familiarity and closeness. We cannot confuse universal principles with historical forms. These principles, which lie behind the forms, are rational and self-evident. They are not always immediate, because one must, behind appearances and beneath the surface, search for them even with effort. This is what causes most believers, who are content with what is more immediate and requires less effort, to remain on the surface of forms and confuse biblical and confessional forms with the substance of faith. If, on the other hand, one perseveres and resists this fascination with immediate forms and puts forth an attitude of rational search, he or she will find that the true principles behind them are the foundations of faith and must be safeguarded. And those principles, once found, are clear and obvious.

To this third form of biblical positivism we have added the expression "ideological inerrantism." The "positivist" tendency to identify the sense of truth with an unambiguous, clear, and transparent sense has not disappeared. Truth and principles are reduced to sense. Only sense gives meaning to truth. Truth cannot have a double sense, a broken sense, a seemingly senseless sense, a mysterious sense. Truth and principles must by nature be clear and distinct.

The desire for clarity and the obsession with unambiguousness have not disappeared; they are always there. Nor has the tendency of truth and principles to erase the possibility of error (inerrancy) disappeared. Inerrancy is still there. Clarity and inerrancy have simply been transferred from the form of the text (letter) and the "confession" *of* belonging to the rational form of conceiving truth and principles.

"Ideological inerrantism" is a sophisticated and refined form of "biblical-theological positivism" because clarity, transparency, and unambiguousness are placed to it no longer at the level of the textual form nor the community, but at the level of the abstract theological reason that interprets the Bible.

---

twentieth centuries, such as Friedrich Schleiermacher, Albrecht Ritschl, Adolf Von Harnack, and Wilhelm Herrmann. Cf. Pannenberg, *Storia e problemi della teologia*, 9–51; Barth, *Protestant Theology*, 1–15.

In this ideological inerrantism, a principle cannot carry both clarity and error at the same time. Every principle must be compactly true. If it is not compactly true, it is not true; therefore it is false. The Bible, even if understood no longer according to its form but according to its eternal principles, would thus be the book of faith par excellence, because it enables us to distinguish truth from falsehood. The Bible would be the place of truth.

The distortion lies in this. If the Bible is the book of truth, then it discards, unmasks, rejects, and excludes falsehood and error. This would be its vocation and main function: to unmask the false. This is how the Bible is viewed and read in most Christian denominations, even the liberal ones. This has led us to make two mistakes. The first is to consider true only what is Christian, and the second is to consider false everything that is not Christian.

This hermeneutical disease of truth as exclusion does not belong only to inerrantists. It is the disease of all Protestantism. The problem that we impute to inerrantists (fundamentalists) of constructing on the Bible a truth that is expressed in forms also manifests itself at a more transversal level in Protestantism when it thinks that the Bible is a book of truth.

There has only been a level shift. The grammatical truth of the inerrantists has become the doctrinal truth of the evangelicals and the ethical truth of the liberals. The mechanism has not disappeared; it has only been shifted. Protestantism is traversed in all its components by this biblical positivism that has reduced the Bible to a place of clear and unambiguous truth.

The Bible is not a place of truth when it is read to exclude. A truth that excludes cannot be truth. Even worse, it excludes truth. There is probably more truth in the excluded than in the one who excludes. The Bible cannot best be read with the criterion of truth and error. Not only does it come out an exclusionary book but also a paranoid one. If everything must be sifted and verified, then we are far from life and truth. The truth that has been created in the Bible, and around those who so read it, is a "small" truth. That is a "confessional" truth. A confessional truth is always a small truth that cannot claim to embody the larger truth.

The greatest truth is always inclusive. This is the criterion for differentiating between different types of truth: inclusiveness. Truth, according to biblical positivism, at any level of manifestation, cannot be inclusive. Truth, by nature, distinguishes, clarifies, excludes. It is unambiguous and clear. It tends to defend itself from others. It cannot be contaminated and must create distance. This distinguishing feature alone is sufficient to unmask it and describe it as untrue. The truth of biblical positivism, positivism of the letter, confession, or principle, is a small truth. Big and true truth is always inclusive because it creates life. And life is bonding.

MODERN BOOK-CENTRISM: CULTURAL INERRANCY[14]

As we pointed out in the opening of this chapter, the West has identified itself from the very beginning of its historical emergence with clarity as the goal of all knowledge. This is visible in Descartes, in the Enlightenment: from then on this tendency has only been reinforced. This has then been compounded by the spread and use of the book as the privileged promoter and support of this clarity. Books and rational clarity have created an incredibly productive and efficient mixture, which have radically transformed the contemporary world.

The same sequence occurred in Christianity. In Western Christianity, which is the one in that spread everywhere, the book (Bible) and rational clarity made a winning combination. This changed Christianity from within and from without and made it dynamic until it spread to all latitudes. What came first, the book-centered rationality of Christian clarity or that of modernity? It is difficult to say. Such is the interpenetration of these two phenomena that the contours of one and the other cannot be well-defined. Between Christianity and modernity there seems to be a symbiosis. This is a paradoxical symbiosis because clearly there are very marked differences. Western Christianity is one thing; Western culture is another. More than in the past, when culture and religion were more structurally linked, today the register of rupture has been chosen. The most obvious sign is the process of secularization, which puts religion in parentheses. This is something that has never happened before.

Yet, we probably live in the age when culture and Christianity are more similar than ever. They are not similar in form but in substance. In

14. This positivist tendency to conceive of modern rationality as the only possible rationality, embodied in his books, is what Giacomo Marramao calls "identity universalism," which he proposes to change to an inclusive and polycentric "universalism of difference." Cf. Marramao, *Passione del presente*, 187–205. See also the harsh critique of exclusionary cultural positivism as expressed by postcolonial studies. Cf. Chakrabarty, *Provincializing Europe*, 8–14; Bhabha, *Location of Culture*, 23–35; Chakravorty Spivak, *Critique of Postcolonial Reason*, 25–41. And in a more radical and provocative tone is expressed by de Sousa Santos, *Epistemologies of the South*, 9–23.

some ways contemporary culture, in its essential registers, is completely Christian. Contemporary Christianity is all for the use and consumption of modernity. The shaping of Christianity according to modern culture is masterful. So is the way in which modern culture has gained strength by virtue of certain essential Christian categories. This is not new. It is present in the great founders of modernity. This is the case with Hobbes, for example, who creates a new contract culture by legitimizing it with the Bible. He goes even to the point of conceiving all of Christianity functioning as Leviathan, that is, the modern state. One of the most important points of convergence in substance between Christianity and modernity is this textual positivism, this book-centrism of clarity, this reductionism of knowledge.

Life, reality, nature, others, for the modern and postmodern West, is a matter of truth or falsehood. Technique has reinforced to the nth degree this univocal orientation of the entire West and then imposed it as the only pattern valid throughout the world. The truth of instrumental, human, or organizational technique has become even more perverse. Everything is filed, ordered, catalogued, differentiated, specified. It is the absolute realm of clarity and order. The alternatives of mystical meaning, accompanying sacredness, or spiritual escapism continually emerge. We would otherwise be swallowed up by the overwhelming flow of linear technique. In reality, these alternatives change nothing. They serve only as moments of pause and respite to continue in the compulsive rhythm of univocal and flattened production toward consumption.

Faith and market have become, in seemingly alternative forms, homozygous twins. There has been no real secularization in this respect. There has been a secularization of forms, not of substance. Even secularization strictly applies to all levels of life the same criterion of efficient univocity that faith applies within the church. Secularization has as its prototype the clarity of the book, whether religious or secular.

To this fourth form of biblical positivism we add the qualification of "cultural inerrantism." The "positivist" tendency to identify the meaning of life with an unambiguous, clear and transparent sense has not disappeared. Life has been reduced to meaning. Only sense gives meaning to life. Life cannot have a double sense, a broken sense, a seemingly senseless sense, a mysterious sense. Life must be clear by nature. The desire for clarity and the obsession with unambiguousness have not disappeared. They are always there. Inerrancy is still there.

In this univocal drift of the West and current theology, the predominant, though not exclusive, model is the univocal model of Aristotelian logic. We owe to Aristotle the full understanding of the importance of three principles of our reasoning: the principle of identity, non-contradiction and the excluded third.[15] These three principles are actually traceable to each other and form the backbone of univocality. Inside the church, we read the Bible this way. Outside the church we read the newspaper and other books the same way.

Modern exegesis and hermeneutics arose as critical strategies in the face of sloppy and exuberant (allegorical) medieval reading. The typical rationality that characterizes across all modern hermeneutics stigmatized immediate readings as superstition and fideism. For a long time, modern hermeneutics was right to curb through its rationality the unwarranted excess of meaning derived from the Bible. But the Bible can be distorted not only by excess, according to a typical human mechanism of distortion, but also by deficit.

Modern hermeneutics thus sins from what represents its true strength, rationality. The same rationality that corrected the excess of superstition has over time caused the deficit of mystery. Cultural positivism in all its forms expresses, in a not so veiled way, its allergy to mystery. Modern hermeneutics is to all intents and purposes a hermeneutics of the deficit. A disenchanted, reductive hermeneutics.[16] Moreover, this mechanism of "rationality" and "disenchantment" increase proportionally. Max Weber sees it in action not only in hermeneutics but in all modern culture. It has constructed itself as a rational culture. In a directly proportional way, it has become in a disenchanted.

This is what we call "cultural inerrantism." The inerrancy of biblical literalism, religious confessionalism, and theological rationalism, which focus on the clarity and unambiguousness of concepts and events, has simply moved out of the church and out of faith to be situated in culture, in technology, in the most essential registers of contemporary living.

---

15. Aristotle (*Metaphysics* IV, 1005b, 19–20). Cf. Fromm, *Arte di amare*, 71–84.
16. Cf. Introduction to Drewermann, *Psicologia del profondo e esegesi*, 7–19.

VIII

Neutralizing the Paradox by a "Deficit of Text"
Anthropocentric Subjectivism

ALTHOUGH EATING IS A pleasure, it also includes a long list of eating disorders. Likewise, although reading the Bible is a blessing, it also includes a long list of anomalies, deviations, and even real hermeneutical pathologies. In the previous chapter we described some of the most frequent anomalies related to the "text." In this chapter, again following the structure of the hermeneutic circle, we will instead consider some anomalies related to the "reader" pole. While those related to the text tend to be more visible, structural, and direct anomalies, those related to the reader tend to be more invisible, rather functional, and indirect anomalies. Both introduce operational short-circuits and one-sided applications of the categories that ground the hermeneutic circle into the hermeneutic circle. Between "structural" and "functional" anomalies there is the same parallelism, contrast, and conditioning that exists in the field of medicine between "anatomical" and "physiological" anomalies.

The former involves disproportion and asymmetry in structure and architecture, while the latter involves imbalance and one-sidedness in practical operations and strategies in the process of reading and interpretation. It is not "textual positivism" (described in the previous chapter) but rather "textual subjectivism" (described in this chapter) that is the basic, frequent, and characteristic form of the anomalies that have a strong hold today and often end up unbalancing the interpretive process. This is our basic thesis that we have been articulating since the first part. In reality, hermeneutic anomalies, as in the physical organism, always involve all sectors and all components of the system and, as such, are always systemic anomalies. As is also the case in medicine, at some point in the process, pathologies as systemic anomalies always include an anatomical-structural and a physiological-functional component. This fact does not prevent a pathology, although conditioned and related to these two dimensions, from depending on and involving more of one of them. The same thing happens in hermeneutics. When the hermeneutic circle is unbalanced by an excessive weight given to the text, synchronically the other pole, that of the reader, will also be deformed, will suffer a deficit. Conversely, when it is the reader who is given excessive attention, synchronically the text will also be deformed and will suffer a deficit of attention.

As we mentioned in the previous chapter, text-related anomalies are common currency in our time. These depend on an even more central, primary, and basic anomaly: "biblical subjectivism." Our hypothesis is even more paradoxical because it advances the idea that "biblical subjectivism" is actually at the root of biblical fundamentalism (biblical literalism), which instead appears and presents itself as a real anomaly related to the biblical text. Even the most extreme forms in defense of the Bible as a sacred text (biblical inerrancy) are actually produced by a basic "biblical subjectivism" typical of modernity. "Biblical subjectivism," however, is expressed on various levels. Let us briefly consider some of these levels.

At a first level, between "textual (biblical) subjectivism" and "modern individualism," there is a clear relationship of contiguity and belonging. Both bet on the individual as subject. At this first level, textual subjectivism appears as an extension and application of socio-cultural individualism, as a more global and generic phenomenon, characteristic of our time. To the question, "How did 'biblical subjectivism,' in its various forms, come to be so widespread among Christians today?" the answer is straightforward and immediate: "Because 'biblical subjectivism' is the child of modern individualism." It could not be otherwise. The trends and orientations of a historical epoch influence and effect by determining, in the short or long range, all manifestations, all levels and all processes within that culture. Modern individualism could not spare or leave untouched our way of reading and interpreting. Biblical subjectivism is thus a direct and emblematic manifestation of modern individualism, which is one of the most characteristic features of our historical period.

At a second level, the degree and nature of the implication and dependence that exists between "textual subjectivism" and "modern individualism" not only varies but is reversed. From another perspective, we could say that "modern individualism" is actually the child and extension of "textual subjectivism." In other words, "modern individualism" is born as "textual subjectivism." The equation behind this statement is as follows. Faced with strong, stable texts that were the embodiment of group power, including the Bible itself as a sacred book, the first locus of assertion of an autonomous subject was the claim of prerogative to introduce new, unique, innovative meanings into the reading of those traditional texts. This de facto claim automatically relativized the power of those texts and their claims on the individual. At the same time it pointed to a new locus of affirmation of the individual that originated in the realization of free readings and innovative experiments in meaning.

This second-level implication not only highlights the real engine of modern individualism, which is not, at least initially, pragmatic and applicative but ideational and theoretical. It is when the individual is able to think, through new readings, new scenarios and alternative worlds to the existing one, that individualism is truly born. Individualism is not born, then, when one finally arrives at a serious and rigorous application of things that one already knows and that the individual merely concretizes. It is born from the introduction, through a new way of reading and thinking, that has the individual as the undisputed protagonist of new worlds in rupture with the traditional texts of the past.

This revolutionary vision of individualism as a creator of new horizons we see applied to the modern book and texts. Modern texts are the first examples of the force of modern individualism, even though it would seem the opposite. It would seem that texts limit, hinder, and moderate modern man's endless drive for freedom. Our age is the age of books. There have never been so many books for all ages, for every subject and of every nature. These pose a challenge to contemporary man in that they highlight the limitation of his knowledge, the arbitrariness of his choices and the partiality and one-sidedness of the information he possesses. This is partially true because books represent this challenge to man. On the other hand, though, these very books, which highlight the limits of modern man, are at the same time a production of modern man. Conceived in this way, they did not exist before. The status and social role that we contemporaries attribute to books is not the same status and role that premodern cultures attribute to them. As mentioned in the previous chapter, the modern book is a different kind of book, all produced by the dynamism of the modern individual. Even the ancient books that we read today, because they are for us classics that we respect and accept as cultural reference points, including the Bible, we read them as if they were modern books, fluid and partial in their meaning that we individuals are called upon to complete. They do not in the least represent absolute mandates, much less complete mandates of what needs to be done today. Premodern books were highly prescriptive and connected to a fixed and stable reality. The books we moderns create and the classical books we read are books best conceived as suggestions scattered within a highly experimental and deliberative individual reading process, where the emphasis is on choice, not on the application of various possible meanings. This is modern individualism on the hermeneutic side.

This implicitly new understanding and definition of ancient processes and categories occurs not only for the book, but also, for example, for science. Modern scientific knowledge, which purports to be objective, is actually anthropocentric. It is this subjectivist, anthropocentric orientation, hidden and sublimated at the root of the environmental crisis, which is an anthropocentric anomaly from beginning to end. The same thing can be said of modern totalitarianisms. We would like to think that they are the reminiscences of past, premodern and primitive eras which we would minimally consider related to an age of freedom such as ours. Actually, they are typical modern phenomena that did not and could not exist in the Middle Ages. Similarly, biblical positivism, even in its most extreme forms, such as biblical inerrancy, which we would think of as reminiscences of past, obscurantist eras, is actually a typical modern phenomenon related to and giving birth to a subjectivist and individualist age like ours.

This textual subjectivism, which characterizes our age, at first involves the Protestants, because they are the ones who have made *sola Scriptura* their cardinal principle but still making it pass through the filter of the conscience of the individual believer. Actually, in *sola scriptura* Protestantism, despite appearances, it is not the text (the Bible) that predominates but the individual who reads that text, because the alternative is not between Bible and individual. In this case Bible and individual are at the same level. The alternative is between church and individual. The Bible will actually be found in both cases, on the side of the church if I choose the church, as in the Middle Ages but also on the side of the individual, if I choose the believer, as in the case of Protestantism. Protestantism is not in the first instance a religion of the book. It is only secondarily so. Protestantism is primarily a religion of the individual. Biblical subjectivism is not a late drift in Protestantism. It is present from the beginning in its basic structure.

In a second moment, textual subjectivism involves all of Christianity, because Christianity has tied religious experience to a text read and metabolized by the believer. Faith comes through the continuous and diligent reading and study of that book. The believer is responsible for understanding and applying that meaning. Modern Christianity has only radicalized this tendency. It has emphasized the reliability of that text more than in the past. It has also made its reading one that is more related to the awareness, freedom, and self-determination of the subject.

In a third level, the West has invested heavily in the subjectivity of the individual and his autonomy and self-determination. This strongly anthropocentric project has radicalized the role of the subject even more.[1] Textual subjectivism is not just a hermeneutical trait or just the expression of a widespread tendency in present-day Christianity. It represents the direction of our entire historical period. Historical periods are never monolithic. Like other historical periods in the past, ours manifests a diverse and contrasting set of phenomena that compose and determine it. But textual subjectivism is undoubtedly a hallmark of the historical period in which we live and of which biblical subjectivism is an extension.

Finally, we come to a final introductory consideration regarding hermeneutic anomalies in general, which applies particularly to modern individualism. There is a tendency to regard anomalies as deviations that take over later and, more importantly, to regard them as the result of misapplication of the virtuous criteria of the system. More often than not, this does not hold up to thoughtful analysis. Often the deviations are present from the beginning and are latent in the system's virtuous categories themselves because of their one-sidedness. The same unilateralism of vision prompts one to consider the onset of the anomalies as the product of misapplication of the categories that ground the system. This causes the anomalies to worsen as, in order to solve them, the same categories that caused them are more convincingly applied. This is what happens with individualism. Extreme subjectivism, self-referentiality, narcissism,

---

1. Taylor, *Disaggio della modernità*, 5–21.

or anthropocentrism do not take over later, at a later time, but are from the beginning present in the modern project. They are so not tangentially but structurally, because they arise from the same virtues that found modern individualism. The analytical gaze cannot stop at considering only the anomalies. It must also consider, describe, and know best the virtues and the very structure of modern individualism.

A THEOLOGICAL-CULTURAL LOOK AT INDIVIDUALIST HERMENEUTICS[2]

Interpretive reductionism, which we have also called "textual positivism" and which widely involves all of Christianity and all of contemporary culture, creates, at some point, its own alternative. This alternative is identified and built around the subject. Textual positivism, in its natural evolution, pushes, almost naturally, toward "textual subjectivism" as a kind of obligatory alternative. These are those typical ping-pong movements of history where it proceeds by provocation and counter-reaction. An excessive emphasis on the text is naturally followed by a radical claim to the relevance of the subject-reader. We shall see that, in reality, the relationship between these two phenomena is more complex and that

---

2. Hermeneutic individualism (hermeneutic subjectivism), which is the phenomenon that claims to reduce the complexity of (written) texts to the narrow and preferential registers of individual subjectivity, is certainly not only a linguistic or literary phenomenon. See Taylor, *Disagio della modernità*, 65–81; *Sources of the Self*, 285–302. More underlying it is a cultural phenomenon that Louis Dumont describes as the ideology of modernity. He writes, "(Individualism) . . . moves from individuals, as is natural for moderns, and only later sees them brought together in society; sometimes it even gives rise to society from the interaction between individuals" (*Saggi sull'individualismo*, 14). However, this social and not just hermeneutical individualism is not negative. On the contrary, it is the basis of modern efficientism, part of its DNA and conscious project. Referring to the *Oratio de hominis dignitate*, a passage by Pico della Mirandola, the starting point of modern individualism, Cavicchia Scalamonti writes, "This oration seems to be a manifesto in which it is clearly established that man's dignity is no longer to be found in the place he had been assigned in the pre-established cosmic order, but, as the oration demonstrates, in his ability to self-define himself autonomously," (*Morte*, 10). If this had not brought undoubted benefit, modernity, greedy for results, would not have chosen and maintained it at all. But what modernity had not calculated for are the adverse side effects of this social and hermeneutic individualism, which occur not only in the isolation and uprooting of the subject, but also in its implosion and in the manipulation of everything external to it: the world, reality and, consequently, texts as well. Cf. Taylor, *Disagio della modernità*, 3–16; Finkielkraut, *Noi, i moderni*, 251–59; Pulcini, *Cura del mondo*, 31–112.

textual subjectivism not only follows but precedes and grounds textual positivism in a kind of hermeneutical somersault.

For the time being, however, let us try to describe the importance for biblical hermeneutics of contemporary (modern and postmodern) individualism and how this conditions it. Textual subjectivism and modern individualism appear as two different and parallel processes. Looking more closely, they are closely related. On the one hand, textual subjectivism is but an extension and application of modern individualism to the reading of texts. On the other hand, social individualism arises from the claim to create new meanings that arise only in the subject. Modern individualism from the beginning is hermeneutic and cognitive.

There is much more proximity, coincidence, and interdependence between these two phenomena than one might see at first glance. Actually, they are essentially the same thing. It could not be otherwise. A cultural tendency, as in this case individualism, hardly spares areas of a culture. It tends to be cross-cultural and widespread. There is much more solidarity than one might believe among the diverse spaces of a culture in a given historical period. The characteristic social individualism of our times could not spare hermeneutics.

Our reading hypothesis (already in chapter two, in the brief historical review on hermeneutics), was clear and specific in its basic direction. The tendency of contemporary hermeneutics, we said, is not the centrality of the "text" but the centrality of the "reader." Contemporary hermeneutics is "reader-centric." Here, the "reader-centeredness" typical of today's hermeneutics is simply the extension of social individualism into the interpretive area. This tendency is not so much hidden in the founding manifesto of hermeneutics made by Schleiermacher. His motto was that philosophical hermeneutics aims at understanding "the understanding," that is, the reader in his understanding. The understanding takes place not in the text but in the reader's head.

Antonio C. Scalamonti[3] further specifies the solidarity between individualism and modern knowledge, Reversing the terms, he says that individualism is first and foremost a theory of knowledge, the claim that knowledge is guaranteed by the individual who innovates and not by the group that preserves it. Social individualism was only possible because of this cognitive and interpretive individualism. The relationship in favor of the group, consolidated for millennia through a knowledge that from the

---

3. Cavicchia Scalamonti, *Morte*, 39–47.

group imposed itself as destiny on the individual, who had to limit himself only to repeating and passing on is now overthrown only in favor of the individual. This occurs when the individual claims for himself and asserts his ability to create new knowledge (readings), solely from himself. It is when the individual is recognized as having the ability to introduce new knowledge that individualism is truly born. The relationship between social individualism and interpretive individualism is much closer than what it might appear at first glance.

Let us pause to briefly consider individualism as a mass cultural phenomenon, as, for example, Charles Taylor describes it. Taylor thinks that individualism is the defining characteristic of the contemporary world.[4] For centuries and centuries man lived with a self that he calls a "porous" self, but recently the self has become a "shielded" self (buffered self). Until about five hundred years ago, man felt confronted with external events having mysterious dimensions beyond him: natural disasters, good or bad spirits, miraculous formulas and potions, various miracles, vital fluids and relics. A colorful "enchanted" easily and unhindered penetrated that "porous" self, which, being nurtured from the outside, identified with it. Between self and external world there was absolute continuity; they were one and the same. The natural world represented the self well, just as the self was also perfectly describable in natural terms. Meaning filtered from the world outside to us automatically. Everything changed with the arrival of modernity, helped in this by Christianity in its Latin-Western version and, above all, Protestantism, as Weber suggests. What counts now is inwardness, personal faith, living prayer hidden in the intimate, in the heart. Soon after, with the Enlightenment the same rejection takes on a new face: the world, which had been obvious to porous man for centuries, is condemned as a false world. The external world, described by the pre-modernists, is the enchanted and illusory production of a world that is not there and is forged by a still immature

---

4. Taylor writes, "The buffered, disciplined self, seeking intimacy (although discipline and intimacy can be in tension), also sees him/herself more and more as an individual. We saw this clearly reflected in the understanding of society implicit in what we called the Modern Moral Order. The social orders we live in are not grounded cosmically, prior to us, there as it was, waiting for us to take up our allotted place; rather society is made by individuals, or at least for individuals, and their place in it should reflect the reasons why they joined in the first place, or why God appointed this form of common existence for them. These reasons in the end come down to the good of human beings, not qua fillers of this or that role, but just simpliciter, a human good which is that of all of them equally, even if they don't achieve it in equal measure" (Taylor, *Secular Age*, 540).

interiority. Such a diagnosis marks the victory of the new well-shielded self, that is, by a self that is critical and distrustful of all exteriority. Thus individualism is born. It carries with it the idea, obvious to us, of history as development or progress. Western man perceives himself as superior to that of other ages and cultures. He declares himself autonomous and finally free from the ancient fears that bound him to nature. One of the great differences between us and our precursors is that we live with a much firmer perception of the boundary separating the self from the rest (i.e., the non-self). We are *shielded* selves. The perception of ourselves and the world has totally changed.

According to Taylor, the individualism that is born with the shielded self has a positive but also problematic trait. He thinks that the unease that marks our period is connected with individualism because this social attitude has become a moral task in what he calls the birth of the ethics of authenticity.[5] Individualism has become not only a fact but a moral task. The social fabric is gradually crumbling because of the erosion, at its base, of the very matrix that guarantees the survival of every individual. This is the strength of the bond. We will try to see how this individualist tendency has also taken the path of contemporary hermeneutics.

Suddenly, however, a paradox appears, for not one but two would be trends in contemporary hermeneutics. On the one hand, there is cognitive reductionism, visible in "biblical-hermeneutical positivism." On the other hand, there is social individualism, with its extension in "biblical interpretive subjectivism." Which of the two is more important? Is it the more decisive or the more visible? It is both. We have a concomitance of cultural dysfunction. How are we to understand this polarization of two opposing but mutually sustaining phenomena? How are we to grasp the hidden complicity between objectifying reductionism and relativizing subjectivism, which characterize our age and our hermeneutics? Let us follow philosopher Giacomo Marramao's description of this.

He holds that the present time[6] is characterized by two sociocultural trends. One of these is techno-economic-consumerist homogenization, which destroys differences and particularities; the other is, especially in more recent times, the defense and proliferation of differences. It is the flight from universalism. It is the feeling of strongly belonging to communities that promise to safeguard a strong and particular identity.

---

5. Taylor, *Disagio della modernità*, 31–36.
6. Marramao, *Passione del presente*, 56–86.

Universalist homologation and identity differentiation, in other words universalism and particularism, according to Marramao, are not two alternatives. They are the two sides of the same coin. At the center we find the paradoxical short circuit of both the global and the local (glocal), of both globalization processes and localization processes, coexisting together. The more technology tends to standardize ways of living in some respects, the more cultural differences seem to deepen. This is at least the demand for differential treatment, the rediscovery of small homelands, small communities.

The idea of the historical becoming the image of a scientific reason, of a rationality, which gradually and progressively extends to all spheres of life, parallels the emergence of thrusts to the claim of one's own cultural specificity, thrusts even going in the direction of the demand for a cultural autochthony. The return of community, is produced not only through the rebellion of cultures other than Western culture. It is also generated within the where it results in a denunciation of Western democratic institutions which have become cold institutions. These are reduced to being purely technical-procedural institutions. They are incapable of motivating individuals, social groups, social aggregates. They are cold, insensitive institutions which are indifferent to communal warmth. The most conspicuous aspect of this critique turns out to be that of the claim for a democracy. It begins to decline away from important needs. These are the demands for forms of life and forms of association which in some way claim the rights of the warm current against the cold current of democratic procedure.

Democracy in the postmodern era, with its obsession with formal procedures and rules, appears unable to account for and respond to its members' need for symbolic identification. According to the critique of communitarians, for example, the element of belonging cannot be entirely resolved in the logic of citizenship. Individuals cannot find symbolic identification simply in the fact that they are citizens, equal before the law, having, along with other fundamental rights, the right to vote. They must somehow also be regarded as socially and culturally specific subjects, subjects who live a real life and for whom it is necessary to feel part of a cultural community.

With Marramao, we realize that opposing cultural dysfunctions, which may coexist on the surface at the base, are instead similar. They keep alive, albeit in different ways, the same underlying mechanism. Similarly, textual positivism, described in the previous chapter, and "biblical subjectivism" that we will describe in this chapter, on the surface appear to be opposites. Further investigation reveals that at their base they are similar. They feed off each other and represent two sides of the same coin. Our reading hypothesis is to bring together these two phenomena, the cultural and the hermeneutical. The description of a cultural polarization (see Marramao), which characterizes our time, is not only an example of how this is possible. That description has a hermeneutic significance. This is because the opposition between textual positivism and textual subjectivism is an extension of that cultural polarization into the sphere of reading texts. We think that the hermeneutic biblical objectivist positivism is actually the religious transcription of the ethical-cultural identity tendency. It seeks to compensate for the objectifying homogenization of our time with the defense of closed and ideological communities. On the other hand, biblical interpretive subjectivism is the religious transcription of the technical-efficient, consumerist, and homogenizing tendency of rampant and unlimited individualism, as described by Marramao.

BIBLICAL SUBJECTIVISM: PSYCHOLOGICAL ANTHROPOCENTRISM[7]

Understood in a philosophical sense, subjectivism is the characteristic of a doctrine that denies the existence of criteria of truth and value independent of the thinking subject. A corollary of this assumption is the extreme and radical denial of what is real and objective. In this sense, subjectivism is a relativist view. In ancient philosophy, which aimed at the search for an objective foundation of knowing, subjectivism was a rare phenomenon. It is found, for example, in the thought of the Sophists. It is also in Protagoras, who elaborates a philosophy based on the useful, where man becomes "the measure of all things." There are for him no criteria other than human sensations to distinguish the true from the false. But subjectivism, not only as a philosophical current but also as a widespread anthropological attitude, took over only with modernity.

---

7. Christopher Lasch gives a pertinent reading of psychological anthropocentrism, calling it "narcissism," and moves it from a purely personal dimension to a cultural tendency. Cf. Lasch, *Culture of Narcissism*, 71–103. Still on narcissism, but from the point of view of an individual, at a later stage, who is more vulnerable because he is over-exposed and over-stressed, Alain Ehrenberg has made some very pertinent observations from a psychosocial perspective. Ehrenberg, *Weariness of the Self*, 15–19.

Modern philosophy takes its cue from Augustine's affirmation of the value of interiority as the starting point for understanding God and the world, which in him still remained in an initial and non-pervasive state. Later on, beginning with Descartes, an increasingly positive value to human subjectivity emerged. It resulted in Leibniz and Berkeley attributing the entire macrocosmic reality to thinking consciousness. Kantian criticism, with its "Copernican revolution," gave the transcendental activity of the subject itself a central role. This paved the way for subjectivism and its affirmation of self-consciousness as the absolute principle of reality. Depending on the areas, one can further distinguish ethical, aesthetic or religious subjectivism, in which the sole norm of the right, the beautiful or the religiously true is attributed to the individual.

In biblical subjectivism the same shift occurs. The reader becomes the determining element in the creation of meaning. The connection to the text does not lapse because Christian hermeneutics would hardly go as far as total denial of the text. But the consideration and reading of the text is completely conditioned by the situation, goals, and motivations of the reader. Since this is not moral but textual subjectivism, there is no lack of reference to the text. One always returns to the text. It is quoted; it is consulted. One talks about it; one comments on it. One praises the text and glorifies it. The text is always the center of attention. Yet it is not the text itself that one has in mind. One projects in the text one's own image, one's own situation, one's own experience. The text does not exist as otherness. It does not possess its own consistency. The text must limit itself to reflecting the reader's issues. If it contradicts it, or if it simply does not talk about it, the text does not count; it does not exist. The text, in textual subjectivism, must be a pure reflection of the reader. This is what we call "psychological dogmatism." It is the decisive and peremptory character of the subjective component in Bible interpretation. A double weakness emerges here. It is that of the text, which in this view is justified only by the reader. It is also that of the reader, because in order to claim the value and relevance of his agenda, he must resort to the authoritativeness of the text.

In biblical subjectivism what really creates the problem is not the presence in itself of personal motives, even in their most extreme subjective form. A biblical reading must be able to make room for these kinds of elements as well because these are part of the life we want to illuminate from the gospel. The problem arises when these subjective elements become the filter that conditions the whole substance of the Bible and imprisons its meaning, no longer allowing the perception of its broader horizon. Subjective motives are not only legitimate; they are also necessary and powerful for the articulation of meaning. But here, in biblical subjectivism, they have taken over everything else.

The legitimate pre-comprehension that the reader carries within, and cannot do without, becomes prejudice and imposition on the text. The text no longer intervenes as an element of confrontation, much less provocation. There is no longer any surprise, except solely the obsession with noting and verifying that the text reflects the reader's agenda. Pre-understanding has disappeared and has become prejudice and manipulation of the text. The reader, like Narcissus, in the water of the pond, sees only his own reflection. The text has been reduced to a mirror, embodying no otherness and carrying no message. Textual subjectivism, by ignoring the text, neutralizes it and finally kills it. By killing the text, however, it also neutralizes the reader, for it condemns the reader to feed on a lifeless object with no real and alternative meanings. Neutralizing the text becomes depowering to the reader himself.

BIBLICAL CONFESSIONALISM: ECCLESIOLOGICAL ANTHROPOCENTRISM[8]

On a more political and social level, confessionalism is that system in which members of a certain religion are advantaged over others. On the more religious and internal level, confessionalism represents that intent to unify the faith and make it compact. It embodies the peremptory intent to reduce the "sense of faith" to the "sense of one's own faith." It proceeds by privileging the compactness and homogeneity of religious experience. Confessionalism is an intent to domesticate faith. Confessing one's faith and convictions is a natural and even necessary exercise in the economy

---

8. In biblical confessionalism we find hidden an individualism expanded to community and elevated to a primary criterion. Apparently the emphasis on community breaks down and criticizes individualism; it criticizes it at a first level and defends it at a subsequent level. And it defends it in two ways: first, because with communitarianism, individualism does not disappear but is maintained through its radicalization and opposition to the group. Second, because communitarianism, like the individualism to which it is opposed, stops the reality of what matters only at the reference identity, which in this case is the group and no longer the individual. Communitarianism appears to many as group individualism. Both are and remain heavily anthropocentric realities and claims. Cf. Etzioni, *Spirit of Community*, 163–206. See also Sandel, *Justice*, 244–69; MacIntyre, *Whose Justice? Which Rationality?*, 349–69.

of religious experience. In the confession of one's faith we are faced with a testimony of faith. In religious confessionalism, this testimony becomes a peremptory affirmation that is intended to be universal, valid for all, from a form that is instead particular and relative. In confessionalism the true confrontation with any external reality is skipped. This is what drives faith communities to modulate the profile and substance of their statements in a more inclusive sense.

There is a hermeneutical version of confessionalism. We could even say that every religious confessionalism is initially a hermeneutic confessionalism where the positively pluriform sense of the Bible is reduced to the univocal compact sense of one's own group. That every religious group and community needs to interpret the meaning of the Bible from and with a view to reinforcing its own faith profile is not legitimate. It is also inevitable. The problem does not lie here. The problem arises when the meaning of the Bible is imprisoned in the profile of one's own confession of faith, when one too candidly identifies one's understanding of Scripture with Scripture itself.

In biblical confessionalism the same shift occurs. The reading community becomes the determinant of meaning-making. The connection to the text does not lapse; Christian communities cannot openly deviate from the text of Scripture. But the consideration and reading of the text is completely conditioned by the situation, motivations, and goals of the reading community. Since this is a Christian community, reference to the text is not lacking—one always returns to the text; one quotes it; one consults it. It is talked about; it is commented on. One praises the text and even glorifies it. The text is always the center of attention. Yet it is not the text itself that one has in mind. Rather one projects in the text the image, the situation, the experience of one's community. The text does not exist as otherness, does not possess its own consistency. It must reflect only the issues of the community. If it contradicts them or if it simply does not talk about them, the text does not count, it does not exist. The text, in biblical confessionalism, must be a pure reflection of the community. This is what we call "ecclesiological dogmatism." It is the decisive and peremptory nature of the community component in the interpretation of the Bible.

In biblical confessionalism, we are faced with a collective biblical subjectivism in which the objective sense of the Bible is lost. Furthermore, it does not give the diversity within the group its due. This, we have seen, reduces the possibilities for qualitative growth of the group itself. Reading the text is nothing more than reading itself by validating its own certainties and anomalies. Biblical confessionalism creates an undue symbiosis between group and Bible. It also creates this undue symbiosis within the group, between member and member. Biblical confessionalism takes away any possible alternative within the group itself. The voices have been reduced to one. A mutual re-solidification is articulated between a text and the group that no longer says anything new. It is reflection of the group. This is a group that, reading that kind of text, no longer creates alternatives within it.

In hermeneutical confessionalism, there appears to be an objectivity of faith. Yet, by virtue of being a purely internal objectivity, it is nothing but group subjectivism. This objectivity of faith is too narrow. The true objectivity, the broad and universal one, transcends each individual group. The call, then, for an objectivity of faith based on the Bible, which claims to be the steadfast truth on which the group is founded, is a false objectivity because it is too narrow. That purported objectivity is actually subjectivism in disguise. A group reality speciously elevated to the status of objective universalism. Biblical confessionalism, in its various versions, is a sophisticated version of modern subjectivism.

BIBLICAL PRAGMATISM: EXPERIENTIAL ANTHROPOCENTRISM[9]

Pragmatism is a philosophical current that emerged as a reaction to the intellectualism of the nineteenth century. In the face of the failure of reason to solve metaphysical problems, it made practice the criterion of verification. Pragmatism developed between the late nineteenth century and the first two decades of the twentieth century, particularly in the American and Anglo-Saxon cultural area. In a more cultural and anthropological sense, pragmatism, understood as attention, care, and obsession with the practicality of life, is an accompanying and distinctive

---

9. Pragmatism has various faces and manifestations. However, it represents the trend of an era and not just a school of thought. As such it still presents itself today in sublimated and refined guises. The typical efficiencyism of our contemporary societies is an example of this. The triumph of technology is another. Cf. Galimberti, *Psiche e techne*, 293–304. In the victory of pragmatism as an anti-humanist phenomenon, Günther Anders sees not a moment, but a constant in modern culture. Anders, *L'uomo è antiquato*, 55–120, 84–90. On pragmatism and its hold on all contemporary societies, which Byung-Chul Han calls the "performance society" (*Achievement Society*), the Korean-German author pauses to consider mainly the nefarious effects in what he calls pragmatism in the period of late modernity. Cf. Han, *Società della stanchezza*, 5–6.

feature of modernity and postmodernity. According to this pragmatism, which is more anthropological, what matters in what we do and how we live is the efficiency and result achieved. Everything must be able to give and guarantee results. If the results are not there we are faced with something unnecessary and useless that can easily be eliminated or skipped without compromising the health and survival of the system.

This view of the world and life, in different proportions and forms, is the most widespread cultural form today. The extent of its imprint, even on churches, is visible in the typical "managerialization" and "technification" of life. It includes not only the more objective and quantitative aspects, but also the more subjective, qualitative, and intimate dimensions of human living.

The prototype of this anthropological orientation is given, according to Hannah Arendt, by the obscuring of the different forms of human activity that in the past it was possible to distinguish. She mentions three of them: labor, work, action. If in the past, for example in the Greek world, action (activity) in any of its forms was preferred to contemplation, nevertheless there remained an awareness that the noblest activity was "action." "Work" represented the least noble activity because it was too closely tied to need and necessity. The free man, on the other hand, was capable of "action" among his peers and left the strenuous work to the slaves in the *oikos* (home). In the modern world this differentiation tends to obscure and everything becomes work. From being a despised activity, work becomes the only worthy activity. This, according to Arendt, marks the birth of the anthropological pragmatism of the moderns. One of the prophets of this pragmatic revolution was Karl Marx. He elevated the model of *Homo faber* to an anthropological model. The basis and justification of modern pragmatism is the prototype of *Homo faber*.

The social and public dimension of this pragmatic shift is provided by the emergence of the economy as the central dimension of modern politics. For the Greeks, Arendt continues, this would have been a contradiction in terms. What is political belongs to the dimension of free and creative action; economics, on the other hand, is the domain of the necessary, of the *oikos* (home), of work, not action. Pragmatism is not a school of thought, and neither is the practical orientation of a part of the population. It represents the matrix of thought and action of the entire modern world. Pragmatism is a disenchanted, mechanical—though very functional expression—of modern subjectivism.

Pragmatism, involving an entire era, did not spare biblical hermeneutics. It has taken hold as reading pragmatism. It probably represents the most widespread form of hermeneutical anomaly. Not the speculative subjectivism of the liberals nor the aesthetic subjectivism of the charismatics, but the concrete subjectivism of the pragmatists today threatens to obscure more the nature and scope of the Bible by reducing it to an application strategy.

Biblical pragmatism discharges as unnecessary and superflous all those interpretive passages that ground and articulate meaning in its various nuances. This is especially because they are guilty of dilating the time of meanings. The pragmatic reader has no time; he is in a hurry. According to his thought pattern, it must be so, on pain of unnecessarily burdening the sense. Sense must be light, functional, and immediate. Consequently, the slowness of true sense, that which characterizes its establishment and manifestation, appears to the pragmatist as a waste of time. All sense must be applicable. It must serve only to construct and elaborate on a sense that can be applied. Everything else has no justification. The typical exuberance of sense, given by plurivocity, is a dead and useless burden. If we have, in our interpretation, accompanying meanings that we do not use, then what good are they? Better not to have them. The pragmatist's is a thrifty, essential war economy interpretation. The pragmatist thinks he knows the only sense that matters. He dispenses with the other possible senses. He destroys them if they already exist. He does not create them because they waste resources on meanings that would remain unused. They dissipate the energy that is needed to promote the only valid sense.

In biblical pragmatism the same shift occurs. It is the practice that becomes the determining element in the creation of meaning. The connection with the text does not lapse because Christian communities cannot openly depart from the text of Scripture. But the consideration and reading of the text are completely conditioned by the concreteness and practicality of the situation. Since it is a Christian community, reference to the text is not lacking. One always returns to the text. It is quoted; it is consulted. It is talked about, commented on. One praises the text and even glorifies it. The text is always the center of attention. In reality it is not the text itself that one has in mind.

The benefit, the result, the effect expected by the pragmatic reader is projected into the text. The text does not exist as otherness. It does not possess its own consistency. The text must limit itself to offering the concrete results that the reader expects. If the text does not accomplish this, then it does not count; it does not exist. The text, in biblical pragmatism, must be a pure guarantor of results. This is what we call "experiential dogmatism," because of the decisive and peremptory character of the pragmatic component in Bible interpretation.

This pragmatic view fails to grasp the characteristic of biblical language. Going further, it proposes a model of biblical language that is actually opposed to it. This model is a child of modernity. There is nothing biblical about it. It, too, is not perverse in itself as long as one does not elevate it to an ideology above criticism. Above all, as long as one does not identify it with biblical language. In modern interpretive pragmatism, the typical technical univocity is transferred to the reading of the biblical text. In divine transcendent language, or divine language embodied in human language, for pragmatism the important thing is its univocity and compactness. Very differently, what characterizes biblical language is its unavailability of meaning, its mystery, its polyvalence.[10]

Hermeneutic pragmatism is a fast track that distrusts mediations. It distrusts them because they slow down any interpretive process. This is not the most problematic element of hermeneutic pragmatism. The bigger problem is the clearance of univocity that leads to an obsession with accuracy and clarity in the Bible. Hermeneutic pragmatism dismantles biblical complexity and its language. It cages biblical plurisense in a clear, monolithic, and immediate sense.

MODERN RATIONALISM: CULTURAL ANTHROPOCENTRISM[11]

Anthropocentrism is the tendency to regard the human being, and everything about him, as central to the universe. Originating very early,

---

10. Rizzi, *Pensare dentro la Bibbia*, 28–37.

11. That social subjectivism, together with interpretive subjectivism, are dependents of a structural anthropocentric tendency of all contemporary culture is a fact that can hardly be disavowed today. And the word-category that best expresses the drift of this modern subjectivism and individualism even in its non-human effects, on nature and the cosmos, is the word "anthropocene." Cf. Crutzen, *Benvenuti nell'antropocene*. On the genesis and a broader description of the anthropocene also at the cultural and political level, Pellegrino and Di Paolo have proposed a recent work; see Pellegrino and Di Paola, *Nell'antropocene*. On the more immediate problems of the Anthropocene and the constraint they impose on today's politics, Bruno Latour has devoted important pages. Cf. Latour, *Sfida di Gaia*, 73–116.

it is clearly visible as early as the Renaissance in a marked way. From a medieval theocentric view, where man's destiny and positioning was predetermined by God, the group and the cosmos, we move to a view where man is the determining factor of his own destiny. This implies that the precondition for being able to affirm himself lies in the autonomy and detachment he claims vis-à-vis God and all that is transcendent. Man becomes the ultimate goal and, at the same time, the starting point for considering, looking at, describing, evaluating and determining everything else. It is here that the defense of human exceptionalism is born and articulated. All other species and entities that make up the cosmos are lesser realities because they do not possess the rationality, awareness, elective will, and determination to guide human and historical processes to their fulfillment.

This radical bet on man conceals two reductions. The first is an anthropological reduction: man becomes detached from the cosmos that until then had been the guarantor of his survival. The second is an individualist reduction: it is no longer the group, which until then had been the extension and prolonger of the stability of the cosmos, that determines man's place and role in the world. It is the individual, alone, through his freedom and self-determination.

From being an elitist vision, anthropocentrism will become fully democratic and expand across all strata of contemporary societies. The various crises that have occurred in recent years—environmental, demographic, and multicultural crises—have given rise to a strong contestation of the validity of this humanist claim. Post-humanism or transhumanism embodies these contestations and claims some success. But looking at the data, results, and orientations, it can be said that anthropocentrism has not disappeared. It has even been reinforced. It has changed in some of its traits, replacing, for example, its initial optimism with a cynical pessimism, which continues in the scene to determine the main rhythm and direction of our age.

The problem of anthropocentrism does not lie in the consideration of human beings as part of the ecosystem that we must consider. This is legitimate, necessary, and inevitable. The problem is that thinking of life from our own gaze has become the only possible gaze which we have imposed on all other species. Anthropocentrism has triggered in chains other reductivisms such as Eurocentrism, speciesism, and machismo, which still heavily condition our globalized reality. It is what we call "cultural dogmatism," because of the decisive and peremptory character of the anthropic component in the formation and articulation of today's culture, which then has a strong spillover effect on the way we interpret the Bible.

All these distortions have taken hold in biblical hermeneutics. We find readings today that are, unbeknownst to them, specist, masculinist, Eurocentric Bible readings. Today most Christians continue to read the Bible in these terms. Today's Bible readings tend to be almost exclusively anthropocentric readings. The paradox is that intentions to correct, balance, or refresh Bible readings, several times, resort to new anthropocentric motives. The result is the reinforcement of biblical anthropocentrism through its updating. The effect of renewal is short-lived and deceptive, because the attrition that was merely delayed by the apparent novelty soon resurfaces. More importantly, is not perceived as the product of that anthropocentrism, so they try to curb it with what actually produced it.

CONCLUSION
Reasonable Doubt: Learning How to Prolong the Power of Questions

THUS, DOUBT, IN A hermeneutics of paradox, is not a deformation or an anomaly that creeps in and takes hold at a late stage of the interpretive process. It is present from the very beginning and is the driving element that triggers and guarantees that whole process. It is therefore not a derivative element because it does not arise from the reader's uncertainties and hesitations but from the text itself, from its plurivocity and irreducible complexity.[1] In this sense we could differentiate it from the kind of doubt that is instead related to the individual and that arises in the natural process of elaboration of meanings that the reader tries to articulate. This doubt is a subjective doubt. The doubt we refer to instead as a "foundational doubt" is a more structural doubt and has an objective character, in that it does not depend on the reader, but precedes the reader because it is articulated in the very structure of the text the reader reads. This foundational, pre-subjective doubt, we call "textual doubt" because it is inscribed in the very structure of plurivocal texts.

Multifaceted texts, which guarantee this structural doubt, certainly require interpretation on the part of the reader, not only to grant the interpreter a clarity and specificity prompted by his or her own context and personal experience but especially to bring out those hidden and latent meanings in the text itself. Only a shrewd reading is able to make manifest the greatness of a text and thus to honor those latent meanings that without that reading would remain truncated and incomplete. But the legitimate and necessary interpretation that each reader is prompted to make by the text itself nevertheless has a constraint that consists in

1. Alter, *Art of Biblical Narrative*; *Art of Biblical Poetry*.

maintaining the plurality to which the text has become a witness. To the semantic plurality of the text, the interpreter will therefore add the plurality of interpretations. When this does not happen, then what we have called "hermeneutic positivism" occurs, which is the reduction of interpretations to a monolithic and compact interpretation that is often intended to be definitive. Here doubt has disappeared at the interpretive stage because it has actually already disappeared at the textual level.

The primary task, then, of a sound and correct interpretation is to guard, preserve, and prolong this doubt through the maintenance of the plurality of meanings that coexist together both in the text and in the interpretations that are worked out of that text. The plurality does not disappear with the interpretations, but is reinforced. This doubt thus becomes the telltale of a healthy interpretive process.

For this reason, any interpretation must be provisional and partial. Wanting to make an interpretation valid by making it final and complete is nonsense, as this ambition leads not only to detachment from the multifaceted reference text (Bible), which is considered confusing and opaque, but mainly because it stops the interpretive process through the conversion of something provisional into something definitive.

Thus, doubt is an ally in the interpretive experience, not a threat. Doubt must be able to coexist with truth. A truth without doubt easily becomes an idolatrous truth because it wants to pass off one part of the truth as the whole truth. What opposes truth is not so much falsehood but partial truths that have become overbearing and bulimic of meaning. The false is not to be sought far from the true but in its nearest and most intimate backyard, precisely because the latter is always nourished by absolutized partial truths. For this reason, doubt, thus conceived, is not only reasonable but is itself part of truth. Truth is only in the search for truth, and the engine of that search is reasonable doubt.

Trying to inscribe this reasonable doubt related to interpretation in a broader cultural perspective, we could say that today human experience, and therefore consequently also religious experience, is torn apart by two strong and opposing stresses. On the one hand by the fragmentation and analytical rationality that underlies it and that today has become transversely corrosive in all spheres of human living and on the other hand by the identity temptation of an absolute security that feels the need to build and ground life and existence on absolutely certain bases. The one refers back to the other. The one is provoked by the other. Thus a polarization is created where one pole fights but at the same time supports and perpetuates the opposite pole.

Ernst-Wolfgang Böckenförde described the global direction of our time well in the phrase "the secularized liberal state lives *on* assumptions it cannot guarantee,"[2] thus calling for a recovery of religion as a basis from which to start. But the reclaiming of religion is still complicated because it could solve some problems and create others at the same time. For this reason, Jürgen Habermas reintroduces as a necessary element, for the survival of Europe, a certain kind of religion, which precisely he calls "a reasonable religion." A state, like a culture and like a society, cannot survive solely on the basis of organizational policy assumptions or purely economic and social management criteria.

With this kind of argument Habermas introduced a post-secular vision of European societies, which points to the value of the "reasonable"[3] and its validity not only for religion but also for ethics and politics. A viable ethics today is not that of the all-out relativism prevalent today, but neither is the ethics built on true and absolute values that try to replace it. Habermas's third way defends not absolute rationality but the reasonableness of "ought to be." The same third way applies it to politics, which in him will take the form of a "deliberative politics" and discursive politics that arises not from secular absolutes but from the reasonable dialogue among various political options. And again in the same way, the social structure must be built on the "reasonable" and not on the social "ideal."

It is in this context that the singular and extraordinary dialogue between the philosopher Jürgen Habermas and Cardinal Joseph Ratzinger fits. These two significant intellectual figures—not only in Germany but internationally as well—engaged in dialogue at the beginning of this twenty-first century, an event organized by the Katholische Akademie in Munich on January 19, 2004. The dialogue was an event in itself because of the meeting and discussion between two such singular personalities who are so influential in the intellectual world of secularists and believers, but it takes on even greater significance when one carefully analyzes the contents of the two talks. Amidst the secularist temptation that brands all forms of religious culture as irrational regression and the fundamentalist temptation that wants to authoritatively impose the truths

---

2. Böckenförde, *Formation of the State*, 13–21.

3. In this regard, consult especially the third chapter of his text on a new political theory entitled "Reasonable versus True. The Morality of Worldviews," in Habermas, *Inclusion of the Other*, 88–115.

of a single religious faith, Habermas and Ratzinger open up the prospect of a postsecular society[4] in which secularists and believers discover dialogue not only as a tool for necessary compromise but as a method for self-discovery.

The Habermasian third way, built on the value of "reasonable," as overcoming relativism and fundamentalism, not only sobers religion or the state but more importantly makes them "inclusive." In both fundamentalism and relativism, the typical exclusionary absolutism is configured and survives intact, though reversed. In fact, a deliberative politics of the "reasonable" has as its first characteristic that of inclusiveness. And in many ways inclusiveness precedes reasonableness because in the face of societies and churches that have become structurally heterogeneous, multicultural, pluralistic, the sin not to be committed is that of worshiping the true and the absolute. The need to recognize those lives, those ideas, which do not resemble our own but have the same right to life and recognition, automatically leads us to decline the true as truthful and the rational as reasonable. The bond of human and religious respect for the other forces us to a change of register. This is theological wisdom and human wisdom.

From a militant call that makes the truth compact automatically follows the exclusion of others. The paradox is that this exclusion of the other occurs through a sincere but myopic call to truth. As in Jesus, truth, which structurally is inclusive, halves and flexes precisely because the center of its essence is not doctrinal propositions but others, concrete persons.

"Reasonable doubt," as an essential component of any interpretive process which we have tried to describe in this text, is thus not a race to the bottom and the watering down of the spiritual meanings derived from a text such as the biblical one but is, on the contrary, the defense of their relevance and foundational force. The plurality, inherent in the text and in the readings of that text, is simply a guarantee against the overbearingness of partial meanings that want to absolutize themselves.

The constraint of plurality only brings out the dialogical, flexible, and inclusive nature of truth. If truth is not inclusive, what kind of truth would it be? If truth is therefore inclusive because it is plural, then not only doubt but also truth is reasonable. Our secularized and minimalist

---

4. Ratzinger and Habermas, *Ethics, Religion and the Liberal State.*

historical time[5] has paradoxically helped us more than religions themselves to understand the true nature of truth. This is thus formed not only of certainties but also of doubts. In this sense there is an unconscious convergence between religion and contemporary society.

Doubt, then, comes not from the subject nor from his or her eventual desire to flee from the truth but from the truth itself. From how, for example, this is configured in the biblical text. When one abandons certain ideas built on the Bible or on the rational and sovereign individual, then one discovers a common fabric that binds, even in differences, faith and life, religion and the world. And this common element is reasonable doubt.

It is therefore the Bible itself that generates legitimate doubts, not about the wrong readings but about the good readings one makes of the Bible. It is above all the good readings, the successful readings, that must be constantly monitored because it is precisely by virtue of their initial success that they feel tempted to become definitive (first error) but above all because they want to substitute themselves for the Bible (second error).

Therefore, good interpretations of the Bible are not true but verisimilar, that is, reasonable. Interpretations of the Bible are legitimate, good, necessary but certainly not sacred, so they have a transitory and provisional character and therefore need to generate new interpretations all the time to avoid their fossilization.

The biblical hermeneutics of paradox does not aim at the answer but at the extension and enrichment of the question. Biblical hermeneutics is not and cannot be a synthetic and resolving instance of meaning. It is not a hermeneutics of clarity but of complexity. Indeed, of dynamic complexity, that is, of paradox.[6] The meaning sought thus always remains an elusive meaning, both in the text from which one starts (Bible), in the account taken of its structural ambivalence, and in the interpretation to which the reader arrives because that legitimate and necessary interpretation nevertheless remains partial and transitory, capable of touching the meaning only tangentially and provisionally.

---

5. Cf. "A Disturbing Hypothesis," in MacIntyre, *After Virtue*, 29–33.
6. Galimberti, *Footsteps of the Sacred*, 35–61. See also Galimberti, *Body*, 11–27.

Bibliography

Adorno, Theodore, and Max Horkheimer. *Dialectic of Enlightenment*. New York: Verso, 2016.
Alter, Robert. *The Art of Biblical Narrative*. London: George Allen & Unwin, 1981.
———. *The Art of Biblical Poetry*. Edinburgh: T&T Clark, 2000.
Anders, Günther. *L'uomo è antiquato: Considerazioni sull'anima dell'epoca della seconda rivoluzione industrial* [*Man is Outdated: Considerations on the Soul of the Age of the Second Industrial Revolution*]. Vol. 1. Turin: Bollati Boringhieri, 2003.
Aquinas, Thomas. *Somma contro i gentili: Libro primo e secondo* [*Summa Against the Gentiles: Book One and Two*]. Bologna: Edizioni Studio Domenicano, 2000.
Audi, Robert. *Epistemologia: Un'introduzione alla teoria della conoscenza* [*Epistemology: An Introduction to the Theory of Knowledge*]. Macerata: Quodlibet, 2016.
Auerbach, Erich. *Mimesis: Il realismo nella letteratura occidentale* [*Mimesis: The Representation of Reality in Western Literature*]. Turin: Einaudi, 2000.
Augé, Marc. *Genio del paganesimo* [*Genius of Paganism*]. Turin: Bollati Boringhieri, 2002.
Augustine. *Confessions*. London: Penguin, 1997.
Barker, Chris, and Emma A. Jane. *Cultural Studies: Theory and Practice*. London: Sage, 2016.
Barr, J. *Old and New in Interpretation: A Study of the Two Testaments*. London: SMC, 1966.
———. *The Semantics of Biblical Language*. London: Xpress, 1983.
Barth, Karl. *Anselm: Fides Quaerens Intellectum: Anselm's Proof of the Existence of God in the Context of His Theological Scheme*. Pittsburgh: Pickwick, 2004.
———. *Der Römerbrief*. Zürich: Theologischer Verlag, 1922.
———. *Protestant Theology in the Nineteenth Century: Its Background and History*. Grand Rapids: Eerdmans, 2001.
Benjamin, Walter. *L'opera d'arte nell'epoca della sua riproducibilità tecnica* [*The Work of Art in the Age of its Technical Reproducibility*]. Turin: Einaudi, 2014.
Benveniste, Émile. *Problemi di linguistica generale*. Milan: Il Saggiatore, 2010.
Berkhof, Louis. *The History of Christian Doctrines*. Grand Rapids: Baker, 1992.
Bettelheim, Bruno. *Un genitore quasi Perfetto* [*A Good Enough Parent: A Book on Child-Rearing*]. Milan: Feltrinelli, 2013.

Bettini, Maurizio. *Elogio del politeismo: Quello che possiamo imparare dalle religioni antiche* [*In Praise of Polytheism: What We Can Learn from Ancient Religions*]. Bologna: Il Mulino, 2014.

Bhabha, Homi K. *The Location of Culture*. London: Routledge, 2007.

Bloesch, D. G. *Holy Scripture: Revelation, Inspiration, and Interpretation*. Christian Foundations. Downers Grove, IL: IVP Academic, 1994.

Bock, Darrell L. *Luke, Vol. 1: 1:1—9:50*. Baker Exegetical Commentary on the New Testament. Grand Rapids: Baker Academic, 1994.

———. *Luke, Vol. 2: 9:51—24:53*. Baker Exegetical Commentary on the New Testament. Ada, MI: Baker Academic, 2010.

Böckenförde, Ernst-Wolfgang. *The Formation of the State as a Process of Secularization*. Brescia: Morcelliana 2005.

Bonhoeffer, Dietrich. *Pregare i salmi con Cristo: Il libro di preghiera della Bibbia* [*Praying the Psalms with Christ: The Prayer Book of the Bible*]. Brescia: Queriniana, 2019.

———. *Widerstand und Ergebung: Briefe und Aufzeichnungen aus der Heraft*. München: Kaiser Verlag, 1990.

Bonomi, Andrea, ed. *La struttura del linguaggio* [*The Structure of Language*]. Milan: Bompiani, 1973.

Brueggemann, Walter, and William H. Bellinger, Jr. *Psalms*. New Cambridge Bible Commentary. New York: Cambridge University Press, 2014.

Bultmann, Rudolf. *Foi et Compréhension: Eschatologie et démythologisation, Vol. 2*. Paris : Seuil, 1969.

Bordoni, Carlo. *Società digitali: Mutamento culturale e nuovi media* [*Digital Societies: Cultural Change and New Media*]. Naples: Liguori Editori, 2007.

Calvin, John. *Commentary on the Psalms*. Carlisle, PA: Banner of Truth Trust, 2009.

Campbell, M. W. *1919: The Untold Story of Adventism's Struggle with Fundamentalism*. Nampa, ID: Pacific, 2019.

Cassirer, Ernst. *The Individual and the Cosmos in the Renaissance Philosophy*. New York: Angelico, 1963.

Cavicchia Scalamonti, Antonio. *La morte: Quattro variazioni sul tema* [*Death: Four Variations on the Theme*]. Santa Maria Capua Vetere: Hypermedium, 2007.

Cerasi, Enrico. *Dire quasi la verità: Per una filosofia del linguaggio religioso* [*Saying Almost the Truth: For a Philosophy of Religious Language*]. Rome: Città Nuova Editrice, 2014.

———. *Il mito del cristianesimo: Per una fondazione metaforica della teologia* [*The Myth of Christianity: For a Metaphorical Foundation of Theology*]. Rome: Città Nuova Editrice, 2011.

Cevolanti, Gustavo, et al. "Dalla filosofia alla scienza, e ritorno: L'analisi della conoscenza tra epistemologia e scienze cognitive [From Philosophy to Science and Back: The Analysis of Knowledge between Epistemology and Cognitive Science]." In *Teorie della conoscenza* [*Theories of Knowledge*], edited by Jean-Michel Besnier, 5–14. Soveria-Mannelli: Rubbettino, 2013.

Chakrabarty, Dipesh. *Provincializing Europe: Postcolonial Thought and Historical Difference*. Princeton: Princeton University Press, 2000.

Chakravorty Spivak. Gayatri. *A Critique of Postcolonial Reason: Toward a History of the Vanishing Present*. Cambridge, MA: Harvard University Press, 2003.

Charles, Sébastien. *L'hypermoderne expliqué aux enfants* [*Hypermodernity Explained to Children*]. Montreal: Liber, 2017.

Childs, Brevard S. *Biblical Theology of the Old and New Testaments: Theological Reflections on the Christian Bible*. London: Xpress, 1996.

Cole, Ross, and Paul Petersen, eds. *Hermeneutics, Intertextuality and the Contemporary Meaning of Scripture*. Cooranbong: Avondale Academic, 2014.

Craddock, Fred B. *Luca* [*Luke*]. Turin: Claudiana, 2002.

Croce, Benedetto. *La storia come pensiero e come azione* [*History as Thought and Action*]. Napoli: Bibliopolis, 2002.

Crocombe, Jeff. *Hermeneutics, Intertextuality and the Contemporary Meaning of Scripture*. Adelaide: Avondale Academic, 2014.

Crutzen, Paul. *Benvenuti nell'antropocene: L'uomo ha cambiato il clima: La terra entra in una nuova era* [*Welcome to the Anthropocene: Man Has Changed the Climate: The Earth Enters a New Era*]. Milan: Mondadori, 2005.

Cullmann, Oscar. *Il nuovo testament* [*The New Testament*]. Bologna: Il Mulino, 1968.

———. *Le salut dans l'histoire: L'existence chrétienne selon le Nouveau Testament* [*Salvation in History: Christian Existence after the New Testament*]. Neuchatel: Delachaux et Niestlé, 1966.

De Certeau, Michel. *L'écriture de l'histoire* [*Writing History*]. Paris: Gallimard, 1995.

Dederen, Raoul, ed. *Handbook of Seventh-Day Adventist Theology*. Hagerstown, MD: Review & Herald, 2000.

Della Stella, Isacco. *Sermoni* [*Sermons*]. Vol. 2. Milan: Edizioni Paoline, 2007.

De Lubac, Henri. *Exégèse médiévale: Les quatre sens de l'Ecriture* [*Medieval Exegesis: The Four Meanings of Scripture*]. Paris: Aubier, 1959.

Derrida, Jacques. *Della grammatologia* [*Of Grammatology*]. Milan: Jaca Book, 1968.

De Saussure, Ferdinand. *Corso di linguistica generale* [*Course of Linguistics*]. Rome: Laterza, 2009.

Descartes, René. *Meditazioni metafisiche* [*Metaphysical Meditations*]. Rome: Laterza, 1997.

De Sousa Santos, B. *Epistemologies of the South: Justice Against Epistemicide*. Boulder: Paradigm, 2014.

Dilthey, Wilhelm. *Die Entstehung der Hermeneutik*. Berlin: 1900.

Di Sante, Carmine. *Dentro la Bibbia: La teologia alternativa di Armido Rizzi* [*Inside the Bible: The Alternative Theology of Armido Rizzi*]. Verona: Gabrielli Editori, 2018.

Drewermann, Eugen. "La verità delle forme" ["The Truth of Forms"]. In *Psicologia del profondo e esegesi: La verità delle forme: Sogno, mito, fiaba, saga e leggenda 1* [*Depth Psychology and Exegesis: The Truth of Forms: Dream, Myth, Fairy Tale, Saga and Legend 1*]. Brescia: Queriniana, 1996.

———. *Wozu Religion? Sinnfindung in Zeiten der Gier nach Macht und Geld: Im Gesprach mit Juergen Hoeren* [*What Use is Religion? Finding Meaning in a Time of Greed for Power and Money: In Conversation with Juergen Hoeren*]. Freiburg: Herder, 2012.

———. *Heilende Religion: Uberwindung der Angst* [*Religion That Heals: Overcoming Anxiety*]. Freiburg: Herder, 2013.

Dumont, Louis. *Saggi sull'individualismo: Una prospettiva antropologica sull'ideologia moderna* [*Essays on Individualism: An Anthropological Perspective on Modern Ideology*]. Milan: Adelphi, 1983.

Eco, Umberto. *Lector in fabula* [*The Reader in the Plot*]. Milan: Bompiani, 2006.

Ehrenberg, Alain. *The Weariness of the Self: Diagnosing the History of Depression in the Contemporary Age*. Montreal: McGill-Queen's University Press, 2016.

Erickson, Millard J. *Christian Theology*. Grand Rapids: Baker Academic, 2013.

Etzioni, Amitai. *The Spirit of Community. The Reinvention of American Society.* New York: Touchstone, 1993.

Fabris, Rinaldo. *Luca [Luke].* Assisi: Cittadella, 2003.

Ferraris, Maurizio. *L'ermeneutica [Hermeneutics].* Rome: Laterza, 1998.

———. *Storia dell'ermeneutica [History of Hermeneutics].* Milan: Bompiani, 1997.

Finkielkraut, Alain. *Noi, i moderni [We, the Moderns].* Turin: Lindau, 2006.

Forte, Bruno. "Sacred Scripture and Theology." *Adventus* 22 (2012) 30–42.

Fosnot, Catherine T. *Constructivism: Theory, Perspectives and Practice.* New York: Teachers College Press, 2005.

Fromm, Erich. *L'arte di amare [The Art of Loving].* Milan: Mondadori, 1996.

Fry, Paul H. *Theory of Literature.* New Haven: Yale University Press, 2012.

Funk, Robert W. *Language, Hermeneutic and Word of God.* New York: Harper & Row, 1966.

Gadamer, Hans-Georg. *Truth and Method.* London: Continuum, 2004.

Galimberti, Umberto. *The Body.* Milan: Feltrinelli, 2002.

———. *Cristianesimo: La religione del cielo vuoto [Christianity: The Religion of the Empty Sky].* Milan: Feltrinelli, 2012.

———. *The Decline of the West [Il tramonto dell'Occidente].* Milan: Feltrinelli, 2006.

———. *Footsteps of the Sacred: Christianity and the Desacralization of the Sacred.* Milan: Feltrinelli, 2000.

———. *Psiche e techne: L'uomo nell'età della tecnica [Psyche and Techne: Man in the Age of Technology].* Milan: Feltrinelli, 2004.

Galli, Carlo. *Contingenza e necessità nella ragione politica moderna [Contingency and Necessity in Modern Political Reason].* Rome: Laterza, 2009.

Gauchet, Marcel. *Il disincanto del mondo [The Disenchantment of the World].* Turin: Einaudi, 1992.

Geffré, Claude. *Credere e interpretare: La svolta ermeneutica della teologia. [Believing and Interpreting: The Hermeneutical Turn in Theology].* Brescia: Queriniana, 2002.

Gettier, Edmund. "Is Justified True Belief Knowledge?" *Analysis* 23.6 (1963) 121–23.

Gisel, Pierre. *Verité et Histoire: La théologie dans la modernité.* Paris: Beauchesne, 1985.

Gonzalez, Justo L. *Christian Thought Revisited: Three Types of Theology.* Nashville: Abingdon, 1990.

Gourevitch, Aron J. *La naissance de l'individu dans l'Europe médiévale.* Paris: Seuil, 1997.

Grondin, Jean. *Introduction to Philosophical Hermeneutics.* New Haven: Yale University Press, 1994.

Habermas, Jürgen. *The Inclusion of the Other: Studies in Political Theory.* Milan: Feltrinelli, 2008.

Jürgen Habermas, et al. *An Awareness of What Is Missing: Faith and Reason in a Post-Secular Age.* Translated by Ciaran Cronin. Malden, MA: Polity, 2010.

Han, Byung-Chul. *L'espulsione dell'altro: Società, percezione e comunicazione oggi [The Expulsion of the Other: Society, Perception and Communication Today].* Milan: Nottetempo, 2017.

———. *Società della stanchezza [Society of Weariness].* Rome: Nottetempo, 2012.

Hasel, Frank M. *Biblical Hermeneutics: An Adventist Approach, Vol. 3.* Silver Spring, MD: Biblical Research Institute, 2021.

———., and Michael G. Hasel. *How to Interpret Scripture.* Oakland: Pacific, 2020.

Heidegger, Martin. *Basic Writings*. Edited by David Farrell Krell. San Francisco: Harper, 1992.
Heussi, Karl. *Kompendium der Kirchengeschichte* [*History of the Church Compendium*]. Tübingen: Mohr, 1988.
Hillman, James. *Re-visione della psicologia*. [*Re-visioning of Psychology*]. Milan: Adelphi, 2008.
Hjelmslev, Louis. *Essais linguistiques* [no info in fns].
Hobbes, Thomas. *De Cive: Elementi filosofici sul Cittadino* [*De Cive: Philosophical Elements on the Citizen*]. Rome: Editori Riuniti, 2014.
———. *Leviatano* [*Leviathan*]. Milan: Rizzoli, 2013.
Janowski, Bernd. *Konfliktgespräche mit Gott: Eine anthropologie der psalmen* [*Conflict Dialogues with God: An Anthropology of Psalms*]. Neukircher-Vluyn: Neukirchener Verlag, 2003.
Jeanrond, Werner G. *L'ermeneutica teologica: Sviluppo e significato* [*Theological Hermeneutics: Development and Meaning*]. Brescia: Queriniana 1994.
Jenkins, Phillip. *The New Faces of Christianity: Believing the Bible in the Global South*. Oxford: Oxford University Press, 2006.
———. *The Next Christendom. The Coming of the Global Christianity*. Oxford: Oxford University Press, 2002.
Jennings, Willie James. *The Christian Imagination. Theology and the Origins of Race*. New Haven: Yale University Press, 2011.
Jensen, Alexander S. *Theological Hermeneutics*. London: SCM, 2007.
Jeremias, Joachim. *Gesù e il suo annuncio* [*Jesus and His Proclamation*]. Brescia: Paideia, 1993.
———. *The Parables of Jesus*. New York: SCM, 1963.
———. *Teologia del Nuovo Testamento: La predicazione di Gesù, Vol. 1* [*New Testament Theology: The Preaching of Jesus, Vol. 1*]. Brescia: Paideia, 2000.
Jung, Carl G. *Psychologische Typen* [*Psychological Types*]. Dusseldorf: Walter-Verlag, 1995.
Kant, Immanuel. *Prolegomeni ad ogni futura metafisica che potrà presentarsi come scienza* [*Prolegomena to Any Future Metaphysics That Would Be Able to Present Itself as a Science*]. Rome: Laterza, 1996.
Kärkkäinen, Veli-Matti. *Christian Theology in a Pluralistic World: A Global Introduction*. Grand Rapids: Eerdmans, 2019.
Keil, C. F., and Franz Delitzsch. *Ezra, Nehemiah, Esther, Job*. Peabody, MA: Hendrickson, 1989.
Kierkegaard, Søren. *Timore e tremore* [*Fear and Trembling*]. Milan: Mondadori, 2016.
Kraus, H. J. *L'Antico Testamento nella ricerca storico-critica dalla Riforma a oggi* [*The Old Testament in Historical-Critical Research from the Reformation to the Present*]. Bologna: Il Mulino, 1975.
Kuhn, Thomas. *The Structure of Scientific Revolutions*. Chicago: University of Chicago Press, 1996.
Kümmel, Werner G. *Il nuovo testamento: Storia dell'indagine scientifica sul problema neotestamentario* [*The New Testament: History of the Scholarly Investigation of the New Testament Problem*]. Bologna: Il Mulino, 1976.
Kundera, Milan. *L'arte del romanzo* [*The Art of the Novel*]. Milan: Adelphi, 1988.
Lakoff, George, and Mark Johnson. *Metaphors We Live By*. Chicago: Chicago University Press, 1981.

Lane, Tony. *A Concise History of Christian Thought*. Grand Rapids: Baker, 2006.
Lasch, Christopher. *The Culture of Narcissism: American Life in an Age of Diminishing Expectations*. New York: Warner Books, 1979.
Latour, Bruno. *La sfida di Gaia: Il nuovo regime climatico* [*The Gaia Challenge: The New Climate Regime*]. Milan: Meltemi, 2020.
Le Goff, Jacques. *La civilisation de l'occident medieval*. Paris: Flammarion, 2008.
———. *Le Dieu du moyen Âge. Entretiens avec Jean-Luc Pouthier*. Paris: Bayard, 2003.
———. *Pour un autre Moyen Âge. Temps, travail et culture en Occident*. Paris: Gallimard, 1977.
Levinas, Emmanuel. *L'au-delà du verset: Lectures et discours talmudiques* [*Beyond the Verse: Talmudic Readings and Speeches*]. Paris: Minuit, 1982.
Lewis, Jeff. *Cultural Studies: The Basics*. London: Sage, 2008.
Lindbeck, George A. *The Nature of Doctrine: Religion and Theology in a Postliberal Age*. Philadelphia: Westminster, 1984.
Luther, Martin. *Reading the Psalms with Luther*. St. Louis: Concordia, 2007.
MacIntyre, Alasdair. *After Virtue: An Essay on Moral Theory*. Rome: Armando Editore, 2007.
———. *Whose Justice? Which Rationality?* Notre Dame, IN: Notre Dame University Press, 1988.
Magno, Gregorio. "Scriptura crescet cum legente." In *Commento morale a Giobbe*, 86–87. [*Moral Commentary on Job*]. Rome: Città Nuova, 1998.
Marguerat, Daniel, and Yvan Bourquin. *Per leggere i racconti biblici* [*To Read Bible Stories*]. Rome: Borla, 2011.
Marramao, Giacomo. *La passione del presente: Breve lessico della modernità-mondo* [*The Passion of the Present: A Brief Lexicon of Modernity-World*]. Turin: Bollati Boringhieri, 2008.
Massarenti, Armando. *Il filosofo tascabile: Dai presocratici a Wittgenstein: 44 ritratti per una storia del pensiero in miniature* [*The Pocket Philosopher: From the Presocratics to Wittgenstein: 44 Portraits for a History of Thought in Miniature*]. Parma: Ugo Guanda Editore, 2010.
McLuhan, Marshall. *La galassia Gütenberg: La nascita dell'uomo tipografico*. Rome: Armando Editori, 2011.
———. *The Gutenberg Galaxy. The Making of Typographic Man*. New York: Signet Books, 1969.
———. *Understanding Media: The Extensions of Man*. New York: Signet, 1964.
McWilliams, Nancy. *Psychoanalytic Diagnosis: Understanding Personality Structure in the Clinical Process*. New York: Guilford, 2019.
Metzger, Bruce M. *Il canone del Nuovo Testamento: Origine, sviluppo e significato* [*The New Testament Canon: Origin, Development and Meaning*]. Brescia: Paideia, 1997.
———. *Il testo del Nuovo Testamento* [*The Text of the New Testament*]. Brescia: Paideia, 1996.
Mura, G. *Ermeneutica e verità: Storia e problemi della filosofia dell'interpretazione* [*Hermeneutics and Truth: History and Problems of the Philosophy of Interpretation*]. Rome: Città Nuova Editrice, 1990.
Nitti, Silvana. *Lutero* [*Luther*]. Rome: Salerno Editrice, 2017.
Nolland, John. *Luke 1–9:20*. Word Biblical Commentary. Dallas: Word Books, 1989.
O'Brien, Daniel. *Theory of Knowledge*. Cambridge: Polity Press, 2017.

Ong, Walter J. *Orality and Literacy: The Technologizing of the Word*. London: Routledge, 2012.
Otto, Rudolf. *Il sacro* [*The Sacred*]. Milan: Se, 2014.
Palmer, Richard E. *Hermeneutics: Interpretation Theory in Schleiermacher, Dilthey, Heidegger and Gadamer*. Evanston, IL: Northwestern University Press, 1969.
Pannenberg, Wolfhart. *Storia e problemi della teologia evangelica contemporanea in Germania: Da Schleiermacher fino a Barth e Tillich* [*History and Problems of Contemporary Evangelical Theology in Germany. From Schleiermacher Until Barth and Tillich*]. Brescia: Queriniana, 2000.
Pascal, Blaise. *Pensieri* [*Thoughts*]. Milan: Rizzoli, 1999.
Pelikan, Jaroslav. Christian Tradition, Vol. 1: The Emergence of the Catholic Tradition. Chicago: The University of Chicago Press, 1971.
Pellegrino, Gianfranco, and Marcello Di Paola. *Nell'antropocene: Etica e politica alla fine di un mondo* [*In the Antropocene: Ethics and Politics at the End of a World*]. Rome: Habitus, 2018.
Piazza, T. *Che cos'è la conoscenza* [*What is Knowledge*]. Rome: Carocci, 2019.
Plato. *The Republic*. London: Penguin Classics, 2007.
———. *Symposium*. Milan: Adelphi, 1979.
Prosperi, Adriano. *Lutero: Gli anni della fede e della libertà* [*Luther: The Years of Faith and Freedom*]. Milan: Mondadori, 2017.
Pulcini, Elena. *La cura del mondo: Paura e responsabilità nell'età globale* [*Caring for the World: Fear and Responsibility in the Global Age*]. Turin: Bollati Boringhieri, 2009.
Ratzinger, Joseph, and Jürgen Habermas. *Ethics, Religion and the Liberal State*. Brescia: Morcelliana, 2005.
Ravasi, Gianfranco. *Il libro dei Salmi: Commento e attualizzazione* [*The Book of Psalms: Commentary and Actualization*]. Vol. 1. Bologna: Edizioni Dehoniane, 1999.
Reid, George W., ed. *Understanding Scripture: An Adventist Approach*. Vol. 1. Hagerstown, MD: Review and Herald, 2006.
Rengstorf, K. H. *Il Vangelo secondo Luca* [*The Gospel according to Luke*]. Brescia: Paideia, 1980.
Ricœur, Paul. *Il conflitto delle interpretazioni* [*The Conflict of Interpretations*]. Milan: Jaca Book, 1995.
———. "The Act of Interpretation." *Esprit* 27.7–8 (1959) 48–59.
———. *Finitude et culpabilité: Philosophie de la volonté, Vol. 2* [*Finiteness and Guilt: Philosophy of the Will*]. Paris: Aubier, 1988.
———. *Hermeneutics and the Human Sciences*. Cambridge: Cambridge University Press, 2016.
———. "The Hermeneutical Function of Distanciation." In *From Text to Action: Essays in Hermeneutics, II*, 72–85. London: Continuum, 1991.
———. *Interpretation Theory: Discourse and the Surplus of Meaning*. Dallas: Texas Christian University Press, 1977.
———. *Philosophical Hermeneutics and Biblical Hermeneutics*. Brescia: Queriniana, 1983.
———. *Le volontaire et l'involontaire: Philosophie de la volontè, Vol. 1* [*The Voluntary and the Involuntary: Philosophy of the Will*]. Paris: Aubier, 1988.
Rieff, Phillip. *The Triumph of the Therapeutic: Uses of Faith After Freud*. Wilmington: ISI, 2006.
Rizzi, Armido. *Pensare dentro la Bibbia* [*Thinking within the Bible*]. Rome: LAS, 2010.

Robbins, Richard H. *Cultural Anthropology: A Problem-Based Approach*. Belmont, CA: Wadsworth, 2013.
Sandel, Michael J. *Justice: What's the Right Thing to Do?* New York: Farrar, Straus and Giroux, 2009.
Schleiermacher, Friedrich. *On Religion: Speeches to its Cultured Despisers*. Cambridge: Cambridge University Press, 1996.
Schökel, Luis Alonso, and Cecilia Carniti. *Salmos, Vol. 1*. Navarre: Verbo Divino, 1992.
———., and J. M. Bravo Aragon. *Appunti di ermeneutica: Comprendere e interpretare i testi biblici e letterari* [*Notes on Hermeneutics: Understanding and Interpreting Biblical and Literary Texts*]. Bologna: EDB, 2014.
Schürmann, Heinz. *Il Vangelo di Luca, Vol. 1: 1–9:50* [*The Gospel of Luke, Vol. 1: 1–9:50*]. Brescia: Paideia, 1983.
Sciolla, Loredana. *Sociologia dei processi culturali* [*Sociology of Cultural Processes*]. Bologna: Il Mulino, 2007.
Tannehill, Robert C. *Luke*. Abingdon New Testament Commentaries. Nashville: Abingdon, 1996.
Tasso, Torquato. *La Gerusalemme Liberata*. Milan: Mondadori, 1993.
Taylor, Charles. *Il disaggio della modernità* [*The Malaise of Modernity*]. Rome: Laterza, 2003.
———. *A Secular Age*. Cambridge, MA: Harvard University Press, 2007.
———. *Sources of the Self*. Cambridge, MA: Harvard University Press, 1989.
Throntveit, Mark A. *Esdra e Neemia* [*Ezra and Nehemiah*]. Turin: Claudiana, 2011.
Tillich, Paul. *The Courage to Be*. Glasgow: Collins, 1979.
———. *A History of Christian Thought: From Its Judaic and Hellenistic Origins to Existentialism*. New York: Touchstone, 1972.
Toulmin, Stephen. *Cosmopolis: The Hidden Agenda of Modernity*. Chicago: University of Chicago Press, 1990.
Trias, Eugenio. *Pensar la religión*. Barcelona: Galaxia Gutenberg, 2015.
Ullmann, Walter. *Individuo e società nel medioevo* [*Individual and Society in the Middle Ages*]. Rome: Laterza, 1974.
Vassallo, Nicla. *Teoria della conoscenza* [*Theory of Knowledge*]. Rome: Laterza, 2015.
Vattimo, Gianni. *Essere e dintorni* [*Being and Surroundings*]. Milan: La Nave di Teseo, 2018.
Ward, Graham. *Barth, Derrida and the Language of Theology*. Cambridge: Cambridge University Press, 1998.
Weber, Max. *La scienza come professione* [*Science as a Profession*]. Turin: Einaudi, 2004.
Wittgenstein, Ludwig. *Ricerche filosofiche* [*Philosophical Investigations*]. Turin: Einaudi, 2021.
———. *Tractatus Logico-Philosophicus* [*Tractatus Logico-Philosophicus*]. Milan: Feltrinelli, 2022.
Zimmermann, Jens. *Hermeneutics: A Very Short Introduction*. Oxford: Oxford University Press, 2015.
Žižek, Slavoj. *Il cuore perverso del cristianesimo* [*The Perverse Heart of Christianity*]. Rome: Meltemi, 2006.
Zoja, Luigi. *Contro Ismene: Considerazioni sulla violenza* [*Against Ismene: Considerations on Violence*]. Turin: Bollati Boringhieri, 2009.

Author Index

Adorno, Theodor, 179
Aeschylus, 116
Alter, Robert, 118, 216
Anders, Günther, 210
Aquinas, Thomas, 89
Aragon, Bravo J., 10, 93, 97, 99, 111, 112
Arendt, Hannah, 211
Aristotle, 68, 116, 125, 126, 195
Audi, Robert, 4
Auerbach, Erich, 114, 115
Augé, Marc, 152
Augustine, 34, 207

Barker, Chris, 87
Barr, James, 13, 115
Barth, Karl, 42, 43, 145, 191
Barthes, Roland, 50
Beck, Ulrich, 49
Bellinger, Jr, William H., 165
Benjamin, Walter, 66
Benveniste, Émile, 76, 138
Berkhof, Louis, 32, 33
Besnier, Jean-Michel
Bettelheim, Bruno, 184, 185
Bettini, Maurizio, 56
Bhabha, Homi K., 193
Bloesch, Donald G., 106
Bock, Darrell L., 30, 74, 95, 99
Böckenförde, Ernst W., 218
Bonhoeffer, Dietrich xv, 162
Bordoni, Carlo, 65

Bourquin, Yvan, 61, 83, 112
Brueggemann, Walter, 165
Bultmann, Rudolf, 108, 109

Calvin, John, 158
Campbell, Michael W., 58, 188
Carniti, Cecilia, 157, 158, 160, 162, 164, 165
Cassirer, Ernst, 23
Cavicchia, Scalamonti Antonio, 23, 66, 67, 88, 201, 202
Cerasi, Enrico, 122, 143
Cevolani, Gustavo, 4
Chakrabarty, Dipesh, 193
Chakravorty, Spivak Gayatri, 193
Charles, Sebastien, 49, 50
Child, Brevard S., 115, 120
Cole, Reece, 58
Craddock, Fred B., 30
Croce, Benedetto, 23
Crocombe, Jeff, 188
Crutzen, Paul J., 213
Cullmann, Oscar, 109, 116

Davidson, Richard M., 188
de Certeau, Michel, 23
de Lubac, Henri, 34
de Saussure, Ferdinand, 76, 87, 137
de Souza Santos, Boaventura, 193
Dederen, Raoul, 188
Delitzsch, Franz, 28
Della, Mirandola Pico, 201

Derrida, Jaques, 127, 145
Descartes, René, 23, 24, 89, 207
Di Paola, Marcello, 213
di Sante, Carmine, 109, 119, 131
Dilthey, Wilhelm, 41, 43, 44
Dornisch, Loretta, 112
Drewermann, Eugen, 143, 144, 195
Dumont, Louis, 201

Eco, Umberto, 50, 51, 85, 89
Ehrenberg, Alain, 206
Erickson, Millard J., 106, 186
Erasmus of Rotterdam, 35, 39
Etzioni, Amitai, 208

Fabris Rinaldo, 72, 93
Ferraris Maurizio, 9, 26, 43, 45, 46, 65
Finkielkraut Alain, 201
Fish Stanley, 50
Forte Bruno, xv
Fosnot Catherine T., 88
Frege Gottlob, 75
Freud Sigmund, 177
Fromm Erich, 106, 125, 195
Fry Paul H., 50, 62
Funk Robert W., 112

Gadamer, Hans G. xvii, 41, 44, 46, 47
Galimberti, Umberto xviii, xxii, 142, 143, 146, 150, 151, 168, 179, 210, 220
Galli, Carlo, 68
Gauchet, Marcel, 66
Geffré, Claude, 3, 4, 11, 14, 18, 19, 51, 52
Gettier, Edmund, 4
Giddens, Anthony, 49
Gisel, Pierre, 125
Gonzalez, Justo L., 32, 33
Gourevitch, Aron J., 23
Grondin, Jean, 3, 43, 45, 46

Habermas, Jürgen, 218, 219
Han, Byung-Chul, 182, 210
Hasel, Frank M., 188, 189
Hasel, Michael G., 188, 189
Heidegger, Martin, 41, 44, 45, 46, 47, 179

Herrmann, Wilhelm, 191
Heussi, Karl, 32, 39
Hillman, James, 143, 181
Hjelmslev, Louis T., 76, 137
Hobbes, Thomas, 68, 69
Holland, Norman, 50
Homer, 114
Horkheimer, Max, 179

Iser, Wolfgang Jürgen, 50

Jane, Emma A., 87
Janowski, Bern, 163, 164
Jauss, Hans-R., 50
Jeanrond, Werner G., 7, 12, 14, 21, 35, 39, 42, 61, 63, 83, 85, 98, 101, 108, 111
Jenkins, Philip, 58, 59.
Jensen, Alexander S., 16, 20, 38, 39, 40, 41, 45, 46, 50
Jeremias, Joachim, 118
Johnson, Mark, 127
Jung, Carl Gustav, 105

Kant, Immanuel, 89, 90, 207
Kärkkäinen, Veli-Matti, 51
Keil, Carl F., 28
Kierkegaard, Søren, 42, 150
Kraus, Hans J., 40
Kuemmel, Werner G., 40
Kuhn, Thomas, 58
Kundera, Milan, 112

Lakoff, George, 127
Lane, Tony, 32, 33, 38, 39
Lasch, Christopher, 206
Latour, Bruno, 213
Le Goff, Jacques, 22, 36
Lessing, Gottohold E., 40
Levinas, Emmanuel, 29
Lewis, Jeff, 87
Lindbeck, George A., 127, 143, 147, 148
Lonergan, Bernard, 148
Luther, Martin, 39, 157

MacIntyre, Alasdair, 208, 220
Magno, Gregorio, 132
Marguerat, Daniel, 61, 83, 112

AUTHOR INDEX

Marramao, Giacomo, 193, 204, 205, 206
Massarenti, Armando, 149
McLuhan, Marshall, 66, 117
McWilliams, Nancy, 177
Melanchton, Philip, 39
Metzger, Bruce M., 67, 120
Milbank, John, 145
Mura, Gaspare, 122

Nicholas of Lyra, 34
Nitti, Silvana, 38
Nolland, John xvi, 72, 93

O'Brien, Dan, 4
Ong, Walter J., 2, 22, 65, 87, 88
Origen, 32, 33
Otto, Rudolf, 150

Palmer, Richard E., 37, 41, 43, 45, 46
Pannenberg, Wolfhart, 191
Pascal, Blaise, 4, 5
Pellegrino, Gianfranco, 213
Petersen, Peter, 58
Philo, 32
Piazza, Tommaso, 4
Pickstock, Catherine, 145
Plato, xvi, 4, 5, 6, 7, 45, 65, 116
Prosperi, Adriano, 39
Pulcini, Elena, 59, 201

Rahner, Karl, 148
Ramsey, Ian, 143
Ratzinger, Joseph, 218, 219
Ravasi, Gianfranco, 157, 158, 160
Reid, George W., 58
Rengstorf, Karl H., 77, 97
Ricœur, Paul, xvi, 1, 6, 7, 26, 41, 44, 47, 54, 61, 62, 65, 67, 70, 71, 73, 75, 76, 84, 91, 92, 93, 96, 98, 109, 110, 112, 116, 117, 138, 143, 158, 160
Rieff, Philip, 180
Ritschl, Albert, 191
Rizzi, Armido, 62, 109, 114, 213
Robbins, Robert H., 87

Sandel, Michael J., 208
Sartre, J. P., 45
Schleiermacher, Friedrich, 38, 41, 42, 43, 44, 50, 191
Schökel, Luis Alonso, 10, 93, 97, 99, 111, 112, 157, 158, 160, 162, 164, 165
Schürmann, Heinz, 74, 95, 99
Sciolla, Loredana, 87
Spinoza, Baruch, 40

Tannehill, Robert C., 30, 77, 97
Taylor, Charles, 200, 201, 202, 203, 204
Theodore of Mopsuestia, 33
Tillich, Paul, 32, 33, 105, 106
Toulmin, Stephen, 179
Touraine, Alain, 49
Trias, Eugenio, 109
Throntveit, Mark A., 27

Ullmann, Walter, 22

Vassallo, Nicla, 4
Vattimo, Gianni, 46
von Harnack, Adolf, 191

Ward, Graham, 145
Weber, Max, 56, 57
Wittgenstein, Ludwig, 148, 149

Zimmermann, Jens, 1
Žižek, Slavoj, 146, 147
Zoja, Luigi, 179, 181, 182, 186

www.ingramcontent.com/pod-product-compliance
Lightning Source LLC
Chambersburg PA
CBHW051052230426
43667CB00013B/2263